Fred Van Bennekom

Customer Surveying

a GUIDEBOOK for
SERVICE MANAGERS

Dr. Frederick C. Van Bennekom

Customer Service Press

Bolton, MA

Published by Customer Service Press, 421 Main Street, Bolton, MA, 01740.

Produced by Nicolin Fields Publishing, Inc., 3 Red Fox Road, North Hampton, NH 03862.

Printed in Canada.

Cover design by Joyce Weston
Book interior design and layout by Linda Chestney

**Publisher's Cataloging-in-Publication
(Provided by Quality Books, Inc.)**

Van Bennekom, Frederick C.
    Customer surveying : a guidebook for service managers
/ Frederick C. Van Bennekom. -- 1st ed.
    p. cm.
    Includes bibliographical references and index.
    ISBN: 0-9713406-0-9

    1. Consumers--Research--Methodology. 2. Market surveys--Methodology. I. Title.

HF5415.32.V36 2002   658.8'34'0723
                             QBI01-201129

Dedication

*To Chris,
Who has tolerated many evenings
where I was glued to my laptop,
encouraging me to achieve my professional goals.*

*To my Parents,
Who instilled in me the work ethic
to stay glued to the laptop
until the job was done right.*

What They're Saying...

"**A** customer satisfaction survey seemed almost dangerous — I was really afraid of putting a lot of work into a project and getting misleading or unusable information. Now, though, I've got enough understanding of both good design and the perils and pitfalls of surveying that I'm confident my time and effort will be well-spent."

    ~Martha Lundgren, Manager, Information Center,
    Texas Association of School Boards

"**T**he art of crafting surveys and analyzing their results provides, arguably, the most important application for statistics. I learned how to avoid pitfalls and biases in this concise but lucid presentation."

    ~Mark D. Joseph, IT Manager, New Jersey Department
    of Environmental Protection

"**A**fter discovering Dr. Van Bennekom's survey workshop and unique approach to survey design, our entire company adopted his sound methodology. His thought provoking and well-organized survey workshops, complemented with the *Customer Surveying Guidebook*, should be attended by anyone who is serious about understanding the power of a well-crafted survey."

    ~Chase Fraser, President, MarketQuiz. Inc., Dallas, TX

"**A**s an officer of a not-for-profit organization, I was tasked to research member wants and attitudes. I've found Customer Surveying Guidebook book to be a valuable guide in designing and executing the survey project so as to obtain usable, accurate results. The book answers questions I would never have thought to ask."

    ~Doug Markley, Treasurer, Landlords, Inc., Overland Park, KS

"Fred's thorough, rigorous approach to survey design and analysis is clearly presented in the *Customer Surveying Guidebook*. He asks the right questions to prompt deeper thinking about the design of the questionnaire and the interpretation of results. Reading his *Guidebook* will help you develop those inquisitive traits that add so much value to a survey program."

~Paul Kowal, President, Kowal Associates, Inc., Boston, MA

"As manager of Network Technology for the Bank of Montreal's Corporate University, Fred's survey methodology has been instrumental in my annual success. The improved understanding of my clients and business challenges has helped my team focus its improvement efforts. All of this has enhanced my team's reputation for being current and insightful which always contributed to my clients' business successes."

~Dan Simonini, Manager, Network Services Institute for Learning,
Bank of Montréal, L'Academie de la Banque de Montréal,
Scarborough, Ontario

"Your book identifies all the keys aspects of a successful survey project — proper planning, designing the survey instrument, the process of administering the survey, gathering the results, analyzing the results, reporting the results, and taking action. I see the information in this book helping us a great deal in developing proper questions for the surveys we are developing for various aspects of our customer relationships we are measuring. The wisdom in your book demonstrates that if we don't invest the time in developing an exceptional survey instrument we'll be making decisions on bad data and possibly taking action on the wrong things."

~Kevin Ritter, Customer Support Manager, Firstlogic, Lacrosse, WI

"**D**r. Van Bennekom's experience is real and he clearly communicates his message so that any support manager will understand who, how, and why to survey their customers, and how to get useful results that will make a positive impact on their organization."

~**Richard Reiter, Director, Technical Support,
NetManage, North Andover, MA**

"**I** was a complete novice, but was asked to do the cutomer satisfaction surveys for our department. I attended a workshop conducted by Dr. Van Bennekom, and with the help of his guidebook our survey efforts have been a great success."

~**Sandee Kennedy, Manager,
Data Resources, Sabre, Ft. Worth, TX**

"**I** just have to express my gratitude for your *Customer Surveying* book! I train our customers on the **e-talk** Survey product, including "consultative training" on designing effective questions, when to survey, what to do with the information gathered, etc. I have read large amounts of information on the subject of surveys and by far, yours is the most straight forward, easy to understand, and comprehensive. Thank you for making my job easier, and my customers happier!"

~**Carol Leonetti, Instructional Designer and Instructor,
e-talk Corporation, Irving, TX**

"**T**he *Customer Surveying Guidebook* covers important topics in step-by-step detail, helping the novice survey project manager learn how to develop a customer survey program. Beyond the excellent content, the book's real strength lies in Dr. Van Bennekom's presentation of otherwise dry material in a very easy-to-understand, approachable way — with a touch of humor. The book is a pleasure to read."

~**David Keifer, Manager, Global Customer Support Services,
Eaton Cutler-Hammer, Pittsburgh, PA**

Table of Contents

Table of Figures
and Exercises

Introduction

This guidebook is written to help you, the customer service manager, effectively plan and manage a survey project. It is not meant to be either an encyclopedia on the subject of surveying, or a textbook on survey theory. My aim is to provide you with the information you need so that you can collect real and useful information about your customers, from your customers. Along the way, I'll introduce some theories and concepts, but always with a focus on practical application. By the same token, I use some of the terminology employed by survey researchers, so that you will have a working knowledge of "insider" language. When I use these terms, however, I do so in context, and I provide clear, easily understandable definitions. Knowing the terminology will help you communicate with survey researchers, should you choose to work with them. There are many books that go into greater detail on specific aspects of surveying. A bibliography is presented at the end of this guide.

We use the term *guide* here very explicitly. A guide in the classic sense shows you the path through unknown territory, helps you avoid pitfalls, and points out features that may enhance the value of the trek. Often, there is more than one path that can lead to the same destination. When that is the case, I will present the options and issues associated with each path, so you can decide which fork best meets the objectives of your research journey.

A guide is also someone who can answer questions that arise along the way. In many sections we anticipate the questions that a novice might have and organize the material under those questions as headings.

This book is organized to walk you through the various stages of a survey project in logical fashion. As a visual aid, Chapters 2 through 7 open with a "trail map" of a survey project, highlighting the topics to be addressed in that chapter.

For each stage, I spell out both the objectives and the steps that must be taken and highlight any forks in the trail. I will lay out the decision criteria for choosing one (or more!) forks over another. There may also be side trails, short excursions that you could bypass but ones that could add to the survey experience. I have tried to present each step in concise but comprehensive detail.

We begin the journey by explaining the essential basics of customer surveying. In Chapter 1, we examine the role of surveying within a customer loyalty program and describe the common types of surveys. Chapter 2 outlines the key "pitfalls" to which a novice surveyor may fall prey. This chapter could serve as a checklist for someone completing a survey project for the first time. In Chapter 3, we turn to the stages of a survey project, starting appropriately with project planning and management.

Next, the design of the survey questionnaire is covered in Chapter 4, with a discussion on how to generate the items to include in the questionnaire and how to design the questions that pose those items. The following chapter explains the administration of the questionnaire, comparing and contrasting the many techniques now available. With the data collected, Chapter 6 discusses the analysis and presentation of the data. Chapter 7 presents how to take action with the analyzed survey data. Chapter 8 falls a little out of sequence. It covers survey automation software in more detail than is covered in Chapter 5. Since this is a new area, it deserves special treatment.

I have written this book from the standpoint of a specific audience — service managers who need to survey customers. This gives the book the freedom to address concerns particular to that venue. However, the concepts and techniques of customer surveys can also be applied to other research ventures, such as surveying employees or surveying customers about issues beyond service.

My hope is that this guide will help you start your project correctly and answer your questions thoroughly as they arise. If you don't find your answers, please be in touch. This is a book about how to gather customer feedback, and your feedback is most welcome. Please write to the author at surveyguide@greatbrook.com or complete the online survey about the book at www.greatbrook.com/guidebooksurvey.htm.

CBCBCB

1 The Basics of Customer Surveying

By the end of this chapter, you will learn:

- The distinction between a survey and a questionnaire or instrument
- The power of sampling
- The role of surveys within a Customer Loyalty Program (CLP)
- How to calculate the Return On Investment (ROI) for a customer surveying program
- The marketing aspects of surveying
- Different types of surveys
- Appropriate uses for each type of survey

Surveying has become a commonplace tool on the business landscape. The driving force behind this phenomenon has been the quality management movement, which has transformed companies from technology-focused entities, developing solutions looking for problems, to customer-focused entities, devising solutions for specific problems. In these customer-focused times, most businesses strive to "get close to the customer" or to help articulate the "voice of the customer." These are goals that can only be achieved by listening to your customers, and surveys are a valuable listening tool.

Customer service organizations by their nature should be customer driven. We in customer service interact with customers on a moment-to-moment basis, which means our organizations may be in touch with customers' needs, wants, and concerns. However, we may also fool ourselves into thinking we truly understand what the customer base is thinking. As we move up the organizational hierarchy in customer service organizations, the likelihood of not really understanding the customer grows. Surveying is one means of listening to customer concerns objectively and scientifically.

Surveying is not the only means for listening, and despite — or perhaps because of — its recent popularity, surveying is often misunderstood and misapplied. For that reason, the best way for us to begin is with some definitions.

What is a Survey? What is Surveying?

Surveying is a term applied to a range of information-gathering activities. Broadly speaking, surveying is a *process* of examining some area of interest. We survey a field of job applicants for their qualifications, and we survey a tract of land for its vegetation, mineral outcrops, animal inhabitants, and other characteristics. Asking your friends and neighbors about some political or social issue is surveying. An election is a particular type of survey. In all these examples, surveying starts with identifying what you want to learn, devising a means to gather the necessary data, then gathering that data, analyzing it, and drawing some conclusions. Thus, surveying is a process.

One element in the surveying process is the *questionnaire* or *instrument* that contains the questions devised for collecting data. In common everyday usage, *survey* is frequently used to denote the instrument. In this guide we will use *questionnaire* and *instrument* interchangeably, but we will use *survey* to describe the overall process.

In our customer surveying process, our purpose is to gather data about some large group of interest, known as a *population*. We likely will pose our survey instrument to a portion of the customer population, which is our *sample*. (More on sampling below.) Not everyone in the sample will participate in the survey, so those in the sample who actually provide us data we call *respondents*.

At a high level, the purpose of our customer surveying efforts is to draw a profile of some group of customers and subsets of that group. While we may ask questions about the respondent (e.g., job title, nature of responsibilities, proficiency in some area, etc.), the major intent behind most surveys is to profile the *perceptions* held by the respondent about the service delivered by our organization. You will *not* be measuring objective reality. In fact, it's likely there's a gap between perceptions and objective reality. For example, customers tend to overestimate how long they are on hold when they telephone for service. It's also possible that customers who are generally unhappy about the quality of service may complain indiscriminately.

While the perceptions held by your customers are not objective reality, *they are reality to your customers*. And that's what matters. Based upon the views they express, you may want to reset customer expectations, change the way customers form their perceptions, or you may need to change the underlying operations that led to those perceptions. At the very least, if there is a substantial difference between customer perceptions and reality, it may mean that your organization is not communicating the level of service it actually provides. The purpose of survey research is to identify reality as perceived by customers to give you the information to form good action plans to improve those perceptions.

In addition to profiling the customer base, we may also use survey data to identify relationships between our actions as a company and the reactions or attitudes of that group. For example, we may want to learn the effectiveness of different service recovery tactics or the impact upon satisfaction of the level of service delivered.

Sampling

Let's say our purpose in conducting a survey is to ascertain how our customers regard the quality of our service delivery and we want to be absolutely, positively certain that we know the feelings held by the entire customer base, or *population*. In that case we would need to talk with every single customer, which we call a *census*. Clearly, this may be difficult if not impossible. No matter how diligently we try, not everyone will respond to a survey request. (Even in dictatorships only 99.9% of the population votes.) It would also be costly to conduct a census, although the advent of survey automation software makes attempting a census more affordable. If we can't conduct a true census, then how can we know what customers really think about our service?

The science of statistics provides a solution to this dilemma. Instead of a census, we can talk with a subset or *sample* of our customers and develop a profile of the entire customer base from that sample. (See Figure 1.1.) Statistically speaking, we are drawing inferences — *statistical inferences* — about the population from the sample. The value of statistical theory is that it tells us the *accuracy* and *confidence* of our inferences.[1] That is, statistics tells us the degree of faith we should place in the survey data as an accurate portrayal of the population. Conversely, statistics will also tell us how large a response group we need in order to attain some desired level of confidence in the results. I have heard presenters at service industry conferences say that as long as you have "a lot" of surveys, then your results will be reasonably accurate. Statistics is a bit more precise than that! By the end of the chapter on survey administration you'll know how to define "a lot."

Sampling is especially important for telephone and postal mail surveys, where the cost of administering the survey is strongly driven by the number of people surveyed. Sampling statistics allow us to examine the trade-off between the confidence in results

Figure 1.1
The Concept of Surveying

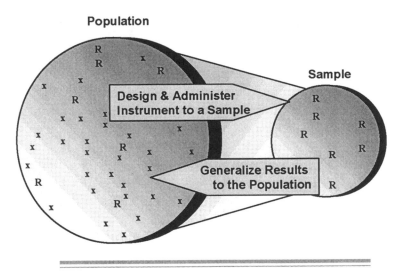

versus the cost of collecting additional survey data. Electronic surveying software has changed this trade-off analysis because of its cost dynamics. These tools are far more scaleable. That is, the cost

---

[1] This discussion of statistical terminology may be releasing well-repressed memories of a college stats class, which is the bane of many a student. Statistics is really just another language for interpreting events in the real world, but too often we get lost in Greek letters and *z* tables. This guidebook will help you learn the value of statistics to your work life, and we'll try not to rekindle a fear of numbers.

of surveying 10 or 10,000 people is about the same. Nonetheless, statistics still are valuable in telling us the confidence and accuracy of the results, based upon the number of respondents.

The method used to generate the sample is important for ensuring that the inferences or conclusions we draw are valid, and a randomly generated sample is typically the best technique to follow. The mechanics of sampling will also be discussed later, but for now it's important to understand the role that sampling plays in the survey process.

> Statistics tells us the degree of faith we should place in the survey data as an accurate portrayal of the population.

Why the focus on sampling theory and statistical measures of the confidence when drawing inferences from a sample to the customer base? Because this is what distinguishes a *scientific survey process* from anecdotal surveying, such as asking your neighbors and friends about a political issue. Scientific surveying demands a rigorous, disciplined approach to a survey project. Following such an approach generates data that can reasonably be applied to critical business decisions. The prime purpose of this book is to teach you how to conduct these scientifically valid surveys.

The advent of the internet, which has made surveying very simple, has also made understanding the issue of scientific surveying more critical. Just post a survey form on a web page and let people who surf to your web page tell you what they think, right? This is surveying, but it is not *scientific* surveying because the administration method is passive. Who's completed these surveys? Only people who have surfed to the web site, and those people likely share some distinctive characteristic. Here's the critical question to ask: are the respondents likely to be representative of the entire population? That's unlikely with a passive survey on a web page. This method introduces a *bias*. (Get used to that term — much of the discussion in this book focuses on how to avoid biases.)

Conducting a passive survey on a web page is not all that different from surveying only your neighbors about, say, a school-related issue in your town. You cannot be certain that the sample group is representative of the entire population of parents in town. You *can* use a web form as a means of administering a survey, but to

make it scientifically valid you must actively solicit a randomly selected sample to complete the survey.

Why Conduct A Customer Survey?

Let's be honest. Organizations, like people, follow fads. Companies sometimes implement new initiatives, such as quality circles
or 360-degree feedback, for much the same reason that a family buys
an SUV — because the neighbors have one. Surveying is a bit of a
fad. Many organizations conduct surveys because they hear that
everyone else is doing it. Does this mean that we think you shouldn't
conduct customer surveys? Not for a minute. All it means is that it
is very important to understand *why* you are conducting a survey
and *what* you hope to achieve from it.

There are good and valid reasons for any organization, and particularly a customer service organization, to survey customers. The
long-run success of an organization depends upon continuous improvement. The key to effective improvement initiatives lies in listening to what's happening within *and* outside the operation, identifying the operation's strengths, weaknesses, opportunities, and
threats — so called SWOT analysis. That means listening to all elements in the value-added chain: suppliers, employees, the process,
and customers. (See Figure 1.2.) Simply taking internal measure-

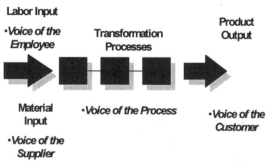

Figure 1.2
The "Voices" of an Enterprise —
The Sources of Continuous Improvement

Labor Input

•*Voice of the Employee*   Transformation Processes   Product Output

Material Input   •*Voice of the Process*   •*Voice of the Customer*

•*Voice of the Supplier*

Based on Ishakawa's "Three Voices"

ments of the operation may tell us how *efficiently* we're using our resources, but listening to customers is key to learning how *effectively* we're applying our resources.[2] Survey results thus are a valuable component of a Balance Scorecard[3] performance measurement system. In fact, surveys provide the balance of the external perspective!

Learning how effective we are in the eyes of our customers is the central reason for a customer surveying effort. But there is a bit more to it than that. What drives effective customer relationships — ones that bond customers? Customers consider a number of factors when assessing service delivery, and these factors relate to the points where the service operation "touches" a customer. Jan Carlson of SAS coined the term "moments of truth" for these touch points.[4] *Service blueprinting*, first advocated by Lynn Shostack, is a process-mapping technique that identifies these customer contact points and the internal processes that contribute to the success or failure of each contact.[5] It's the outcome of these contact encounters that surveying can help us understand.

Most all service transactions result in some *technical outcome*. For example, a computer is fixed; a customer's order is expedited; or the customer learns how to use some computer application. With surveys we're measuring a different outcome. We measure *customers' perceptions* of various attributes of a service operation, such as speed of response, quality of the solution, professionalism of the service representatives, and concern shown for the customer's situation. Measuring these perceptions provides critical input to quality improvement projects, since it targets weak areas to be improved — and strong areas to be replicated. In essence, we're measuring the customer outcome. (See Figure 1.3.)

Measuring perceptions is clearly valuable, but we aren't getting full value from a customer survey if we stop there. Perceptions are the raw material for *attitudes* that customers come to hold about a service business. Examples of a customer attitude are the confidence that customers have in a service business as a long-term provider of technology solutions, the extent of our satisfaction with a

---

[2] *Efficiency* and *effectiveness* are frequently used interchangeably. The author views them as contrasting, but complementary, concepts. Effectiveness is doing the right things well. Efficiency is doing those things with the fewest resources.

[3] See Lynch and Cross (1995), and Kaplan and Norton (1996).

[4] Kao (1987).

[5] Shostack (1984). The concept has been expanded by others. For example, see Zeithaml and Bitner, (1996).

Figure 1.3
The Outcomes of a Service Event

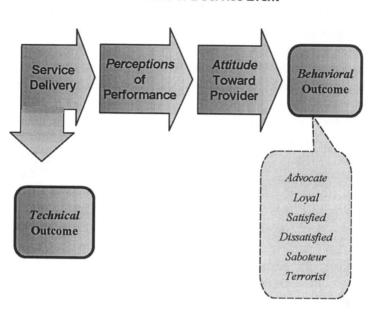

service provider, or the willingness to serve as a reference. Surveys can also be used to assess these attitudes.

But the chain of effects doesn't stop there! Just as perceptions drive attitudes, attitudes drive *behavior,* and understanding the customer behavior driven by service experiences yields the true pearls of knowledge from a customer research program. But it's also the hardest to assess. The most important behavior to understand is the degree of loyalty that customers show toward a company. Have we created company advocates and evangelists or have we created dissatisfied malcontents and terrorists?[6] Research has shown there's a big distinction in customer purchasing behavior driven by satisfaction levels. *Highly satisfied* customers are much more likely to

[6] Scott Cook, CEO of Intuit, is credited with coining most of these terms. I used the term *terrorists* when relating a story to a training class about a full-page ad placed in my local paper by a town resident who was disgusted with the cable company's phone and internet service. *Bolton Common,* March 10, 2000, page 16.

repurchase or to give positive recommendations than *merely satisfied* customers.[7]

An in-depth customer loyalty program would link the perceptions and attitudes measured by surveys in the past, say, a year ago, with the purchasing behavior exhibited by customers today. That purchasing data would be sourced from a customer relationship management (CRM) system. Measuring the behavior induced by our service tells us how truly effective we have been in bonding customers to our company. This loyalty information is also critical to determining prices, arguing for more resources, or marketing to potential customers.

If you're the manager of an internal help desk, you might be saying, "So what? My customers are a captive audience. Measuring loyalty behavior doesn't matter." True, future purchase intent is not relevant, but what if the survey could tell the impact of the help desk upon users' productivity? This information could prove invaluable at budget time — or to counter an outsourcing initiative.

Customer Loyalty Research Portfolio: Surveys and Beyond

Before we lead you down the primrose path, surveys are not the panacea for all that ails you. Nor are surveys the only, or necessarily the best way to research customers to meet certain business needs. Surveys are very good at taking specific, customer-reported measurements that paint a picture of how the customer population feels.

Surveys are *not* good at exploring for new customer concerns or delving, in fine detail, into specific issues. Other research tools are better equipped for that. Some of these techniques will be described later as we cover tools for generating the survey questionnaire, but they can also be used to examine issues identified by surveys. Any time we're doing customer research — or any type of research — we need to arm our quiver with the full array of arrows, employing multiple means of listening. That's why an effective customer loyalty program is a *portfolio of research techniques and action programs*. Each listening technique provides different and complementary types of information that, when combined, provide the information needed to ensure we hit the target.

---

[7] See for example Hart et al. 1990. They report research at Xerox that completely satisfied people are six times more likely to purchase in the next 18 months than are merely satisfied customers.

The purpose of a customer loyalty program is to assess customers' attitudes toward our organization or company and to take appropriate action to foster positive attitudes and bonding. To accomplish this we need *both* quantitative and qualitative research efforts to capture the full breadth of information for assessment and improvement. We need to:

- **Listen Actively.** Customer research should be performed continuously to ensure a consistent quality of service delivery.

- **Listen Broadly.** Listening efforts should reflect the concerns of the entire customer base. That's the role of surveys. Surveys are also very good at providing an overview of our relationships with customers, as well as identifying problem areas for in-depth review.

- **Listen Deeply.** Personal interviews and focus groups allow us to understand the "why" behind the attitudes that surface through broad-based surveys. These research techniques generate the granular data that provide solid footing for improvement efforts.

- **Listen to Extremes.** Comments from those who are highly pleased or displeased may identify strengths to be duplicated or fail points to be corrected. We should actively, not just passively, encourage people to complain — and to compliment. As the title of a recent book aptly puts it, *A Complaint is a Gift.*[8]

Beyond listening in multiple ways, we also must listen *correctly* each time we hear something. Perhaps a greater risk than doing no customer research is performing that research, but doing it wrong. There is nothing magical about data that come from a survey or off a computer. It will only be accurate if the underlying methodology is correct. If the information is wrong, then we may make ill-fated business decisions with unjustified confidence. We may fall prey to delusions of knowledge. Bad data is *worse* than no data.

You have probably heard newscasts present survey research on some societal issue where the findings of one study are diametrically opposite from the findings of some previous study. How can that be? One of the research plans was flawed. Of course, this flaw may have been intentional. "Researchers" have been known to write the conclusions of a study before conducting the research. In our situation of measuring customer loyalty and satisfaction, our concern is to avoid unintentional flaws in our research plan.

---

[8] Barlow and Møller, 1996.

A customer loyalty program is more than just research, though. It's an action program. The research on the front end identifies areas of concern for the operation, whether it's poor training of the service agents, breakdowns in communication, or a seriously aggrieved customer in need of compensation. Collecting data about customer concerns is only half the story. Be prepared to apply the findings of the research to corrective action and service recovery events. The very process of surveying customers sets expectations that their input will be acted upon! You might actually intensify a customer's dissatisfaction if the responses don't drive specific action.

The ROI of Customer Loyalty Programs

Before committing resources to a new program, a legitimate question to ask is: *What is the payback for a customer survey or a comprehensive customer loyalty program? What is the Return on Investment (ROI)?* Some bean counters will argue that simply showing an increase in customer satisfaction measures doesn't prove the value of a program. Bottom-line numbers are, well, bottom-line numbers. More than once I have fielded questions from the person assigned to start a surveying effort only to find out management has allotted a $1,000 budget for the entire program. You don't need to spend a fortune to institute a good program, but such severe under-funding is a recipe for failure.

It's very common for a customer loyalty program to be underfunded, and perhaps one of the reasons for this is the difficulty in measuring the payback. The focus of a customer loyalty program is upon customer retention, and there are myriad factors that lead to the retention or defection of a customer. The real world isn't a scientist's laboratory where one variable can be changed at a time to measure its impact. Is it really possible then to measure the contribution of a customer loyalty program? Yes it is, and some research organizations, such as eSatisfy of Arlington, VA, have done work in this area. Their research studies have compared the cost of gaining a new customer to the cost of retaining a current one. The studies have also measured the impact of quality service upon customer loyalty. These studies show that the cost of a loyalty program is quickly surpassed by the incremental profit from retained customers.[9]

To do your own ROI study and to set a target for the loyalty program, you first want to determine how much of an improve-

---

[9] Goodman (1999).

ment in customer retention rates will justify the program. See the accompanying figure for an example. Look at the revenue and gross profit generated by repeat customers each year. We suggest separating the sales of repeat customers from new customers because long-standing, loyal customers typically buy more each year than new customers. By dividing the operating profit per customer into the estimated cost of the customer loyalty program, you can calculate the number of customers defections you would have to prevent to pay for the customer loyalty program. You can go a step further by calculating the change in the defection rate this represents.

Consider this new defection rate as a goal for your customer loyalty program. Change the defection rate by that amount, and you're at break-even. Here lies an advantage of this approach. You now have a target defection rate, and you have a means to measure the value delivered by the innovation of the customer loyalty pro-

Figure 1.4
Estimating the Breakeven Point for a
Customer Loyalty Program
An Example

Estimated Annual Cost of Customer Loyalty Program (CLP)			500,000
Annual Revenue per Customer	10,000		
Gross Operating Margin	15%		
Annual Operating Profit per Customer		1,500	
Number of Prevented Defections to Pay for CLP			333
Total Number of Customers	200,000		
Number of Defections per Year	12,000		
Defection Rate		6.0%	
New Defection Rate to Pay for CLP			5.8%

gram. Can the entire future change in the defection rate be attributed to the customer loyalty program? Obviously not. Other factors will affect the defection rate, both positively and negatively. (Statistical analysis could be performed to isolate the impact of the different variables.) Most likely you will exceed the target to the extent that the impact of the loyalty program cannot be challenged.

You can also extend the ROI analysis of the value of the customer loyalty program. In lieu of the CLP, marketing would have to replace those lost customers. (Actually, they'd have

> Studies show that the cost of acquiring a new customer ranges from two to 20 times the cost of retaining a customer.

to replace more than that number since new customers typically buy less and are less profitable.) Compare the cost of the CLP to the cost of acquiring a new customer. (Try to get an estimate from marketing.) eSatisfy studies show that the cost of acquiring a new customer ranges from two to 20 times the cost of retaining a customer, depending upon the industry.

There are other ways to calculate the return on investment. You can, for example, calculate the net present value (NPV) of a customer's life-time stream of profits with and without the investment of the loyalty program. This is sometimes called a customer life-time value analysis. These ROI calculations are more precise, but they don't provide a target for the loyalty program that is as intuitively understandable.

What if you're managing an internal help desk or some other service organization that doesn't directly affect revenue? An ROI is more difficult to calculate, but not impossible. You could compare the cost of the internal support organization versus the cost of outsourcing for an equivalent level of service. Ideally, you would like to identify the increased productivity your internal customer's experience resulting from the quality of service delivered. The productivity question would be a good question to pose in the focus groups used to design the questionnaire. (See Chapter 4.) If you can measure productivity changes in some objective manner, do so, but as a fall back, you can survey users for their perceptions of your organization's productivity impact. These survey questions might ask how much less time is lost due to interruptions in computing technology or how much more effectively computer applications are being used due to assistance from your group.

The Marketing Aspects of Customer Surveying

In classic consumer market research, surveys are conducted of a group of people with whom the sponsoring company may have no future contact. For example, the author once participated in a torturous phone survey on the use of cleaning products. The market researcher gets information from the respondent and that's the end of the relationship. It's a one-way or unilateral communication flow. Scientific survey principles are rigorously applied.

In a customer satisfaction survey, we are surveying not just any faceless group — we are surveying *our customers*, whom we hope to keep as loyal customers. The *very process* of surveying our customers communicates something back to our customers, setting expectations for some action, and what we do with the information gathered will deliver a further message. Doing nothing with the information is probably worse than not gathering it in the first place. If we are engaged in an ongoing customer loyalty program, then we will likely be turning to the same customers again for feedback, not to mention future sales. They are not likely to be impressed with an organization that asks for their time and opinions for no apparent purpose, and they certainly won't be motivated to participate in future data collection efforts.

> The *very process* of surveying our customers sets expectations for some action — what we do with the information gathered will deliver a further message.

This bilateral communication flow in a customer satisfaction survey complicates the surveying task a bit. We cannot ignore the marketing aspects of the survey process. That would be foolhardy. But we also don't want to compromise too much on the scientific rigor of our survey work, which can happen if our survey process becomes an interactive discussion of service failures. The survey data may lead to significant changes in the design of the support operation, and those decisions should be based on scientifically valid information. The message here is to keep your eyes on both objectives — the marketing objective and the scientific data-gathering objective, but recognize that you'll best accomplish the marketing objective in the long run by gathering sound data and acting upon it to improve service delivery.

Types of Surveys

For our purposes in customer service we can think about surveys as falling into three categories: special-purpose as-needed surveys, periodic surveys, and transaction-driven surveys.

Specific Purpose Surveys

In service organizations often we have a question we need answered right away or we're engaged in some project for which we need some data from customers. For example, the sales organization may be pushing the support organization to extend the hours of support coverage because sales says they are hearing that need from customers. Your service organization may be designing a new slate of service contract offerings and want to test product bundles and pricing structures with conjoint analysis. Or your help desk may need to revise its service level agreements with internal clients.

These one-time research needs can be met with a survey, complemented by some one-on-one interviews with customers or clients. This is not an ongoing or regular research effort as are the next two survey types. A custom survey instrument would need to be written. Electronic survey tools have made surveys a valuable tool for this type of research due to the ease of conducting such surveys and their speed of response.

Periodic Surveys

A periodic survey is one where a questionnaire is administered on a recurring or periodic basis, for example annually or quarterly. This type of survey is best used to understand issues in the overall relationship between the service provider and the customer. For example, with this type of survey you can examine:

- Ease of doing business
- Value delivered by the service organization
- Overall impressions of service quality today compared to the past
- Key areas needing improvement
- Future needs that customers envision
- How customers make purchasing decisions
- The importance that clients attach to various aspects or attributes of service delivery
- The image customers have of your service organization

There are several key points to consider when designing a periodic survey. Some of these also apply to transaction-driven surveys:

Focus on the overview. In a periodic survey, focus on the relationship between you and your customers at an overview level. Your clients can't remember the details of every interaction they've had with you over the past year. Transaction-driven surveys are better suited for this detail.

Also, be aware how human beings remember and recall events. If you ask questions about the quality of service delivered over a long period of service interactions, say, the last year, what will stand out in a respondent's mind? Two types of interactions will most strongly affect the answer: 1) the most recent interactions, 2) extremely negative interactions.

Let's draw an analogy. You probably buy gasoline for your car about once a week. Think about your overall experiences with buying gas for the past year. Which ones come to mind? The experiences you quickly recall are probably 1) the last time you bought gas or 2) the time nine months ago where the gas pump didn't shut off and you got gasoline all down the side of your car — and on your dress clothes. Do the 50 times when you bought gas with no incident come to mind? Probably not.

Resist the temptation to ask everything. If your group performs a wide range of service functions (e.g., training classes, technology project management, help desk services, and more), then the manager responsible for each business area will want a piece of the survey dedicated to her area. This can make a survey long and unwieldy. Plus, as noted below, some of those areas may not pertain to all respondents. Instead, consider performing a survey each quarter that focuses on different business areas.

Focus on the key topic of concern. Similarly, watch how many new friends you have when you announce the survey program. It's like winning a lottery — without the bounce in the bank account. You may be interested in focusing on ordering and fulfillment processes, but the product marketing manager may say, "While you've got them on the phone..." Resist!

Relevance to the respondent. Another key design issue for this type of survey is to be sure that you pose questions relevant to the respondent. For example, the person who handles billing or contract renewal is unlikely to be the same person who can address the quality of the service delivery. Another example is that senior managers in an organization may consume different types of services from an internal IT group than do the front-line knowledge workers. Senior managers are more likely concerned about a future planning horizon, whereas, the front-line people are concerned with support of today's technologies. This is another reason for following the previous suggestion to conduct multiple surveys. Define your population of interest and be sure all the questions relate to that population.

Separate topics for a transaction-driven survey from the periodic survey. If you're also conducting transaction-driven surveys, don't overlap with those surveys. Earlier we said that a customer loyalty program should be a portfolio of complementary activities. The periodic survey should complement the research accomplished through transaction-driven surveys.

Collect attribute importance and expectation data. To fully understand how effective our service has been, we need to know more than just customer perceptions of different attributes of service delivery. We need to know what customers are expecting and how important each aspect of service is to their overall assessment. Armed with that knowledge, we can target our improvement efforts. A periodic survey is useful for generating these types of data, yet there is a tendency to include these questions in transaction-driven surveys. This can be dangerous, because the importance of an attribute at any point in time will be affected by experiences in the most recent transaction. Research shows that the importance and expectations people ascribe to service traits is fairly stable, so measuring it once a year is sufficient.

> Define your population of interest and be sure all the questions relate to that population.

Let's turn back to the gasoline buying example. What attributes are important in your selection of a gas station? Price, location, convenience, and brand of gasoline probably are in your list. The list doesn't change week to week, although it might change over long periods of time as new innovations come to the market, such as pay at the pump, presence of a convenience store, or now Mobil's Speedpass™. When I was young, we'd expect someone to pump the gas, clean the windshield, and check the oil. Expectations have changed — but slowly.

You can use importance and expectation data collected periodically to contrast to the perception of service delivery quality generated in a transaction-driven surveys. Again, make your periodic and transactional survey complement each other.

Transaction-Driven Surveys

A transaction-driven survey is one where a customer is surveyed as a result of some event.[10] This type of survey is increasingly common in the customer service world, where customers are surveyed after the completion of a service transaction.

Transaction-driven surveys serve primarily as a quality control tool. By constantly listening to the customer base, we can detect changes in performance and hopefully isolate and correct the root causes of problems. We can even construct and use Statistical Process Control (SPC) charts, which is a systematic means of tracking quality levels. (See Chapter 7.)

Following some basic rules will make a major difference in the quality of the information derived from transactional surveys. As with periodic surveys, there are some key points to remember for this type of survey:

Keep it short and sweet. This variation of the KISS acronym can be important to getting people to respond. Remember that the purpose of a transactional survey is to take a quick pulse on the service quality, not to measure everything under the sun.

Don't lose your focus. Just as with periodic surveys, resist the requests from colleagues in other functional groups to ask questions on their behalf. Don't do it! If the introduction to your survey says that the survey relates to the last service transaction and you ask unrelated questions, it will annoy your respondents — who are your customers, after all! In measuring satisfaction, don't create dissatisfaction. Also, this will negatively affect response rates in the long run.

Make sure the survey is comprehensive. While adhering to the KISS axiom, it's also important to be sure that your instrument measures the critical items. Here's a comment frequently heard. "Some of our customers give us high ratings on the individuals items we measure on our survey, but then they give us a mediocre rating on the overall service quality question." Here's what is likely

---

[10] *Event-driven* is another term used for this type of survey. Also, *transaction-driven* is sometimes shortened to *transactional*.

happening. The customer's overall rating is being driven by some attribute *not* in the survey. This is why it is so important to talk with your customers as you construct your questionnaire to be certain that it measures the critical points. (This is covered in depth in Chapter 4.) If you do see responses such as the one described in the quote, those customers would be good persons to interview.

Use more than one instrument. Let's say you've done your job in developing the survey and find that you have 15 questions that you want to ask. What to do? You can probably group these 15 questions into two categories — those of primary and secondary importance. Consider constructing two (or more) instruments, each with the "core" set of questions of primary importance augmented with some of the questions from the secondary group. So, you might have two 12-question survey instruments, each with a common set of nine primary questions plus three secondary questions. Do note that the lower number of responses for the secondary questions means the confidence in those results will be lower, but shorter surveys should lead to greater response.

Complement with customer comment solicitations. Part of the purpose of a transactional survey is to give your customers the opportunity to voice their feelings — pro and con — about a service experience. In a transaction-driven survey you'll likely be applying sampling theory, which means that not every transaction will be surveyed. Yet wouldn't you like to know if a customer has something extremely pertinent to say? Some customers will provide feedback even if you don't solicit it, but research shows that they are the minority. Add to this the fact that a customer who gets surveyed once may be disappointed if not surveyed when they have an experience they would like to share.

Consider complementary research initiatives. Conduct the transaction-driven survey and solicit feedback for all the rest of the completed transactions asking if there was anything extremely negative — or positive! — the customer would like to share with you. This general feedback solicitation can be done through a quick email or by instituting and "advertising" a toll-free customer comment line.

Be prepared to respond. One key value in conducting a survey program is that it shows you care about the customer. This empathy is important in a customer's overall evaluation of a service experience. All that goodwill will be lost — and then some — if a customer tells you something that demands action, and you ignore it. Don't treat this casually. We have recently seen many companies putting "contact us" links on their web sites without allocating resources to respond to the inquiries in a timely manner — if at all. Plan to respond. It's key to bonding with customers. Tools exist to manage complaint handling. Consider using them.

Recognize the complexity of survey administration issues. Although transactional surveys take place in short, frequent bursts, as opposed to the large wave of a periodic survey, there are some distinct administrative issues that you must consider. Procedures to handle these issues must be built.

First, how frequently do you want to survey the same person? If you draw your sample randomly, then occasionally the same person's name may be drawn as frequently as two or three times in a month. The tolerance of users to repeated surveys will vary. A reasonable rule of thumb is to limit surveying an individual to once per quarter. But you should ask your own users how they feel about this. In fact, perhaps your first survey should pose the question: how frequently would customers be willing to provide feedback. This could be included in the note you send out introducing your new surveying process.

Second, some people simply don't want to be surveyed at all or will grow weary of the experience. For them, a show of empathy is an annoyance. Some procedure is needed to eliminate these people from the survey list. For example, you could have an "unsurvey" feature similar to those found in electronic newsletters. Elsewhere in this guide we argue that survey samples should be generated randomly, and these limitations on the survey population just described will create a biased sample. That is true. This is one of those areas where we see a compromise between the scientific and the marketing roles of surveying. Trying to force a response from a customer who doesn't want to be surveyed is foolish and counterproductive, since it is likely to alienate that person.

Third, make sure you identify the transaction for which you want feedback. Since one person may have multiple transactions within a short period of time, you should include the transaction log number and, if possible, a short description of the incident.

Fourth, the survey process is tied to the service management system you're using. The history list of completed survey transactions serves as the population from which a sample is generated, and the contact information resides in the service management system. Obviously, this data transfer process can be done manually, but if the transaction-driven survey effort is an ongoing process, then you may want to automate some or all of the process. This is a feature that is starting to emerge in the electronic survey software tools, but automatic interfaces can be written to handle the job if the feature doesn't exist.

Summary

In this first chapter, critical background material has been presented for those contemplating a customer surveying program. Scientific surveying was defined as a rigorous process of designing and administering an instrument to a properly developed sample of the target population. Then, the survey research was positioned within the broader scope of customer loyalty programs. Surveying won't meet all the needs, and it's important to know what purposes surveys do serve. For those of you who are trying to justify the investment on a customer survey program, I next presented a simple way to calculate the payback on a survey program. This should help you build the case for adding these capabilities. Finally, the three major types of surveys were presented — ad hoc, periodic, and transaction-driven — along with key points to understand about each. Before we move into the details of creating a survey program, the next chapter outlines some of the key mistakes found in survey programs.

CŞCŞCŞ

2 Pitfalls on the Survey Trail

By the end of this chapter, you will learn:

- Characteristics required for a scientifically rigorous survey
- Biases in the survey instrument design that threaten the quality of the results
- Biases from the survey administration that threaten the quality of the results
- Factors, beyond response rate, that can affect a survey's value

Survey research is deceptively simple — with an emphasis on deceptive. After all, a survey instrument is just a bunch of questions strung together, right? But like any research, a survey not done correctly will provide potentially misleading data. At an industry conference prior to leading a discussion group on surveying, the author overheard one person say to another, "Senior management wanted some customer satisfaction numbers. So, we threw together a quick survey. We had to something." Is doing something better than doing nothing? How would you rather make business decisions: based upon data from a poorly designed and executed research project, based upon your gut feeling, or based upon data from a rigorous research project? I'd trust decisions made from gut feeling more than those based on delusions of knowledge. Humorist Will Rogers once said, "It ain't what you know that hurts you. It's what you do know that ain't so."

A couple of absolute requirements for producing good survey research are: 1) *validity* and *reliability* in the survey instrument; 2) *precision* and *accuracy* in all aspects of administration. *Both* requirements must be met if we are to generate solid data for business decision-making. We can have precise and accurate results based upon the statistics of sampling, yet have an instrument that unintentionally measures the wrong things. Or we can employ a solid instrument, but administer it to a biased sample producing skewed results. In either scenario we may operate under delusions of knowledge.

This chapter will outline common mistakes or pitfalls on the survey project trek. Subsequent chapters will describe in detail how to avoid these pitfalls and execute a survey project correctly. This chapter could serve as a checklist for a well-done survey. As you move through the instrument design and survey administration stages of your project, come back to this chapter and make sure you've avoided the pitfalls.

Instrument Design and Survey Quality

Survey designers stress that a good instrument has two qualities: validity and reliability. The validity of the survey instrument is determined by answering one critical question:

➤ Do the questions on the instrument *truly measure* what we *intend* them to measure?

The reliability of a survey instrument is determined by answering another critical question:

➤ Does every respondent *interpret* the questions on the instrument *in the same way*?

A question could be valid but not reliable and vice versa. Here's an example of an invalid but possibly reliable question. A help desk asked its customers on a survey if they received "service of consistent quality." They were ecstatic at the high scores received! Unfortunately, respondents did feel they were receiving consistent — but low — quality service. Of course, the help desk survey intended to measure consistent, *high*-quality service.

If respondents are answering different questions, based upon varying interpretations some of which differ from your intent, then you are actually (albeit, unintentionally) administering *multiple instruments*. Any conclusions based on the resulting data will be flawed even though the administration may be performed properly. Typically, an unreliable question will also produce invalid results, but occasionally they won't occur simultaneously.

Instrument validity and reliability can be compromised by any of the following mistakes in constructing individual questions or the overall questionnaire. These errors lead to *instrumentation bias*, that is, errors introduced into the response data caused by flaws in the instrument. See Figure 2.1 for examples.

- ◆ **Absence of clearly stated criteria for evaluation.** Whenever you ask someone to rate something, you must also give him or her a basis for comparison. For the sake of discussion, let's assume you want survey respondents to rate the quality of a training class. Is the comparison to be made against the most recent training class taken from your organization, all classes taken over the last year, training from other companies, or something else? If you don't provide a benchmark, then each respondent will use his own. How can the results then be interpreted? Think about what you want to understand from the responses to the question, and be sure the question includes the necessary elements. Do not make the respondent infer something.

- ◆ **Questions that do not apply to respondent.** When a question is posed, every respondent should have an option for an answer that fits her situation, even if that option is *Not Applicable*. For example, if you ask someone to rate the various types of services your organization delivers, she may not have consumed some of the services. The respondent may leave the question blank, she may enter a neutral response, or she may make up some other answer. Blanks are easy to interpret, but "invalid" neutral responses distort the findings. Too many inappropriate questions will likely lead the respondent to stop completing the survey. The quick solution is to include "N/A" as a response option — but will people use that as a way of avoiding answering more difficult questions? A better solution is to use branching techniques to direct respondents around a body of questions that don't apply to them.

- ◆ **Examples that lead responses.** Sometimes when we construct a question, we realize that the respondent may not understand the terminology used in the question. We're tempted to then include an example in the question, as a means of helping the respondent to understand it. This is almost always a bad idea. The example narrows the respondent's thinking to that one particular item. Whereas, you probably want the respondent to think beyond that one example. This is particularly important for open-ended questions. Try to reword the question to avoid the need for an example. This can be very challenging. If absolutely necessary, use a very "bland" example, one that won't bias anyone.

Here are a couple of examples. A survey conducted for a training organization posed an open-ended question asking what type of satisfaction guarantee the respondent most preferred, and the examples of repeating the class or getting money refunded were included. Guess what were the common responses by far? The examples skewed the results. In another case, a help desk asked its clients what type of seminars on current technology issues they wanted and included the examples of use of personal digital assistants (PDAs) and the Y2K crisis. "Technology seminars" was not considered a very clear concept to most people. So including those examples was deemed necessary and safe since those seminars had already been given.

◆ **Unreasonable recall expectations.** Ever watch a Congressional hearing where the person testifying is asked, "Where were you on the night of…" Did you think to yourself…, "How can they expect the poor person to remember that kind of detail?" Yet, we have a tendency to do that in our instrument design. As a service manager, you eat, drink, and breathe your business. Respondents for your survey do not! Therefore, don't expect them to recall events that happened a long time ago.

> The events that will drive the composite image are likely to be either the most recent events or the worst events.

If your questions ask the respondent to evaluate the quality of service over the past year, you're asking the respondent to create a mental composite of events (possibly a great many of them!) stretching over a considerable period of time. The events that will drive the composite image are likely to be either the most recent events or the worst events, since those are most prominent in our memories. This is part of the reason why periodic surveys have shortcomings in truly measuring the satisfaction level with service over the entire period.

Choose a recall period that is long enough for respondents to have sufficient experiences to form an impression but recent enough that they can remember. Three months is a good rule of thumb. A technique for bounding recall is to choose some marker date as the start of the recall period. For example, you might say, "Since the winter holiday season…"

◆ **Ambiguous wording.** Use of unclear or imprecise language is the greatest threat to a question's validity and reliability. Always avoid jargon used in your work group, which may not translate clearly for the customers you are surveying. Also, really challenge each phrase or term in the question to see if it can have multiple meanings. "Response time" is perhaps the best example of a service industry term that can have multiple meanings. Does it mean how quickly the phone was answered, how quickly the caller spoke with a real person, or the time until the properly qualified person started working on the issue?

> The order in which you ask questions may bias the response for certain questions.

Two goals in writing questions are to be clear and brief. If you find ambiguous terms, then you have to be less brief to be clearer. Rather than using "response time," substitute a more precise phrase such as "the time from when you called until you first spoke with a technical representative…" Yes, it's wordier, but those additional words are critical.

◆ **Combination questions.** Ask one question at a time. That seems simple enough, but there's always a temptation to make a question clearer by adding another descriptive term. There's also a temptation to shorten the length of a survey instrument by combining two questions. For example, at a recent industry conference, the speaker evaluation form asked attendees to judge the "effectiveness and organization of the speaker." Another question asked about the "topic and content of the session." Are those pairs of attributes so closely aligned that they constitute a single question? Couldn't the speaker be organized but terribly ineffective — or vice versa? Couldn't the topic be great but the content stink? When the respondent answers, which attribute will drive the answer? When you're analyzing the data, you won't know! As a conference organizer, how would take action on data from those questions?

- **Leading or loaded questions.** This shortcoming in question design is more common in surveys on public policy issues or political preferences, but it can creep into customer service questionnaires. One area where this can easily happen is in questions about the degree of empathy customers feel you show them. Here, customers may feel swayed to tell you what they think you want to hear, and therefore, it is particularly important to watch the tone of your words. Use neutral, almost bland, phrasing. Remember, if you want an honest response, don't lead the respondent.

- **Improper sequencing of questions.** The order in which you ask questions may bias the response for certain questions. The most common error of this type is putting demographic questions at the front of the questionnaire. They should always go last. Demographic questions can be viewed as intruding on someone's privacy. By asking them first, you may set up a mental wall for the respondent, who then will be less forthcoming — or may even decide not to complete the survey. Consider this: in the survey introduction you have told respondents how valuable their feedback is, but when the first questions encountered are about their job title or responsibilities, you've killed their motivation to help you.

  Another example of the sequencing issue occurs when asking importance and satisfaction in consecutive questions. If someone is very unsatisfied with some aspect of the service, they will likely exaggerate its importance.

  Sequencing issues may be subtler. In a recent experiment conducted by the author, we changed the order of two questions: "accuracy of information provided by the service representative" and "clarity of explanation of how an issue would be handled." The order of the questions changed the responses significantly. Why? When respondents evaluated the "accuracy of information," they must have included some aspects of the "clarity of explanations." But when asked the "clarity of explanations" first, "accuracy of information" was not subsumed into the "clarity" evaluation. One technique for addressing this problem is to randomize the order of the questions. Obviously, special software is needed for telephone or web-based surveying to accomplish this, and multiple versions of a hard copy survey would be needed.

Figure 2.1
Reducing Instrumentation Bias

Clearly Stated *Criteria* for Evaluation.

Wrong	"How would you rate the ability of the project team to define business requirements?"
Right	"Compared to other projects done for you by our company, how would you rate the ability of the project team to define business requirements?"

Questions *Must Apply* to Respondent

Wrong	"How effective did you find the FAX-Back support system?"
Right	"If you used the FAX-Back support system, how effective did you find it?" (With "not applicable" as an response option.)

Examples Should *Not Lead* Response

Wrong	"Which one of our professional services, for example, installation services, do you feel is most valuable?"
Right	"Which of our professional services is most critical to you?"

Reasonable Recall Expectations

Wrong	"In your support calls over the past year, on average, how many minutes was it before the phone was answered?"
Right	"During the past three months, has the time for a support representative to answer the phone been reasonable?"

Unambiguous Word Choice

Wrong	"In your last support call, was the response time reasonable?"
Right	"Consider your last request for support. How reasonable was the time from when you called until you spoke with a support representative?"

Ask *One Question* at a Time

Wrong	"Was the staff technically competent and courteous?"
Right	"Was the staff member who handled your issue technically competent? Was the staff member who handled your issue courteous?"

Avoid *Leading* or *Loaded* Wording

Wrong	"How did our interest in you, our customer, match your expectations?"
Right	"To what extent did our concern for you match your expectations?"

Overall, there are three objectives for which a survey designer should strive in constructing a questionnaire[1]:

1. **Focus.** Key on one specific attribute or phenomenon in each question.

2. **Clarity.** Keep the syntax simple to avoid confusing the respondent. Avoid using long, dependent clauses to open a sentence and avoid using compound, complex sentence structures. These force the respondent to navigate a maze of logic, which may lead him or her to answer improperly. If this happens, your data will be corrupted. Also, use common vocabulary that everyone will understand. You are not trying to impress the respondent with your vocabulary, nor do you want to insult the respondent. In customer services, especially if business clients are the customers whom we will be surveying, there is general vocabulary that everyone should understand.

3. **Brevity.** Pose the question as succinctly as possible.

Unfortunately, the three objectives may work against each other. For example, in trying to be clear, you may have to be less than brief in writing the question. Avoiding ambiguous terms, such as "response time" or "first time fix," may require longer descriptions to ensure clarity. The key to constructing effective questions is figuring out how to achieve the best possible balance among these objectives.

Survey Administration and Survey Quality

While the design of the survey instrument is important to getting valid responses, the way the survey is administered is also critical to a quality research effort. Survey administration may adversely impact the quality of the data in many ways. These issues will be covered more fully in Chapter 5 on Survey Administration:

♦ **Bias through the administration process.** Some respondents may not give honest answers because of who is sponsoring the survey (known as *auspices*) or because of who is conducting the survey (*acquiescence*). If an internal help desk conducts a telephone survey of its users, the users may fear reprisals for unfavorable responses due to a lack of anonymity. Similarly, if the general manager personally conducts the survey interviews,

---

[1] Alreck and Settle (1985) cover these issues very well.

users may fear giving the "wrong" answer.[2] Some survey designers will argue that you simply shouldn't state who is sponsoring the research. For some types of surveying, this deceit may be acceptable, but since our customer satisfaction surveys are in part a marketing exercise, we must be totally honest with the respondent, our customer.

- **Bias through the administration technique.** Telephone administration is quite prone to introducing bias since each interviewer must consistently deliver the questionnaire script in the same manner. The administration technique may also bias the results if the technique chosen excludes a segment of the population. For example, if you don't have email addresses for every potential respondent, then an email survey could create a bias.

- **Bias from the targeting the wrong population.** If you don't survey the right people, you won't get the business information you want. In customer services, we are less at risk of totally missing our mark than other types of organizations because we are dealing with a familiar population — our customers. We probably know their street addresses, phone numbers, and email addresses. Market researchers for a consumer product goods company would be envious. However, we might still target the wrong population. For example, if you want to understand the purchasing decision for service contracts, you should not be surveying the user who consumes the services. True, we're surveying out customers, but there are different categories of customers.

- **Bias in the sample generation.** Remember that the purpose of surveying a sample is to draw statistical inferences from the sample to the population. Thus, the sample needs to be representative of the population. You might think this requires some complex selection process, but it is actually the opposite! A *random selection* of respondents from the target population minimizes the threat of this bias.

---

[2] In a similar issue, the *Wall Street Journal* (October 6, 2000, page B6) reported that Stuart R. Patterson, CEO of Speechworks, International, Inc. received a phone message from Arthur Levitt, Jr., chairman of the Securities and Exchange Commission (SEC) less than a month after Speechworks completed its initial public offering. He first thought it was a prank, but then found out the call was real. The two played phone tag for a week, all the while Patterson was terrified that the SEC had problems with the newly public company. Levitt was actually making a customer service call, following the advice of getting close to his customers. Perhaps Levitt needs to rethink how the SEC surveys its customers.

- **Bias in the respondent group.** Within the sample, those with the strongest opinions are most likely to respond, so we need to motivate those with more neutral feelings through incentives or follow-up notices.

- **Statistical strength of the generalizations from the sample to the population.** Obviously, the more respondents surveyed, the more confidence we have that the sample represents the population. Statistical strength is composed of two elements: 1) the likelihood of the survey results 2) being within a certain percentage of the results that would be found if a census were taken. These two elements are known as *precision* and *accuracy*, respectively. Thus, the precision and accuracy for a survey may be stated as: "95% certainty of the answers being within a +/- 4% margin of error." Typically, the first element is omitted since 95% certainty is used by convention. In addition to the sample size, the size of the population also affects the statistical strength.

> In customer services, we are less at risk of totally missing our mark than other types of organizations because we are dealing with a familiar population — our customers.

Summary

This chapter has outlined the key threats to producing good data from a survey program. There are two types of biases: bias from the instrument and bias from the administration. Within each category there are multiple sources for those biases. Much of the rest of the book addresses how to avoid these biases. First, we turn to the steps to manage a survey project.

C3C3C3

3 Survey Project Management

By the end of this chapter, you will learn:
- The stages of a survey project
- The resources required for a typical survey project
- The budget you may need for the project
- The typical time frame you should expect for a survey project
- Which task to do first: designing the questionnaire or determining the administration method?

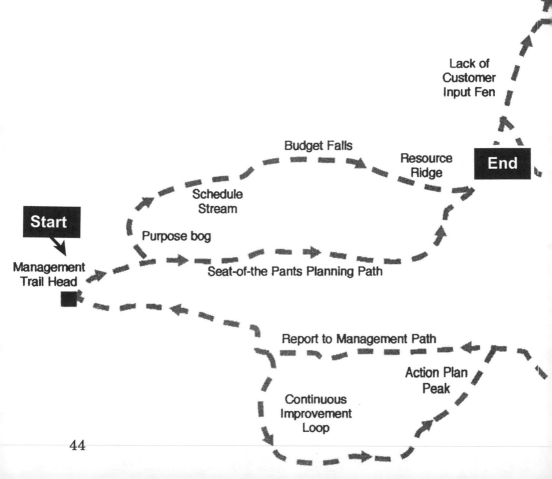

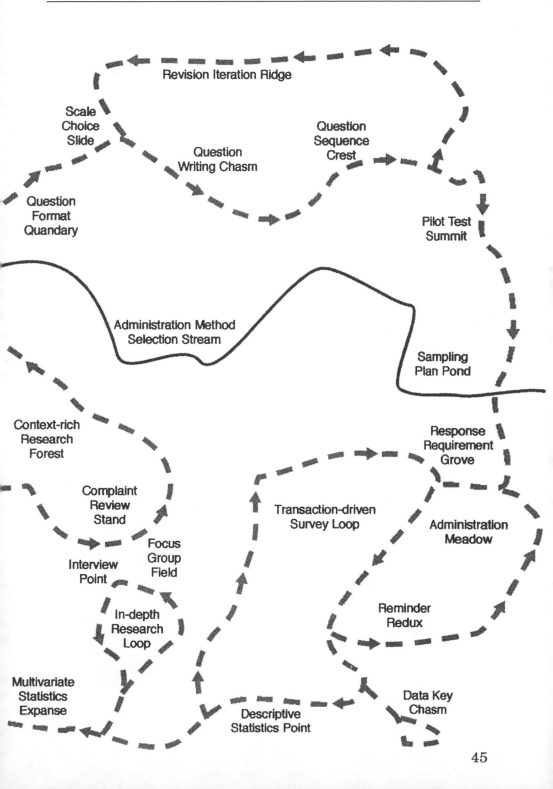

Key Stages of a Survey Project

As with any project, the process of performing survey research follows a series of steps. At a high level they are:

1. Project Planning
- Formulate a statement of purpose
- Identify needed resources
- Create a budget
- Develop a project schedule

2. Survey Instrument Development
- Identify the service attributes for the survey through focus groups or interviews
- Design the survey instrument: question construction, scales, introductions, etc.
- Pilot test: Administer the instrument to a sample to identify flaws

3. Administration (Distribution and Data Collection)
- Determine the administration method
- Identify the target population and develop the target sample

Figure 3.1
Key Stages in a Survey Program

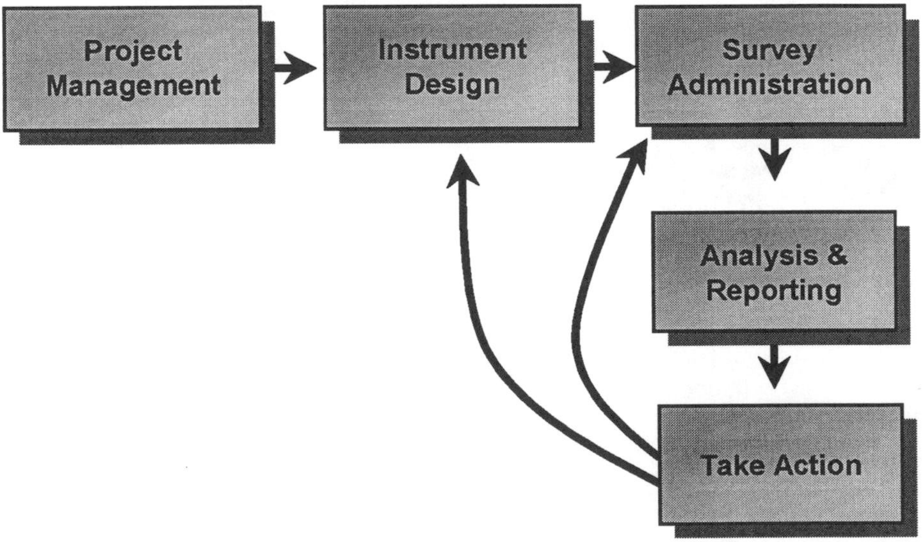

- Send a pre-administration notification
- Distribute the survey
- Send follow-up notes to non respondents
- Gather responses and key into database

4. Analysis & Reporting

- Analyze the data
- Report the results

5. Take Action

- Apply survey data to address specific customer issues and to broader organizational improvement projects

6. Repeat Process for continuous feedback

- Modify instrument, if needed, before future administrations

If you're working with a library of professionally written questions, much of the critical work of instrument design will have been done for you, but you still need to attack survey project management in a rigorous, structured fashion. The remainder of this chapter focuses on the first stage of survey project management — project planning. Subsequent chapters will address each of the remaining stages.

Planning a Survey Project

A survey project should be treated like any other project. Good project management skills are important if the project is to be completed on time, within budget, and with the desired results. A project plan should be developed that identifies the purpose of the survey project, the resources needed, the budget required, and a schedule for the process.

Statement of Purpose. At the very outset of a survey project, the project manager should develop a short statement of the purpose of the project. (See Figure 3.2 for an example.) This is no trivial or proforma exercise. The statement should answer the following questions:

- What's motivating you to conduct a survey? Is the purpose to identify specific strengths and weaknesses in the service delivery operation? To monitor the quality of service delivery at an overview level? To demonstrate the value that your service organization is delivering to its clients?

- Who is the target population? This may sound simple: it's your customers. But there likely are many subsets to your customer base, and the exact purpose of the research effort will dictate who in the customer company is the target population.

47

◆ What actions do you plan to take with the results? Will the results spawn some continuous improvement projects? Will you be providing the results to your customers in some "report card"?

If your only purpose in conducting a user survey is because your boss told you to do one, then stop reading this and apply your energy to more fruitful ventures! Without a well-defined Statement of Purpose the project may meander from the original intent — and it will probably never be completed. As later project stages are described, we will occasionally suggest that you look to your Statement of Purpose as a beacon to keep the project aimed down its original path.

However, this doesn't mean the Statement of Purpose is locked in stone. As you move through the project, your thinking will become more refined, especially as you do the investigatory work on the questionnaire design. Go back and update the Statement of Purpose. Challenge yourself. Is this really where you now feel the project should focus? If so, then amend the Statement of Purpose.

Beware of a purpose that is too broad in scope. A survey can't do everything at once. A survey can't provide a broad overview of the quality of service *and* provide comprehensive granular, actionable data. As stated in the first chapter, a survey should be part of a portfolio of research techniques, each of which serves a role in the

---

Figure 3.2
Example of Statement of Purpose

Project: Transaction-Driven Survey.

The purpose of the survey project is to ensure we're delivering high-quality service to our clients who call for assistance. We will survey a sample of each closed transaction to gauge overall satisfaction with our service and to identify where service has not met expectations. Findings will be tracked on an ongoing basis and the results will be used to improve the service delivery process, representative training, and other areas identified as causing dissatisfaction. The survey data will be combined with other customer research to develop improvement projects.

---

overall goal of improving customer loyalty. You may use surveys to identify a problem area, then use another survey — or perhaps a focus group or interviews — to develop the detailed information.

The author has found that project sponsors may be the people most prone to having unrealistic expectations of a survey project. Setting those expectations straight may require some tactful diplomacy. Earlier, we positioned a survey project as one element in a customer loyalty program. You may make that argument using the logic outlined there.

Resources

A key part of the planning process is identifying what resources will be needed for the various stages of the project. This includes personnel, volunteer assistance, contract labor, facilities, equipment, etc. The following list breaks these components down into finer detail.

- **Project Manager.** One person should have overall responsibility for the project. This person may also perform many of the individual tasks in the project. A survey project will demand about one-third to one-half of the project manager's work time during the development project. If this is an on-going survey effort, then some portion of a person's time will be needed, depending upon the scope of the effort.

- **Project Team.** A cross-functional team, composed of representatives from groups that will use or be affected by the survey's findings, best ensures success of the project. The team should also include the skill sets needed to accomplish the various tasks that are not to be outsourced. The time demands on the project team will be determined by the scope of the tasks taken on by team members, that is, what's not outsourced.

- **Project Sponsor.** While not part of the formal project team, a project sponsor may be the most important resource to ensure the success of the project. Someone in senior management should take ownership of the project. This person will help secure any budgetary needs, gain participation from other functional groups, and be the formal contact for customers in any correspondence. Perhaps most important, this person can help ensure that focus on the project remains, preventing survey team members from being siphoned off for other projects, thus delaying the survey project.

- **Customers or users.** If focus groups or interviews are to be used in the design stages for the instrument, then a number of customers or users will need to be solicited for this activity. Customers or users will also be needed for the pilot tests.

- **Contracted Resources.** Several areas of a survey project are amenable to outsourcing, but these tasks may also be done in-house. Resources that might be contracted include: 1) moderators to conduct focus groups or interviews, 2) a survey expert to design the questionnaire, 3) a mail house for mailings and keying in or scanning the completed surveys, if conducting surveys via postal mail, 4) a telemarketing organization, if conducting surveys via telephone, 5) a web designer to create or enhance web forms if the survey is to be conducted via a web form, and 6) a statistician to analyze the survey data and possibly to write the report. Of course, there are many organizations that will deliver a total solution. See Chapter 8 for a partial listing of outsourcing organizations.

> Advantages of out-sourcing: expertise that may not be available internally and financial incentive to meet a schedule and deliver the product.

There are two advantages to outsourcing. First, the outsourcers will bring expertise that may not be available internally. Second, the outsourcers have a financial incentive to meet a schedule and deliver their product.

- **Facilities.** Rooms for project team meetings are obvious, but you may want to hire a meeting room in a hotel for conducting focus groups. If you are conducting a telephone survey, you may need to set up a telephone calling area.

- **Tools, equipment, and other resources.** Aside from normal office equipment, you may need other resources depending upon the administration method chosen. For example, if you are using an electronic survey software tool, that tool must be acquired and some time may be needed from your system administrator.

It is important that the people assigned to the project be committed to it. That is, their tasks should be part of their job definitions. The author has seen projects where the project managers were supposed to do this "in their spare time." In a service environment, especially in a support service environment, we operate in a fire-fighting mode. Doing the survey project will be a secondary priority that may never get done.

Budget

Elements in a survey project budget include:

- **Salaries** of the project manager and members of the project team.

- **Incentives** provided to customers to participate in focus groups and pilot tests and to respond to the survey questionnaire.

- **Computer usage** and other communication technologies. (This item should be minimal.)

- **Consulting fees** for outside expertise to conduct focus groups, develop instruments, design web forms, perform data analysis, or other services deemed necessary.

- **Survey administration**, which will vary with the administration method chosen, length of survey, and the decision to outsource this work or perform it in-house. For postal mail surveys, the cost categories are copying of the instrument and other customer communications, outgoing and return postage and envelopes, and keying or scanning of the returned instrument. Your postage costs will depend upon the weight of the mailings. Three sheets of 8 ½ x11 inch paper, an outgoing and a return envelope should weigh just under one ounce. Ideally, a postal mail survey will include three mailings. (See Chapter 5.) These costs will be incurred for each survey project conducted.

For telephone surveys, the cost components are: outsourcing the telephone calling or staffing for it, facilities, equipment, and training for the interviewers. These costs, except perhaps for the training, will be incurred for each survey conducted.

Electronic mail or web-form surveys require either the purchase of software to perform this function or internal development of these capabilities. If you are sending a survey by email without such software, then budget for keying the responses of the returned instruments. Surveying software is a one-time cost, excluding product upgrades, since the software can be used for future survey projects. Note that survey software services can be "rented" from a survey software company that has an ASP (Application Service Provider) hosting service.

Schedule

As with any project, the project schedule is concerned with both the person-hours to accomplish tasks and the elapsed time necessary for certain tasks. Here we give a brief overview of the time demands for each task. Each activity will be discussed in far more detail in subsequent chapters. We cannot give you an exact schedule for your project, but we try to give you the information needed for you to plan your project.

- ◆ **Project Planning.** This stage could take a month or more depending upon how politics and approvals are handled in your organization. Do plan on having several meetings with the project team to brainstorm and refine the project plan. The decision-making process for some areas needs to start early, such as evaluation and selection of survey administration method.

- ◆ **Survey Instrument Development.** This is a three-part process. The first phase is the identification of the attributes to be measured in the survey. Focus groups, interviews, and other research activities are typically used. Scheduling each focus group will require two to four weeks notice to the prospective participants of the sessions. The actual session should be scheduled for a two to three hour time slot. Digesting and analyzing the data is very time consuming depending upon how formal the write-up will be. Plan on three to four hours of analysis time for each hour of focus group time. That ratio will diminish as more focus groups are done.

  The second phase is the actual design of the survey instrument. The time required for design will depend on the length of your survey. After all attributes are identified, plan on one to two weeks for the initial draft. If the focus group data have undergone solid analysis, then the design process will be accelerated because much of the thinking about questions to ask will have been done. Plan for two or three review and revision sessions with the project team over the course of two to six weeks. Design is best done in iterations to allow for fresh review of the instrument. The task time for the primary instrument designer will take about one-person-week, longer for a complex survey.

  The final phase of instrument development is the pilot test. This is when you administer the instrument to a handful of people from the respondent group. As with the focus groups, some notice will be needed to schedule these sessions with customers. Three to five pilot tests should be done at minimum, and you should schedule one half hour to one hour, depending on the length of the survey. Note that the results of these tests may lead to revision work for the questionnaire.

Schedule a meeting with the project team after the pilot tests to finalize the instrument.

♦ **Survey Administration (Distribution and Data Collection)**
The timing for this stage is difficult to generalize, because so much depends upon the distribution method chosen and the resources at your disposal. That said, there are some rules of thumb that you can use to gauge your scheduling requirements.

The first step is selecting an administration method. If buying some tool or outsourcing, then a request for proposal (RFP) should be developed. This could take several meetings with the project team to refine.

The second step, regardless of the administration method, is for the project team to identify the target population. After that, plan for a half day or more to clean the distribution list and get it in proper form. The time for this task will depend upon the cleanliness and accessibility of your customer data base.

The time for the third step, the actual administration, will depend upon the administration methods — and whether you outsource this task. For hardcopy surveys by either postal mail or interdepartmental mail, distribution could take several person-days for a large sample, if you choose to do the tasks in-house. Hardcopy surveys require copying the instrument, labeling and stuffing envelopes, and affixing postage. One person can process around 30 mailings per hour, including the set-up time required. Ideally, there should be three mailings: announcement letters, the survey, and follow-up notes. The time to key the data into a file will depend upon the length of the instrument, especially open-ended questions, and the number of responses. Typically, a person can key 15 data points per minute, including set-up time. Keying can begin when the first response is returned. Scanning the instruments will eliminate the variability of data keying, but this introduces a new up-front task, creating a form that can be scanned and contracting for those services.

> The actual administration will depend upon the administration methods — and whether you outsource this task.

For telephone surveys, each interviewer can successfully

complete perhaps four surveys per hour if it is a short survey. Most of the time will be spent trying to get people on the phone. (Obviously, this assumes you're not using a computer to do the dialing as any telemarketing agency would use.) A longer survey, with many open-ended questions, could cut that per-hour completion rate in half. Keying data in a data file should be part of the interview process.

Electronic survey administration will take perhaps 15 minutes — once the system is properly configured and the user has learned how to use the software. As with any application, the project manager or designee can expect to spend about a day or more learning the system. Since this software interacts with email clients, plan for a few set-up and configuration issues that may require the system administrator. Loading the responses into a data file should take about one hour if you are using a survey automation tool. If you are conducting an email survey without such a tool, then the keying time is similar to that for postal mail surveys.

> Whether the survey project comes in on schedule or not, is determined to a great degree by the commitment of the people involved.

If you decide to outsource administration, you don't get away scott-free. An RFP must be developed, potential vendors interviewed, and a decision made. Even then, the project manager will need to work with the vendor to implement the instrument into the vendor's processes. The time for administration will probably range from one to three weeks.

◆ **Reporting** The amount of time required to analyze the data and report the results will depend on the length of the survey and the analysis to be performed. For a large annual survey, plan for one to two days to generate descriptive statistics for the data. If you plan to perform analysis on various sample segments, recognize that analyzing each segment will take about the same time as analyzing the entire data set. Open-ended questions take *considerable* time to analyze if you're planning to codify the responses and make some sense out of all the comments.

Writing a good, thorough report, complete with charts and graphs will take three to four days, if you are dealing with a large, annual survey. Some surveying software will increase productivity in this activity. If you are conducting an on-going transactional survey, the time for analysis and reporting should be far less for each week's or month's reporting.

As with any project, the ability to keep a survey project on schedule will be determined by the degree of commitment you can secure from the people involved. This is particularly important in two areas. First, if you are conducting some focus groups or other customer interviews to gather inputs for the questionnaire design stage, then you need to give sufficient notice to your customers to schedule those sessions. Second, when going through the iterations to refine the questionnaire, you need commitments from all participants within your organization to provide feedback in a timely manner.

We'll conclude this chapter with a discussion that seemingly contradicts the flow of a survey project schedule we've laid out. So far, we've presented a linear flow: plan the project, design the questionnaire, administer the questionnaire, and analyze the results. It's not that simple. There is a critical interdependency between the questionnaire design and the administration method. The questionnaire design sets requirements for the administration, while the administration method sets constraints for the questionnaire design. (We can see a chicken-or-the-egg argument forming here!)

You may be locked into a particular administration method for any number of reasons. Know that when you're designing the questionnaire. Otherwise, early in the questionnaire design stage when you have a sense of the scope and size of the instrument, also determine the administration method. The logistics of implementing an administration method take time, especially if outsourcing, so this lead time is important.

Summary

This chapter has outlined the three major components of a survey project: resources, budget, and schedule. These projects are not overly complex, but a lack of planning can led to missed deadlines or delivering less than the expected results. Good project management skills will help insure a successful survey project.

CBCBCB

Designing the Questionnaire

4

By the end of this chapter, you will learn:

- The steps to take in designing a questionnaire
- How to identify the points you should cover in your questionnaire
- The importance of getting input from the respondent group as part of the design process
- The elements of a questionnaire
- Issues in the sequencing of questions within an instrument
- The advantages and disadvantages of the different types of question format
- How to select scales and anchors for a questionnaire
- Tips for writing good questions and how to hone your question-writing skills
- The critical importance of conducting pilot tests
- How good you are at identifying flaws in a questionnaire

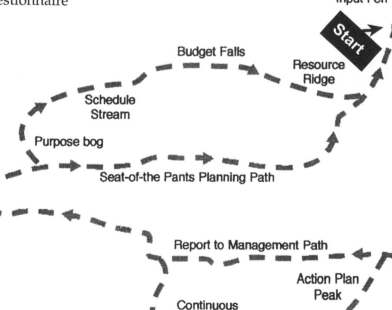

Lack of Customer Input Fen

Start

Budget Falls

Resource Ridge

Schedule Stream

Purpose bog

Seat-of-the Pants Planning Path

Management Trail Head

Report to Management Path

Action Plan Peak

Continuous Improvement Loop

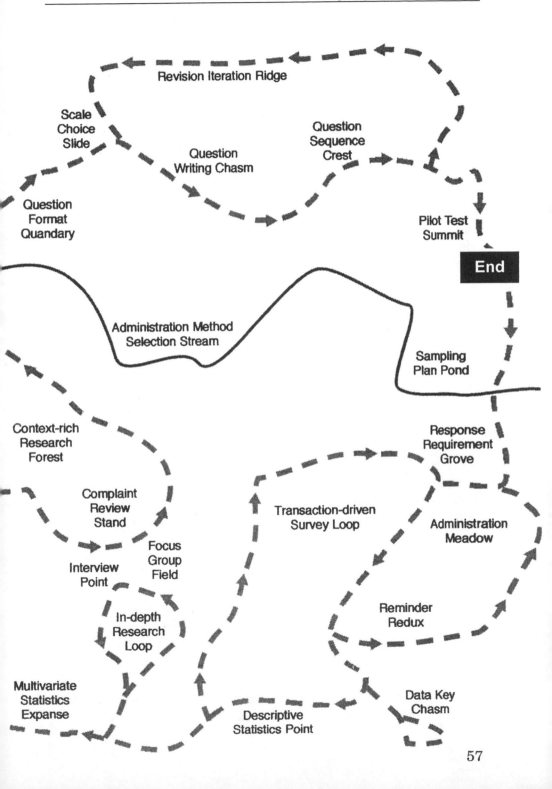

Designing the survey instrument or questionnaire is where many people think a survey project starts. Hopefully, you did not turn straight to this chapter. If you did, please check out Chapter 2, which describes the "threats to validity" caused by a poor questionnaire, before reading any further. You also should not start the questionnaire design process unless you have developed a *Statement of Purpose* for the survey program. (See Chapter 3.)

Identifying the Questions to Ask — Basic Research

Designing a questionnaire is more complex than sitting down and writing a bunch of questions that you think are important. Before you even start to write a single question, you need to uncover what questions you should write. As mentioned before, if you're working from a library of pre-written questions, then the work of writing the individual questions has been done for you. However, you still should follow a rigorous process for developing your instrument, gathering input from different constituencies, determining the attributes for inclusion, and testing the instrument before throwing the switch and sending it out. If you're designing from scratch, then you need the additional focus on the crafting of individual questions.

There are at least two primary constituencies whose input you should solicit in the initial stages of the design process, management and customers. It's to those we first turn our attention.

What are management's concerns and interests? You're reading this book because you're planning to conduct a survey. Most likely someone in the management hierarchy has suggested your organization needs to find out what customers think of your service. Perhaps some complaint calls have made their way to senior management. Clearly, management is willing to fund the survey effort for some reasons. Find out what those reasons are. What you discover may lead to some specific questions for the survey instrument, or may direct the overall tenor of the survey project. For example, if management wants to monitor service quality, then the best means to the desired end is a transaction-driven survey process, as opposed to an annual survey.

Remember that management opinions are not uniform. Different managers will have different concerns. So, talk to all the managers who could be affected by the survey results. But do beware.

The reason for developing a Statement of Purpose in the initial project planning is to have a clear objective for the survey project. This survey should not serve multiple masters! If you throw in a few market research questions along with the operational questions, you could be dooming the entire survey effort.

As discussed elsewhere, all the questions on an instrument must pertain to the respondent who is completing the survey. If the marketing questions are irrelevant to some respondents, they may disregard the entire survey. Or worse, they may complete it with bogus responses. A survey that serves multiple masters will also be long, which will affect response rates.

You may need to interview people in the company beyond management. It's best to interview them separately from their management. The author has interviewed groups where no one spoke other than the manager in the group. Separately, though, the individuals had lots of good ideas and concerns. They just weren't comfortable saying those things in front of management.

What are customers' concerns? Every service manager knows what his customers think, right? That's a natural tendency for managers to have. If absolutely true, then there would be no need to do a survey! Service managers do have a keen understanding of their customers since they interact with them constantly, but customers know customers even better. So, in devising your questionnaire, you must get input from the customer base to be sure that the survey instrument truly asks questions that reflect their concerns.

There are different ways of gathering input from customers, and there are entire books written on each of these methods. The purpose here is to give an overview of two common techniques, personal interviews and focus groups (also known as small group interviews) that are used for this exploratory research. We refer you to the bibliography for specific title recommendations.

Remember that the main purpose of this research may be to help create a questionnaire, but it is also a worthwhile end in itself! Survey data provide high-level information about the customer base as a whole, but data from interviews or focus groups provide detailed, rich information about customer concerns in the service delivery process. These data should be analyzed and included in any management report to complement the survey data. Quotes from customers bring the bland numerical survey data to life. Descriptions of customers' thought processes can be invaluable for improvement projects.

Personal Interviews

Perhaps the most obvious way of gathering input from customers is to talk with them one-on-one. You may speak with customers regularly as part of your job, but for the purposes of the survey questionnaire design effort, you should pursue this piece of research with some structure. (See some of the issues involved in Fig. 4.1.) You might compare this to a candidate's job interview. Neither should be a casual conversation. Devise a set of interview questions that you think will help elicit the concerns customers have with your service and conduct the interview with a purpose in mind.

If you are a hiring manager, you may have heard of an interviewing technique called *behavior-based interviewing*. The idea behind this technique is to get candidates to focus on describing how they have reacted or behaved in specific situations, rather than having them expound theoretical ideas or opinions of how they might conduct themselves. Researchers, both academic and business, commonly use a related technique known as *critical incident studies*. The idea is to get respondents focused on the encounters that truly have defined how they view your organization. These are the critical incidents. We recommend you apply this concept to your interview guide.

In a critical incident study, we ask customers to focus on actual events, recount the chronology of a critical incident, and describe what led them to their conclusions. This technique may get the respondents to recount details that seem trivial to them, but might be crucial to you. As the interviewer, you should push the interviewee to expound in detail and get them to describe their thought processes. (See Exercise 1 for a way to practice this technique. Discussion of the Exercise is in the Appendix.)

When we say "critical," we don't mean "criticize." In fact, the typical critical incident study asks the respondent to describe one positive and one negative incident. Remember, the purpose of customer research is to identify both shortcomings to be corrected *and* strengths to be replicated.

The interview guide will be a great help in ensuring that you get what you need from the interview process, but it should assist you, not shackle you. As distinct from the highly structured questionnaire you'll be devising for the survey, the guide you will be using in the interviews is best described as a *semi-structured questionnaire*. That means that the interviewer has the flexibility to pursue topics as they develop in the flow of discussion. When you conduct the interviews, try to follow the general outline of the interview guide for each interview, but feel free to pursue lines of inquiry when the customer brings up some topic or describes some aspect of your operation.

Also recognize that your initial interviews will likely help you fine-tune your questionnaire — just as these interviews will help you tune the final survey instrument. So, after you conduct each interview, debrief yourself. Think about the questionnaire you used. Should you add some question? Should you alter the sequence of some questions? Did the wording on some questions prove ineffective? Do this debriefing *immediately* after the interview is concluded. If the interview is not taped, then the debriefing must also include the content of the interview. Don't wait. Do it while recollections are fresh!

Figure 4.1
Interviews

✓ *One-on-One Discussion*

Strengths	Issues
— Deep in Context	— How Structured a Questionnaire?
— Explore Unexpected Paths	— How Many Interviewers?
— Paints the Initial Picture	— By Phone or In Person?
	— Length?

Once you have your guide or interview questionnaire in hand, only a few practical decisions remain. These are:

How should notes be taken? The best way to take notes is by automating the process — use a tape recorder. You *must* be open about this with the interviewee. This isn't just a matter of ethics — it may be a legal matter. Don't take a page from Linda Tripp's book of clandestine actions. Taping without consent may well be illegal in your jurisdiction. Tell the interviewee that by taping you can concentrate on the flow of the discussion, which will speed the interview process. (By the way, that's the truth!) Also, tell the interviewee that confidentiality will be preserved.

Address the topic of taping when you set up the appointment, and do that in a voice discussion, *not* as an email exchange, to give

---

Exercise 1
Critical Incident Study and Attribute Identification

Before you conduct interviews or focus groups, you should practice your facilitation technique. Of course, it's much easier to practice a personal interview than a focus group since you only need one person to help out. The skills are similar. Ask a colleague or friend to think about their recent experiences with some service provider, e.g., airlines, and ask them to describe a very positive experience and a very negative experience. Push them to provide more detail and the feelings evoked by the experience.

Now your task is to take those descriptions and identify the attributes of the service experience that were critical to how the customer formed his or her attitudes. Was it the length of time for service to be delivered, the lack of any updates about what was happening, the concern shown for the customer's situation, the willingness to listen? This will take some thinking.

You can also practice these skills without a knowing volunteer. When a colleague or friend complains about – or compliments – something, for example her experience with the support center for her cell phone service provider, listen attentively. Think through the analytical process of identifying the critical attributes.

---

you the chance to allay any concerns. When you start the interview, open with a statement about the topic of the interview and that the interview is being taped, getting the interviewee's verbal consent on tape. If the person is uncomfortable with the taping, then don't do it. Pull out the note pad. If the interview is being done by telephone, you can still tape record if you use a speaker phone or some device that connects to the phone. Otherwise, use a phone with a headset to give you both hands free for note taking. The best notes will be quotes from the interviewee.

How many interviewers should be used? Ideally, only one person should do the interviews. This simplifies the analysis of the data, and it also gives the sole interviewer more freedom to pursue additional lines of inquiry during the interviews. If there are multiple interviewers, then the questionnaire must be followed more tightly.

Who should conduct the interviews? Someone with training as an interviewer should conduct the interviews. Most managers have had training as an interviewer through personnel hiring, so don't sell your capabilities short. This is not rocket science, but it does require a structured, rigorous approach. The person or persons doing these interviews ideally should be the people who will design the survey instrument.

How should the interview sample be generated? In direct contrast to the survey sample, which should be drawn randomly, the sample for interviews should be a *purposive sample.* You should select customers whom you believe will bring out the entire range of issues. You should also be sure to have the most important segments of your customer base reflected in your interview sample. Think about how your customer base breaks down in terms of industry, size, type of service delivered, products supported, etc. Also, do not just pick people whom you know think well of your operation. In fact, you should be certain to select some of your harshest critics. These might be the hardest interviews to conduct, but they could also be the most fruitful. (Interviewing your critics may also be good marketing.)

When you extend the invitation for the interview, be sure to explain in full the purpose behind the interview. Just as with the introduction to the survey instrument, the "introduction" to a request for a research interview is a step that is frequently overlooked.

Where should these interviews be conducted? These interviews are best conducted in person, and they should be done wherever is convenient for the interviewee. Face-to-face interaction is preferable both because interviewees often open up more in direct conversation and because the interviewer can use visual clues to sense when a probing follow-up question is warranted.

The downside of in-person interviews is that using them may introduce a geographic bias to your sample, if your customers are dispersed across the country — unless you can justify a travel budget for this exercise. Of course, you can also conduct telephone interviews. These will likely not be as rich, and they will tend to be shorter just because of the nature of the medium. Do several personal interviews before you do any telephone interviews so that you have your script well developed to make maximum use of the interview time.

How long should these interviews last? The length of the interviews will depend upon the skill of the interviewer and the openness of the interviewee. Most likely, the interview will last for 30 minutes to an hour. Do recognize that some interviewees will be non-responsive. These will be very short — and frustrating — interviews. You, as the interviewer, may feel that you have failed, but there are some people who are just poor interviews.

How many need to be done? "When you stop hearing new things," is the simple answer. Try to do at least a dozen interviews or enough to cover the critical business segments. When you find that no new issues are coming out and the interviews are now confirming what you've already heard, then you'll know you have done enough for the purposes of developing the questionnaire. Don't worry about doing too many. As noted before, such interviews are a worthwhile research effort, independent of their value for development of a survey instrument.

Focus Groups

Focus groups, also known as *small group interviews*, have become a common market research tool in recent decades. While market researchers use focus groups to test out new product ideas, you can use a focus group to generate the issues of concerns held by customers. (See Figure 4.2.)

The concept behind a focus group is to have a *directed discussion* among a small group of people. As the attendees discuss the topic, the dynamic of the interaction may well bring to the surface issues or ideas that would have been missed during personal interviews with the same people. Because you're gathering input from many people at once, focus groups are also more time efficient. If your customers are geographically dispersed but in clusters around major cities, this is also an efficient way to gather face-to-face input.

Focus groups do have their shortcomings. Some people may be intimidated from sharing their true feelings in a group setting, especially if their feelings run contrary to the opinion leaders within the group. In a one-on-one interview these people may be more forthcoming. These concerns may be very real in a focus group to learn consumer reaction to some new product. The concerns are less critical for a business-oriented focus group, but the moderator should still be watchful for the group dynamics.

Focus groups also have cost and scheduling issues. With personal interviews you can go to the interviewee's location or conduct the interview by telephone. With focus groups you're asking a group of people to go to a meeting place for a specific period of time. This obviously presents scheduling issues, and you may need to rent a meeting room at a local hotel. Also, strongly consider providing some incentive or thank you gift for the people to attend. An amount of $50 to $100 is common. Remember, they are customers!

Web-based focus groups are a new research tool that overcomes the geographical issue. With this tool, a "discussion" is held using the internet. It is a threaded discussion much like one would see in a newsgroup — however, it is a restricted discussion. The moderator's job is much different since exchanges aren't happening in real time. Responses are thoughtful, not spontaneous, and the dynamics of a group interaction are greatly diminished. While travel and schedule issues are mitigated, the elapsed time for this type of focus group is much greater, lasting probably one to two weeks.

Figure 4.2
Focus Groups

✓ **A Directed Discussion Among a Selection of Customers**

Strengths	Issues
– Deep in context	– Planning & execution critical
– Explore unexpected paths	– Good moderator critical
– Interaction among participants	– Have one central theme
	– How many to invite?
	– Whom to invite?
	– Time consuming textual analysis

There are six things you need for a focus group: attendees, a moderator, a questionnaire, a means of recording the discussion, a meeting place, and time. These will be addressed while answering a few specific questions.

How many people should be in a focus group? The ideal number of attendees in a focus group is somewhere between seven and 15. Too few and the interaction will be limited — remember, a few people will turn out to be non-responsive. Too many and not everyone will have a chance to participate. As a general rule, it is always best to invite at least 15 people, with the expectation that three to five will cancel. Attending this session may be mission critical to you, but it is not to the attendees. A business issue or personal issue — or bad weather — will easily top your focus group in their priority queue.

The commitment of customers to your business will drive cancellation rates. The author has conducted groups where half the confirmed attendees didn't appear, and others where everyone showed up. I would rather err on the side of having a slightly crowded room than have a room so empty you can hear a pin drop.

Who should be invited? Just as with the personal interviews, the focus group sample is purposive. You want a good cross-section of customers represented. Don't be afraid to include your critics. They will likely provide the most valuable data. If you improve your operations from the survey data so that your critics are pleased, then you have really succeeded and you will likely have created a strong advocate.

If you have dramatically different customer segments, then you may want to hold separate focus groups for each segment. Say you're the service operation for a catalog retailer. You may have both consumer and business clients. Their concerns would likely be very different. Separate focus groups will allow more detailed discussion of concerns specific to the two groups. Consider whether mixing the segments might enrich the discussion or whether the people won't be able to relate to each other.

Who should _not_ be invited? You want a free-ranging discussion among the attendees. Having several members of the project team sit in the session may inhibit the discussion. So, limit the number of "observers" in attendance. This may be particularly true for an internal company survey project, where the attendees will know the observers. In a focus group to design a survey instrument for external customers, observers can also be troublesome. The author ran such a group where the business principals attended. The president engaged the attendees in prolonged discussions. Some incremental information was brought out, but the primary purpose of the session was deflected. So as a general rule, minimize observers, and make sure that observers observe.

What's the role of the moderator? The moderator is _critical_ to the focus group's success. Her role is to ensure that all the important topics are covered, to promote interaction, to guide the discussion, to probe for deeper detail as warranted, and to control the dynamics of the group interaction. A good moderator will help bring out all sides, encourage all members of the group to present their ideas, and control an overbearing opinion leader. It's also very important for the moderator to control the group so that one person speaks at a time. Otherwise, the tape recording will be unintelligible. (The author has learned that the hard way!)

Finding the right moderator can be tricky. Although it is not difficult to find individuals for hire who have group management skills and specialized expertise in conducting focus groups, those specialists may not be knowledgeable about the service industry or service issues. Without knowledge of the general business area, the moderator may lose credibility with the group. Also, if the moderator knows the field, then he can ask better, more probing, follow-up questions. Just as with a training instructor, the ideal moderator is one with deep knowledge of the field and the right "platform skills."

What type of questionnaire should be used? As with personal interviews, the questionnaire for a focus group session should be semi-structured. Know the points that you want to cover and develop questions to elicit those responses. There are various techniques for prompting discussion, such as sentence completion and projective comparisons. The critical incident technique discussed above is very appropriate for focus groups. There are many books that cover these techniques, but perhaps the best way of getting to the details of the core issues is to be like a three-year-old child — keep asking, "Why?" You'll find you're peeling back the layers and eventually you will uncover the fundamental reason why something is important to the respondent. If you hire a moderator, meet with him well in advance to discuss the questionnaire and to develop a strategy for the session.

> The ideal focus group moderator is one with deep knowledge of the field and the right "platform skills."

Where should focus group sessions be held and how should the discussion be captured? Focus group research has achieved high science because of its extensive use to research new product concepts. Dedicated rooms have been created to conduct these sessions. These "laboratories," which are equipped with video taping setups and one-way mirrors, resemble usability labs used by software firms. (IBM recently had a television ad set in a focus group facility.) For our purposes in developing a customer survey questionnaire, using these facilities may be overkill. In fact, some people find the one-way mirrors intimidating. Low tech can be better.

Much of the same value can be reaped with a less sophisticated setup. A good, comfortable conference room in your facility will work well, but do consider renting a meeting room at a hotel if you feel that some customers will be uncomfortable providing negative feedback in your domain. This expense is small and could be important. Have name cards or "name tents" for each attendee. This gives an air of formality to the proceedings and will help the strangers interact. It also allows the moderator to address people by name increasing rapport. Plus, capturing the speakers' names on the tape recording can be valuable for following the progression of one person's comments.

An audio tape should capture all the data you really need. As with the personal interview, discuss taping the session at the outset of the session. Most people will not mind being taped, and after five minutes when engaged in discussion, they will forget the recorder is even on. To open the session, have all the participants introduce themselves. That way you will be able to identify who is speaking later when listening to the tape.

Be prepared to turn the tape recorder off. If the discussion runs hot, and attendees start "naming names," the tape may inhibit their willingness to be candid. Someone may say, "If the tape weren't running, I'd..." or they may look at the tape recorder while talking. Without asking, grab the recorder and offer to turn it off. Later, look for nods of acquiescence that it's okay to turn the recorder back on.

Practice beforehand where best to place the recorder. If the conference room is small, this is no problem. If you're in a larger room, distant people's comments may not be captured. You may need a microphone extension, but the recorder must be within reach in order to switch tapes.

Background noise can also be a problem for the dynamics of the group and for the tape recording. A client once had the author conduct an evening focus group in a lounge area of the client's facility — purportedly because they wanted attendees to see the new facility. The setting was awkward and too informal. Discussion was stilted. Plus, the motors of the nearby vending machines drowned out the comments of folks in the back of the room in real life — and on the tape.

How many focus groups should be conducted? As with interviews, you will know you've done enough when you hear no new issues arise. This is exploratory research. When you find you're confirming issues already uncovered rather exploring new issues, your task is complete. Two to three focus groups should be sufficient for the purposes of developing a customer survey instrument, more if you have multiple customer segments. Again, this is valuable research in addition to identifying attributes to include in the instrument.

How long should the sessions last? This depends on the topic. Focus groups typically last for two hours. Three hours may be necessary to let the discussion truly run its course. Mornings are better than afternoons because there is less chance that invitees will get caught up in a business issue at the office and have to cancel, but evenings are preferable if attendees cannot justify this as part of their work day. Obviously, for a meeting of this length you should provide some refreshments. Consider serving a light snack or lunch. This is part of the "thank you." Food is a cheap way to build rapport.

Having read this section, you might well be saying to yourself, "I've been conducting focus groups for years. I just didn't use that fancy name." The author made that statement years ago when formally studying research methodologies. In my days at Digital Equipment Corporation, I had conducted numerous small group interviews with field managers to develop management reporting systems. This is not rocket science. The logistical details simply need to be planned properly, and a moderator must be found who can truly facilitate a good discussion.

Documentary Data

Interviews and focus groups provide a first-hand, immediate sensing of the customer base, but there are other data sources about customer concerns that you can tap. One good source is customer complaint data. Customer complaints clearly are critical incidents, so review those files. Consider calling those people for interviews. If your organization does not actively solicit customer complaints — and compliments — it should consider doing so as part of a customer loyalty program. Your organization may conduct some informal or less refined form of surveying. For example, there may be customer comment cards soliciting open-ended responses. All of these can serve as fodder for exploratory research, identifying issues of concern for the survey instrument design process.

Analyzing the Data

Now that you've gathered all this rich, contextual data, you have to make sense of it. You may despair a bit, feeling overwhelmed. As you listen to the tape recordings from the interviews of focus groups, look for recurring themes. (Chapter 6 discusses analyzing textual data in more detail.) Organize the comments you hear under those themes. Also, look for relationships across the themes. Analyzing textual data is frequently termed a "distillation process." You're boiling down all this watery text into a rich paste.

Drafting the Questionnaire

Paradoxically, the best place to start drafting the questionnaire instrument may be at the end! Not the end of the questionnaire, but the end product of the survey project: the final report. Obviously, you cannot write the content of the report, but you can draft the format of the report. What kind of graphs and data tables would you include? What data would you envision contrasting against other data? Along what dimensions will you segment the data? What types of actions might you recommend?

This exercise, sometimes called developing an "end-state vision," will force you to think about the information you hope to communicate with the survey research. This in turn will define the kind of data you need to collect and the questions you need to ask. As you're performing this exercise, review the Statement of Purpose for the research project. Do they align? If not, rethink them both, because they should align.

A recurring theme in this book is that writing a good questionnaire is more involved than the novice may at first expect. One of the key mistakes novices will make is believing that they can write an instrument in one sitting. A survey instrument — or any questionnaire used to guide a research project — needs to be attacked in stages. Writing the questionnaire is truly an iterative process for which you should budget several weeks.

Let's draw an analogy to a report being sent to senior management. You would likely want to pass through several read-and-refine iterations before delivering it to the person who controls your professional future. You should be just as concerned about putting a document or questionnaire before your customers.

In drafting the questionnaire, the stages you should follow are:

1. **Organize your essential findings.** Write down the issues and attributes that you found important from the interviews, focus groups, meetings with management, and other initial research. (This may be an outcome of that previous research.) Group them into logical blocks. You may find the five service quality dimensions to be a good framework here. (See Figure 4.3.) These quality dimensions were developed by academic researchers in an extensive study.

Figure 4.3
Service Quality Dimensions

The specific questions you'll want to ask on your survey are best determined by the needs, concerns, and issues of your customer base. However, there are themes that transcend across surveys. The five Service Quality Dimensions are a potential organizing theme.

1. **Reliability** – Delivering on promises, e.g., speed and accuracy of problem resolution

2. **Responsiveness** – Being willing to help, e.g., time on hold, speed of response by technician

3. **Assurance** – Inspiring trust and confidence
   - *Competency:* technical knowledge of support agent
   - *Courtesy:* politeness of the support agent
   - *Credibility:* belief that the support agent is being forthright

4. **Empathy** – Treating customers as individuals
   - *Communication skills:* ability to communicate nature of repair work performed
   - *Understanding the customer:* willingness to get to know customer's work environment

5. **Tangibles** – Representing the service physically e.g., providing verification of resolutions

Sources: Zeithaml, Valarie A., Leonard L. Berry, and A. Parasuraman, *"Communication and Control Processes in the Delivery of Service Quality,"* Journal of Marketing, Vol. 52 (April 1988), pp. 35-48.

Zeithaml, Valarie A., A. Parasuraman, and Leonard L. Berry, *Delivering Quality Service,* New York: The Free Press, 1990.

Try doing this exercise in a conference room on the white board or using post-it notes so that you can move the issues around easily. Don't be surprised if some issues seem to belong to multiple blocks. This may cause you to rethink the dimensions you are using to group the issues. You may also have two sets of dimensions. For example, one dimension set may follow the chronology of a service delivery event (i.e., logging the request, initial response, service delivery, call escalation, etc.), and the second dimension set may follow the service quality dimensions.

2. **Consider the three basic types of questions.** On most surveys, you'll be asking three different types of questions. First, the heart of the survey will contain questions measuring customer perceptions of your organization's performance for the various service delivery *attributes* (See Figure 4.4). These attributes were identified through the interviews and focus groups. Second, you will most likely want to analyze the answers to these questions along some *demographic* variables, such as customer type, department, product type, user expertise, etc. If you have these data in your customer records and the survey is not anonymous, don't waste the space asking the question. Third, you will undoubtedly want some overall measure of the customer's *attitude* toward your service operation. We mentioned this in the opening chapter. These summary attitudinal measures will be the first data reported in the executive summary, and they serve an important role in advanced statistical analysis.

3. **Select question format(s).** Decide the format for the questions you want to use. If you're going to ask for responses on a scale, decide on the scale type or types. (You should limit the number of different scale types since multiple scale types will confuse the respondent.) You may find you will change your mind about the scale type as you develop the questions, but it's good to consider the scale type now. This forces you to write the questions to fit the scale.

4. **Draft some questions.** This may well prove more taxing than you think as you stumble over phrasing.

5. **Take a break.** Put the questionnaire draft down and go back to doing other work! Come back to the questionnaire in a day or two when your mind is fresh.

6. **Repeat steps three and four.** Refining the instrument is an iterative process. Like writing a good report, each time you read

it, you will find places to improve. Look for ambiguous wording. Challenge yourself about whether the concept expressed in the question will be clear to others. It's crystal clear to you, of course! Review the list of common mistakes in questionnaire design in Chapter 2 and look for those kinds of flaws.

7. **Seek other input.** At some point you will say, "Good enough!"— or "I've had enough!" That means it is time to get someone else's input. Get other members of your project team to review the questionnaire. Schedule a meeting with the project team to go over it at a macro and micro level. Ask yourselves whether the questionnaire meets the objectives of the survey research project, and whether the original objectives were correct. In the process of doing the initial research and drafting the questionnaire, some new ideas may well have surfaced.

Figure 4.4
Examples of Attributes of a Service Delivery Experience Within Service Quality Dimensions

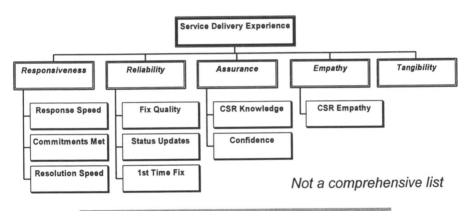

Not a comprehensive list

You may also consider asking some professional colleagues from outside your company — or just plain friends — to read the questionnaire. They will have an eye for jargon or company-specific phrasing that the project team might miss.

8. **Repeat steps three to seven as necessary.**
9. **Pilot test your draft questionnaire with a representative sample of customers.** This is a *critical stage* in the process, so we will come back to it when we finish discussing the mechanics of questionnaire design.

Elements of a Questionnaire

A questionnaire has several components. If you are using survey automation software, the software will have some inherent process that will guide you through each of these elements — hopefully. Each element serves a purpose, but their combined purposes are 1) to increase the likelihood the respondent will complete the survey, and 2) to get the questionnaire completed correctly. Those elements are: an introduction, instructions, initial questions, sections and their headings, summary, and a thank you.

Introduction

The survey questionnaire should open with an introduction. Ideally, this should be personally addressed to the respondent, so a mail merge program is useful. If this is a hardcopy survey, and you want the person to be able to respond anonymously, then put this introduction on a separate page from the instrument. The introduction should reinforce and replicate the message of an introductory note from a senior manager, which the respondent group should have received a couple of weeks in advance of the survey itself — more about this in the next chapter. The main point of both is to explain the purpose of the survey and convey its importance.

Don't underestimate the importance of the introduction in motivating the respondent! In the author's college classes students frequently have to perform survey research, and their introductions are typically very laconic: "Please answer the following questions." The motivational content of that statement is rather slim.

The mechanics of the introduction differ based on the administration method. In a telephone survey, the introduction is the opening of the interview script. (See Figure 4.5.) The motivational message must be concise and clear for a telephone survey. The introductory script must also state who should be completing the survey and ask if the interviewee feels if someone else would be better suited to answer the questionnaire. The interviewer must also ask if this is a good time to conduct the interview, and if not, when should the interviewer call back.

For a hardcopy survey, the survey introduction most likely should be a separate page, but in a transaction-driven survey it may be just a paragraph at the top of the instrument. Use a separate page if putting the introduction with the survey gives it a cramped formatting. For email and web surveys, where the link to the survey web form is sent by email, the elements of the introduction are

Figure 4.5
Sample Telephone Script

Good morning/afternoon. My name is <name> and I'm <title>.

We have been contracted by <company name> to survey its customers about problem escalation services. The goal of this survey is to understand your expectations and experiences when you have a software failure needing escalation.

The survey should take about 10 to 15 minutes to complete. Is this a convenient time?

<If not> When would be a convenient time for me to call back? Could I fax or email you a copy of the survey questionnaire to simplify the surveying when we do talk?

The questions on this survey focus on the escalation process for a software problem and just to be clear about terminology, let me outline the support process.

After a customer reports a problem, the first step is for the front-line field support persons to attempt a restoration of service. If the problem cannot be resolved, then the escalation process to Engineering begins with the delivery of some work-around to provide initial relief. The next step is the creation and delivery of a temporary patch with a short-term code fix. Next, a permanent patch, which has been fully tested in the customer environment is delivered. This leads to the final step of call closure when the customer agrees that the problem has been resolved.

For each stage of the escalation process, I'll ask you for free-form answers about your expectations. Then I'll ask you to rate your experiences on a five-point scale that ranges from minus 2 to plus 2, where plus 2 represents Greatly Exceed Expectations and minus 2 represents Greatly Below Expectations.

Notice the difficulty in setting the respondent's mental frame for a complicated service delivery process. Without that description, the respondent might respond incorrectly. But is it too long? How would you shorten it? Survey design is full of trade-offs – and here's one!

virtually the same as for a postal survey, just reinterpreted for an electronic format. (See Figure 4.6.)

In addition to the motivational aspects of the introduction, the following points need to be addressed.

1. **State who should complete the survey.** This is very important. The exact purpose of the survey will dictate what person in the respondent company should complete the survey, yet your customer database may not properly target the respondent group. Be sure to ask that the survey be passed onto the appropriate person if necessary.

2. **State the expected time to complete the survey.** Set the respondent's expectations for how long the survey should take to complete by saying how many questions are in the survey. This is important for a multiple screen web-form survey.

3. **Emphasize anonymity, if appropriate.** If you are allowing the respondent to remain anonymous, then make that statement. Of course, if you have personally addressed the introductory note, then it must be on a page separate from the instrument.

Figure 4.6
Sample Introduction for Web-Form Survey Instrument

Dear Acme Manufacturing Employee,

As we wrote you in a recent email, the Information Technology Group (ITG) is instituting an annual survey of its user community. The purpose is to identify areas in which we can better serve your computing technology needs. We will make the results available to the Acme community through a future electronic newsletter.

The survey contains about 40 questions and should take about 15 minutes to complete. To access the survey, please visit http://www.acmemanufacturing.pb.tu and follow the instructions there. We will be initiating improvement projects next month, so please complete the survey by Friday, May 19th.

For each completed survey we receive, ITG will make a donation to the charity you indicate at the end of the survey. We value your honest and forthright feedback. Be assured that your responses will be anonymous.

Thank you for your time and interest in helping us serve you better.

---

4. **What to do with the completed questionnaire.** For a postal mail survey you **must** include a self-addressed stamped envelope. This serves a vital purpose. It increases the response rate from the group that is least motivated, that is, those people who do not hold extreme views about your service.

5. **When to do the survey.** The answer to this is obvious from your perspective: as soon as possible. But the necessity of this will be less apparent to the recipients. Pick a date slightly less than a week from when you expect they will get the survey and request (nicely) that they complete the survey by then. Explain that you want it back quickly, so that you can begin to take action on the data to improve the service they receive. The idea is to get them to do the survey now while they have it in their hands. Once it is in the "to do" pile, all bets are off about when — or if — it will get done.

6. **Definition of certain terminology.** You might want to define some otherwise ambiguous terms in the introduction. For example, you may want to use the term *service representative* to describe any person with whom the customer interacts. Notice in Figure 4.6, the introduction defines *computing environment*. Imagine writing questions without that up-front definition. By including definitions in the introduction, you've reduced the possibility of multiple interpretations, and you've allowed writing more concise questions without embedded definitions. Keep this list short, though. We want to get the respondent engaged in taking the survey as soon as possible.

Instructions

After the introduction, instructions will then precede the survey questions. (See Figure 4.7.) The respondent must be told two points.

1. **How to enter answers.** While it may seem silly, tell the person to circle the number, check the appropriate boxes, or click on the radio button.[1] You would be amazed at how inventive people are in creating their own instructions if left to their own devices. You may think you are insulting the respondent's intelligence, but it's better to err on the side of over-instructing. For proof of the need for good instructions, we only need look at the infamous "butterfly ballot" used in Florida in the 2000 election.

   If a series of questions use the same scale type, then instruc-

---

[1] A *radio button* is a term used in web form design. It is a small white circle. By clicking your mouse on it, the circle darkens indicating you have selected the corresponding option.

Figure 4.7
Sample Survey Instructions
(web survey form example for an internal help desk)

The purpose of this survey is to identify areas in which ITG can serve you better. Remember that your responses should reflect your perception of the service delivered to you by ITG. Please exclude your experiences with service delivered by outside technology vendors.

The survey uses the phrases "computing environment" or "computing technology" to refer to the hardware and software that you use to perform your information processing and knowledge tasks.

For each question consider your perception of ITG's performance over the past three months. Many of the questions ask for you to compare these perceptions to your expectations. Please respond by selecting the appropriate number on a scale that ranges from -3 to +3 where -3 means that performance fell well short of expectations, +3 means that expectations were greatly exceeded. Choose 0 if your expectations were just barely met.

When you finish the survey, click the SUBMIT button.

---

tions for this scale probably only need to be stated once, but if you change scale types, then you need to include instructions each time the question format changes. For multiple choice question formats, always state whether the respondent is to select one answer or all that apply. Forced ranking and fixed sum question formats are particularly prone to errors in entering a response, so include clear instructions. More on these later.

For email surveys done in ASCII text with survey automation software, instructions on how to complete the survey are critical. These software packages use special characters to indicate the respondent's answer when processing the response. The software should include examples of the proper instructions. For a web-form survey, survey software may provide some data entry controls to prevent an incorrect entry, but controls without explanations will just anger the respondent and cause him to quit the survey.

2. **How the scale works.** If you are using one scale predominantly throughout the survey, then explain the scale at the start of the instrument. *For a telephone survey this step is especially critical,* and the interviewer should remind the respondent about the scale occasionally throughout the interview. Instructions are critical to getting the data you want. Respondents will have a tendency to rate things on the high side of interval scales, especially the importance of different attributes of service. Your task in writing the instructions is to tell the respondent what should lead them to choose a particular answer. If you are interested in the relative scores across a set of questions, then tell them that you will be using the results for that purpose.

Initial Questions

Now we come to the heart of the survey — asking questions. Pay particular attention to the initial questions. The first question or questions are very important because here you are delivering on the promise set out in the introduction and in any announcement letter. These questions should get the respondents thinking about the subject matter, engage them, and make them want to move ahead through the survey. Open with relatively easy questions to answer. Don't open with some very complex question structure since the respondent may feel completing the survey is not worth the apparent effort. Never open with demographic questions. They are invasive and don't engage the respondent.

Section Headings

Longer surveys should be created with distinct sections. For example, one section of a survey may ask for input about current service levels, while a second section may ask the respondents to prioritize future initiatives. When you transition from one section to another, you should include a brief statement to reset the mental frame. These section headings should be two to three lines at most. The idea is to pace the respondents through the survey and not let them get lost. Respondents feel a sense of accomplishment when they finish a section. Thus, a 45-question instrument with three, 15-question sections will seem shorter than a 45-question survey with no sections.

Summary and Thank You

At the end of the survey, don't forget to thank the respondent. You might also remind them of what to do with the completed questionnaire. If you are using a survey automation tool, it may have a feature to send a thank you note automatically once the "submit" button has been hit. Be brief and to the point, but appreciative.

Sequencing Questions

Your instrument should be designed to meet a limited set of objectives. In the introduction you told the respondents what you want from them. How you sequence the questions will reinforce and maintain that mental frame. In customer service, the concentration of our surveying is upon customers' reactions to events or transactions, asking their perceptions of service performance. Thus, our survey instruments will likely be addressing the various aspects of a service transaction. The questions should probably be sequenced to walk the respondent through a service transaction. To do otherwise might confuse the respondent, and that's exactly what should be avoided.

Beyond that general rule, there are a few other issues to keep in mind as you sequence your questionnaire:

♦ **From general to specific.** Earlier we mentioned that the initial questions should engage the respondent and get the respondent thinking. These questions should be fairly general, and then you can move to more specific questions in the heart of the instrument.

♦ **Demographic questions.** Here's how *not* to start a questionnaire. Don't ever lead off with demographic questions, that is, questions about the respondent's job title, responsibilities, salary, the company's products, or the like. Demographic questions will likely be used for segmenting the survey data in the analysis phase, but these questions won't engage the respondent. They do exactly the opposite. They set up a mental wall because they appear to be prying. This will hurt the response rate and lessen the likelihood of forthright answers, especially in any open-ended questions. They should be placed at the end of the survey when you have gained the respondent's confidence, and they should be kept as brief as possible. Don't ask questions whose data you don't need. If the survey is not anonymous, be sure not to ask questions the respondent thinks you should know from your customer records. So, why do novice survey designers typically put demographic questions first? It's because they're the easiest questions to write.

♦ **Question interaction.** The potential exists for one question to bias the way the respondent thinks about subsequent questions, especially the very next one. The topic of one question may make some aspect more salient to the respondent than it truly is. The respondent will think subconsciously, "This must be important, otherwise, why would they ask it?"

Be particularly aware of question interaction for questions about the service agent. Respondents may be reluctant to give negative feedback about service agents, especially if they believe the fault lies with the service delivery system and not with the people. Suppose you ask about the time to respond to your service request, which is a reflection on the system and not on the agent, and the respondent feels the response time was poor. If the next question is about the service agent's technical competence, dedication, or courtesy, the respondent may then overcompensate for those questions. Consider leading with a question that will likely get positive response, e.g., courtesy, or using section headings that set the respondent's mental set properly.

Sometimes, you may ask a series of related questions where constructs or attributes may overlap in the respondent's mind. This is particularly important in a telephone survey where the questions are presented in a strict linear fashion. On a hardcopy or web-form survey, the respondent can consider several questions at once or go back and change an answer. Not so for a telephone survey. Start with one that is likely to be the broadest, then go to more specific. For example, the *clarity of an explanation* and the *satisfaction with a resolution* are somewhat related. If presented in that order, someone unhappy with a *resolution* may give a more negative answer to the *explanation* question because they don't know that the *resolution* question will be asked. Asking *resolution* first may allow a more objective answer to the *explanation* question.

Rotating questions is a technique that corrects for the bias that may be introduced by question interactions. Here, the order of questions within groups will be changed randomly, which averages out the question-interaction effects. This can most easily be accomplished in telephone and web-form surveys if some software program is automating the scripts. For other types of administration methods, variations of the instrument must be created. This introduces the potential for mis-keying the responses.

One very common instance of question interaction occurs when a survey instrument asks about satisfaction with some service attribute and follows that immediately with a question

81

about the importance of the attribute. If someone is very displeased with the service quality for some attribute, the importance of that attribute is temporarily magnified. Furthermore, many respondents know what you plan to do with that data, that is, compare the importance to the satisfaction in a *gap analysis*. Some respondents may consciously overstate the importance to "send a message" about the intensity of their displeasure. Importance is better measured through statistical analysis of performance ratings and overall satisfaction. Chapter 6 addresses this technique.

◆ **Branching.** Many times you may want only certain respondents to answer some questions, based upon some qualifications. For example, you would not want people to answer questions about the quality of training programs if they have never taken one, although you would still want to get their impressions of the comprehensiveness of program offerings. One technique to handle this situation is to have a *not applicable* (N/A) option for a response. If a respondent is constantly checking N/A, however, the likelihood of completing the survey diminishes.

A better technique is to have *branching,* sometimes called *conditional branching* or *skip and hit*. With branching, a respondent is only posed certain questions if the answer to some other question meets certain conditions. In many cases that conditional question is used only to qualify the respondent for a set of questions. For example, whether the respondent has taken any training courses would qualify them to have questions posed about the training courses. Typically, this question is a binary, Yes/No question, but branching could be driven by a multiple choice or ordinal ranking question. For example, an ordinal question listing choices for the number of courses taken could have each choice lead to a different branch.

Branching may also lead to an open-ended question driven by the response to an interval-scaled question. For example, a score of 2 or lower on a 1-to-5 scale could prompt an open-ended question asking for an explanation. This is a way of generating detailed data on a selected basis.

How to implement branching depends upon the administration technique. On a hardcopy survey, specific instructions must be presented. For example, "If your answer to question 7 is 'no,' then please skip to Question 11." Guiding arrows are useful when formatting the questionnaire. When the data are compiled, the analyst should also verify that respondents did not incorrectly answer those questions. As a rule, if the respondent has to figure out how to follow the branch, then keep the number of branching questions to an absolute minimum.

Implementing branching is simplest with telephone surveys since the interviewer controls the presentation of questions. Use of computer aided telephone interviewing (CATI) software is necessary if there are many branches. Without CATI, an interviewer could easily get confused. For an email or web-form survey, instructions similar to a hardcopy survey should be given. Some survey software tools support transparent branching on web-form surveys. With these tools, responses are processed as web-form screens are submitted, and no instructions are necessary. However, a screen submittal must occur prior to every branch. Too many screen submittals may annoy the respondent because they have to wait for the background processing to occur and the new screen to be downloaded.

◆ **Placing of the summary attitudinal questions.** Every customer satisfaction questionnaire will pose at least one question that solicits the customer's overall satisfaction. This is an important question because it provides a summary number, and the response serves as the dependent variable in regression analysis. (See Chapter 6.) But where should the question be placed, before or after you ask specific questions about performance attributes? Here are the arguments. *Ask it before* because then the response is not biased by the performance questions that will follow. *Ask it after* because the respondent's thinking has been stimulated more fully. There is no clear answer. This is an ongoing debate.

One solution is to ask two related but different overall satisfaction questions, placing one early in the questionnaire and one later. One question might ask overall satisfaction directly while the other might ask future purchase likelihood or service quality compared to the past. If you have an experimenter's spirit, you might alternate the placement, and see if there is a difference in the response.

Question Formats

There are two major question formats: unstructured and structured. The structured format can be further divided into categorical or multiple choice, ordinal scales, interval-rating scales, and ratio scales. (See Figure 4.8) Under each of these formats there are many question types. Each question format and type will be addressed, but first we have to take a brief diversion into the issue of *data types*. Each question format will generate a different type of data, and what you can do, mathematically, with the survey data depends upon the data type. This also determines how you can present the data in charts.

Data Types

Many people might think that "data are data," but in fact there are five different types of data. Notice that the analytical capabilities increase as we move through the list. (See Figure 6.3.) The analysis of each data type is covered more fully in Chapter 6.

1. **Textual Data.** We may not think of text as data, but it really is. It may well be the richest type of data because it can express relationships, details, and nuances, but it is also the messiest type of data from an analytical point of view. Analyzing textual data is addressed elsewhere in this guide, but the obvious statement to make here is that text cannot be manipulated mathematically without first sorting, filtering, and categorizing it. We can then develop *frequency distributions*, but this is time consuming.

> Don't lead off with demographic questions, that is, questions about the respondent's job title, responsibilities, salary, the company's products.

2. **Categorical or Nominal Data.** Nominal data is what results from categorizing textual data. It is also the type of data derived from multiple choice or categorical questions. When we ask a question such as, "Which of the following services have you consumed in the past month?" with a list from which the respondent selects, the response generates *nominal data*. The respondent either has or has not consumed each of the service types presented. There is no relationship identified among the response choices. With nominal data we can only calculate frequency distributions, that is, relating what percentage of respondents chose each item. When we segment our respondent group by customer type, product type, or some other demographic characteristic, typically, nominal data are generated.

3. **Ordinal Data.** Let's change the question used above. Say we asked, "Please rank the services you consumed by the value you received, placing a 1 next to the most valuable, a 2 next to

second most valuable, and so on." We no longer have nominal data since we know something about the relationship among the response choices. We have a *ranked order* along the dimension of "value received." This added information conveys more meaning, slightly extending the analysis we can apply to *ordinal data*. Again, we can calculate frequency distributions showing the percentage of times a certain service type was rated first, second, and so on. But because we have an ordered list, we can also calculate *cumulative frequency distributions*. That is, you can display the percentage of respondents who chose the first or the second most highly ranked services. You might be tempted to take a weighted average of the scores to develop a summary

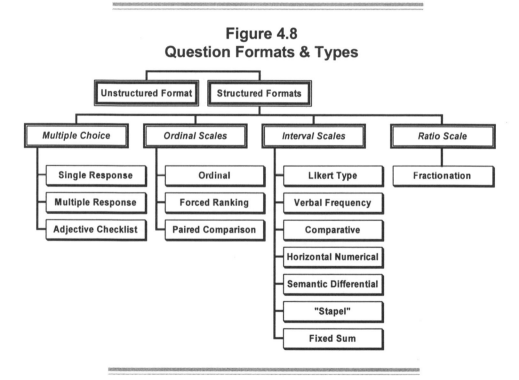

Figure 4.8
Question Formats & Types

score for each service, but in doing so, you are making an unjustified leap of faith that the data are interval data.

4. **Interval Data.** Again, let's change the question. "Please rate the value you received for each service you consumed on a scale of 1 to 5." If the question is properly constructed with good anchors, then we can reasonably assume that the difference be-

tween a rating of 5 versus 4 is the same difference as between a 4 versus 3, 3 versus 2, and 2 versus 1. In other words, the intervals between each rating point are the same, yielding *interval data*. We can calculate frequency distributions and cumulative frequency distributions, but now we can legitimately take *averages* of the data. We can also add and subtract interval data.

The distinction between ordinal and interval data is crucial to the analysis that can be performed upon the data. Frequently, the interval assumption is compromised due to the construction of the question. Say we asked respondents to tell us whether the value of each service was *Poor, Fair, Good, Very Good*, or *Excellent*. Are the data from this question nominal, ordinal, or interval? The data are definitely nominal, and since the response choices display a clear ranked preference, we will have ordinal data. But can we assert that the difference between *Poor* and *Fair* is the same as between *Fair* and *Good*? Research shows that those are not equal intervals, so we would not have interval data. Mathematically, it would not be legitimate to assign 1 to 5 numbers for those choices and take averages. You will see this done frequently. It is wrong to do so! There are other design decisions that can compromise interval properties, such as how the response choices are visually displayed. We will cover these later.

5. **Ratio Data**. Let's assume the data from the 1-to-5 scale meet the interval requirements. If the survey responses found the average value of one service was 4.2 and another service's value averaged 2.1, could we say that the former service was twice as valuable as the latter? Hopefully, you have said "no." We can only perform that type of analysis upon *ratio data*. Ratio data have *true zero points*. For example, a salary of $42,000 is truly twice $21,000 — ignoring taxes, of course. We can make this analysis because salaries have a true zero point. With ratio data we can multiply and divide the data. Questions about time on hold, number of service requests, and hours of training could also generate ratio data depending upon how the questions are constructed.

Understanding the nature of data types is important as we construct an instrument and consider the analysis we intend to do upon the data collected. The advantages and disadvantages of each question type are discussed in the next section along with issues in question construction. In customer satisfaction surveys, typically we solicit perceptions on scales and thus generate interval data. We may also have questions that generate the other data types with ratio data being the most uncommon. Let's restate the caveat about interval data: *a poorly designed interval question will unknowingly result in ordinal data, and averages taken of that data will be suspect.*

You may think that interval data are superior to ranking data because we can take averages. But what if you wanted to know the importance of various attributes of service delivery. If you ask respondents to **rank order** the attributes, they cannot equivocate. One will be ranked first, another second, and so on — if the question is completed correctly. Clear rankings will be generated. That would not necessarily be the case if you asked respondents to **rate** the importance of each attribute. Respondents could give every attribute the highest rating. How would you take action on that data? This is not a theoretical question. Respondents will typically show little dispersion of responses when asked about the importance of service delivery attributes. Ranking may provide more meaningful information. Another method of handling the response dispersion issue is with the fixed-sum question format described later.

Unstructured Question Format

Unstructured questions, also known as open-ended, free-form, or "verbatims,"[2] are used when we want an unconstrained answer from the respondent. These are useful at the end of the survey and at points in the body of the survey where you want more complete information. But don't overuse them. Unstructured questions increase the work, both for the respondent — called *respondent burden* — and for the poor analyst who has to make sense out of the textual responses. The time necessary to complete open-ended questions may even lead respondents to abandon the survey.

Tip: If you feel you have to use a lot of open-ended questions, then you're not ready to do a broad-based survey! You probably need to do some basic research through focus groups and interviews. The author once received a four-page survey from a professional organization that had eleven open-ended questions! Worse yet, many of the open-ended questions were redundant.

You may be perplexed. We've said that text is the richest form of data, providing the details necessary to develop improvement projects, but here we are saying to use them only minimally. Survey instrument

---

[2] This is undoubtedly one of the most egregious examples of new word creation spawned by business-speak!

design is replete with trade-offs, and this is one of them. Use open-ended questions judiciously, especially in the body of the instrument.

One technique for judicious use of open-ended questions is to pose them after certain structured questions about key performance attributes, but do it on a conditional-branching basis for each respondent. (See the previous discussion on branching.) This is a key advantage of telephone surveys and web-form surveys where responses are processed as submitted and the flow of the questionnaire is controlled by the surveyor. For example, if a respondent gives a very low rating on a performance question, then an open-ended question can be posed to understand why.[3] For other survey methods, this technique isn't viable. Instead, consider posing an open-ended question after a block of structured questions and ask respondents to clarify or expand on previous answers if they wish. Note the compromise between generating rich textual data and respondent burden.

Structured Question Formats

Structured questions are ones where the response is solicited along some predetermined lines. There are four types of structured questions, and you will notice that they correspond to the data types just described.

- ♦ Multiple Choice or Categorical
- ♦ Ordinal Scales
- ♦ Interval Ratings Scales
- ♦ Ratio Scales

Because structured question formats generate *coded data*, rather than text, they have distinct advantages. They are quicker for the respondent to complete, and the data are much easier to analyze. On the downside, though, structured questions do restrict the response, especially for multiple choice questions. If the respondent has a legitimate response other than those presented, this information will be lost. Also, the way the choices are presented can bias the respondent. It is for these reasons that a proper design of structured questions is so critical.

---

[3] In a recent presentation on the topic, a person in the audience said he had experienced this type of branching on a web-form survey. A new pop-up window would open with the open-ended question. He found this annoying, and recognized what response score would lead to the pop-up box, for example a 4 or below on a 1-to-10 scale. He then changed the way he answered to avoid the pop-up box! Beware of unintended consequences!

Multiple Choice or Categorical

In a multiple choice question format, the respondent is given a list of items and is asked to choose either the one answer that best applies or all the choices that apply, depending upon the situation. Questions using this format generate nominal (or categorical) data. For example, they provide data to segment the respondent base. You might ask the respondent's job title, company size, or frequency of requesting service by giving the respondent a list of options from which to select. Remember, you can only calculate frequency distributions from this type of data.

Note that some of the items just listed could be asked in a fill-in-the-blank format. However, it is easier and less error prone for the respondent to check a box than to write in an answer. Remember respondent burden!

There are a few variations of the multiple-choice format:

Multiple Choice, Multiple Response. Just as the name implies, the respondent is asked to select all the response choices that are appropriate. Recognize that the sum of selected choices across all responses will be greater than the number of responses. Summing the percentage that select each option will be greater than 100%.

Multiple Choice, Single Response. Just as the name implies, the respondent is asked to select the one most appropriate response. Be sure that the question and instructions are worded to direct the respondent to select the most appropriate response, not just any response that might apply.

Binary Choice. This is the Multiple Choice, Single Response format with only two choices. Typically, these choices are *yes, no* or *true, false*.

Adjective Checklist. This is a variation of the Multiple Choice, Multiple Response where the choices presented are adjectives. (See Figure 4.9.) This format is useful when you want to know how the respondent perceives a product or service or the image of an organization.

There are several *critical design considerations* when writing multiple choice questions. These are:

◆ **Range of choices in response sets.** The choices offered should cover the entire range of possible choices. You should include an *Other* category and ask the person to specify the *other* in a space provided next to it. In the section covering open-ended questions we made the point that too many open-ended questions indicate a survey effort that was premature. Similarly, if you find that more than 10% of respondents choose *Other*, then you did not do your homework in designing the survey. The range of response choices can be identified during the up-front research effort, including the pilot test. If you're going to use this survey instrument in the future, update your choices based upon the *Other* responses.

♦ **Distinctions among choices**. When asking the respondent to choose the most appropriate response from a set, be sure that choices don't overlap. This will make it more difficult for the respondent to make a clear choice.

♦ **Number of choices.** Respondents will not go through a long list of choices to find the best one or even to select all that apply. If you have more than 10 choices, they probably overlap. For telephone surveys, the number of choices is particularly important, because the respondent has to remember them all. Six to eight is the maximum number of choices for a telephone survey. With telephone surveys especially, you should look for the *primacy* and *recency* effects. Respondents tend to choose either the first or the last choice offered, since those stick in their memories best. If you find that is happening, either shorten the list or rotate the order in which the choices are presented to the respondent to minimize the bias.

♦ **Sequencing of choices.** The sequencing of the choices may affect response. Most of the time this is a result you want to avoid. Say you were asking a question about service agent's professionalism. Ask yourself if one choice would influence a

Figure 4.9
Adjective Checklist
Useful for Measuring Images

Please place a check mark next to the items that describe your job.

__ Easy	__ Risky
__ Boring	__ A Hassle
__ Challenging	__ Aggravating
__ Dead End	__ Tiring
__ Rewarding	__ Frustrating

respondent's reaction to the following items. There are, however, occasions when you will want to employ sequencing to achieve a particular end. For example, you may have a choice that you want to be sure people consider, even though few might pick it. By putting that one early in the list, ahead of the more likely choices, you ensure that people will read it.

To recap: the choice list should be comprehensive, short, mutually exclusive, and properly sequenced. It may take some thought to achieve all those characteristics.

Ordinal Scales

With an ordinal question format, the respondent is asked to sort a group of items into an order applying some criterion. The relative difference between the ordered items is *not* captured. There are three types of ordinal scales one of which is called *Ordinal*.

Basic Ordinal Scale. This scale can be used when the relationship of an action to some events or milestones is desired. (See Figure 4.10.) The respondent is asked to select one response choice out of a list of ordered choices. Notice that the relationship among the choices is what distinguishes this question format from a multiple-choice question that would generate nominal data.

Ordinal scales are useful when asking demographic data that is potentially sensitive or private. Most people would be reluctant to give a surveyor their exact age or salary, but they are more likely to check a box that fits their answer from an ordered list of choices where each choice covers some range, for example, 41 to 50 years, or $50,000 to $60,000 per year.

The astute reader might recognize that those two examples just given, age and salary, are ratio data, but we are turning them into ordinal (or perhaps nominal) data by using this format. You're right! But it's the best way to get these kind of data. In a situation like this we can relax the rules that apply to ordinal data and take weighted averages using the midpoint of the ranges and consider it ratio data. Using a previous example, $55,000 would be the midpoint of the $50,000 to $60,000 range, and that could be used to determine the weighted average salary of the respondent pool.

Forced-Ranking Scale. With a forced-ranking question, we ask the respondent to take a number of items and place them in order, based on a criterion, such as importance, value, or use. (See Figure 4.11.) This question format is extremely useful when we want the respondent to distinguish among a set of items, such as the impor-tance of attributes of our service delivery. As noted earlier, interval-rating scales allow the respondent to state that everything is equally important. While ordinal data cannot be manipulated mathemati-cally as interval data can, the data may prove more meaningful. The shortcomings of forced-ranking questions, covered below, are severe. For that reason, we recommend you think seriously before using this scale. Consider using a fixed-sum question format.

Paired Comparison. In a paired comparison question, we ask the respondent to rank order two items at a time. If we use every paired combination for all the items, statistically we can develop a very reliable ordering of all the items. This does get to be a lengthy pro-cess, one that would not seem appropriate for a surveying effort that is part research and part customer relationship management. (See Figure 4.12.)

When creating ordinal scale questions, particularly forced-rank-ing scales, there are a couple of *critical design considerations:*

♦ **Clarity and thoroughness of instructions.** Ranking questions aren't very user-friendly. Respondents are very likely to com-plete these questions incorrectly. With forced ranking questions, some respondents will use a "1" ranking twice. They may le-gitimately think two items deserve an equally high ranking, but this causes problems for the analyst. Frequently, respondents won't rank order all the items. If given an eight-item list, they may rank order 6 through 8 and the 1 through 3. The analyst is faced with a dilemma. Do you "complete" the question for the respondent or throw the response out? In the opening sections of Chapter 6 we address the issue of data cleansing.

These problems are unlikely to occur in a telephone survey where the interviewer can politely prod the respondent to com-plete the question properly. If you are considering purchasing a survey automation software package, check to see what edit controls the software has, if any. Ideally, the software should prompt the respondent to complete the question correctly.

♦ **Number of items.** The above problem will be minimized with a reasonably sized list. Rank ordering even 10 items is extremely difficult. About five items is a good number of items. This is particularly critical on a telephone survey where the respon-dent is being asked to recall the items *and* order them without the aid of seeing them written down. That's a tall order.

Figure 4.10
Ordinal Scale
Use When the Relationship of an Action to an Event or Milestone Is Needed

If the service transaction took a protracted time, at what point would you expect it to be escalated to management? (Please check only one.)

___ After the first day of the incident

___ After the second day of the incident

___ After the third day of the incident

___ After the fourth day of the incident

Figure 4.11
Forced Ranking
Provides a Ranked Order of Items

Please rank the following items in their order of importance to you. Please place a 1 next to the most important, a 2 next to the second most important, etc. Do not use a ranking number more than once.

___ Elapsed time for the phone to be answered

___ Elapsed time before speaking with a technical person

___ Total elapsed time to resolve the problem

___ Courtesy of the staff

This format is prone to respondent error. Use very few items.

Figure 4.12
Paired Comparison
Provides Relative Rankings

For each pair of items below, place a check mark next to the one that is most important to you.

___ Courtesy of the staff
___ Technical competency of the staff

___ Courtesy of the staff
___ Elapsed time before speaking with a technical person

___ Technical competency of the staff
___ Elapsed time before speaking with a technical person

Interval-Rating Scales

Interval-rating questions ask the respondent to give a response along some scale that shows the *strength of feeling* about some attribute or phenomenon. The advantage of this can be seen in the following question. Hotel surveys frequently ask: "Will you stay with us the next time you travel to Our Fair City? Yes or no." A respondent may fall into one of the two extremes, but for many, if not most people, our true feelings are not so clear-cut. The real answer is: "it depends…" A more appropriate question might be: "What's the likelihood that you will stay with us the next time you travel to Our Fair City?" Here's where interval-rating scales shed more light since they allow us to see shades of gray.

With an interval scale, the respondent is asked to select an answer along some dimension, such as value received, ease of use, or degree of satisfaction. This dimension is presented in the response scale, which is described using short phrases known as *anchors*. (See Figure 4.13 for the elements of an interval rating question and Figure 4.14 for a list of possible dimensions for a scale.) There are two common types of response scales, each of which has unique design considerations that will be addressed later.

Verbal Scales. In the first type, the response scale is posed as a series of ordered statements. These are called *verbal-scaled* questions. This is sometimes referred to as a *fully-anchored scale*. Typically, a number is not presented along with the statements though in the coding of data from these verbal-scaled questions, numbers are assigned to each statement to enhance the analytical capabilities.

Numeric Scales. In the second type, *numeric-scaled* questions, the response scale is posed as a series of numbers with anchors over the two ends of the numeric scale and also possibly over the midpoint and select other points. These verbal statements are called *anchors* since they anchor the number to a description of some point on the dimension used for measurement.

Interval-rating scales are a commonly used question format because they provide data that can be manipulated mathematically (add, subtract, and average), and they are fairly easy for respondents to complete. If you have a series of questions that all share the same scale, then you can design a very efficient table layout for the questions on a printed page or web form. On a telephone survey, the respondent can more easily remember an interval scale and thus can concentrate on the content of the question.

There are a great many interval scale types, which are covered below. Naming conventions for the scales are not universal. Differences among them relate to: how the scale is presented, the dimension described by the anchors, how the respondent records a choice, and the type of answer solicited. If you are considering using survey automation software, be sure to examine the rating formats supported by the software. You may design a questionnaire and find the software cannot support the format.

Figure 4.13
Elements of an Interval-Rating Scale

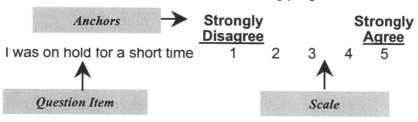

Listed below are several statements. Please indicate your agreement with each by selecting a number from 1 to 5 where 1 represents Strongly Disagree and 5 represents Strongly Agree.

Likert-type Scale. The "classic" scale is the *Likert-type scale*, named after its creator, Rensis Likert. (See Figure 4.15.) Likert scales ask the respondent the *level of agreement with some statement*. Thus, the anchors typically are *Strongly Disagree — Disagree — Neither Agree Nor Disagree — Agree — Strongly Agree.* This is a very flexible scale since almost any phenomenon can be made into a statement. For example, "The time on hold when I call for service is too long." With other anchors, you may find it hard to write all your questions to fit the dimension in the anchors. The Likert-type scale may be your answer.

Verbal-Frequency Scale. This scale identifies how frequently some action is taken or should be taken. The anchors for this scale are *Never* and *Always.*[4] (See Figure 4.16.)

---

[4] Terminology can get confusing. Notice that the *Verbal* Frequency Scale is a numeric scale, not a verbal scale!

Figure 4.14
Measurement Dimensions for Interval Scales

There are many, many dimensions that you might find appropriate for a scale. Here are some dimensions with possible endpoint anchors. Notice the last three are more generic; whereas, the first ones are more tied to the description of an attribute.

Concern:	Extremely Concerned – No Concern At All
Clarity:	Extremely Clear – Extremely Hard to Understand
Accuracy:	Extremely Accurate – Not Accurate At All
Difficulty or ease:	Extremely Easy to Use – Extremely Difficult to Use
Likelihood of some action:	Extremely Likely – Extremely Unlikely
Importance:	Extremely Important – Not Important At All
Value:	Extremely Valuable – Not Valuable At All
Frequency:	Always – Never
Superior/Inferior:	Very Superior – Very Inferior
Criticality:	Extremely Critical – Not Critical At All
Level of Use:	Always – Never or High – Low
Satisfaction:	Extremely Satisfied – Extremely Dissatisfied
Degree of expectations met:	Falls Well Short – Greatly Exceeds
Strength of agreement:	Strongly Agree – Strongly Disagree

Comparative Scale. When you want to compare the performance of a group to some benchmark, the comparative scale is appropriate. The anchors for this numeric scale might be *Highly Inferior* and *Highly Superior* though other anchors might be more appropriate to describe the nature of the comparison. (See Figure 4.17.) With this scale it is very important to provide the benchmark or standard in the question. If you don't give the basis for comparison, then every respondent will apply a unique one.

Horizontal-Numerical Scale. Though very similar to the above scales, the layout of the horizontal numerical scale presents the anchors on the same line as the scale but beyond the two scale end points. The scale is not presented next to each question. Rather, respondents are asked to fill in their response. (See Figure 4.18.)

Semantic Differential. Like the Stapel scale that follows, the semantic differential scale can be used to develop a composite image held of an organization. A series of paired adjectives are presented to respondents along with a scale, and they are asked to determine what number matches their view of the organization along the dimension in the paired adjectives (See Figure 4.19.) Care must be taken that the paired adjectives reflect the same phenomenon, and they should be polar opposites. Consider presenting some pairs with the positive adjective on the left and other pairs with the positive adjective to the right. This will force respondents to read each pair. As a means of benchmarking, you could use this scale to develop a profile of your organization and use the same set of paired adjectives in a question that asks respondents to rate the best in the industry.

Stapel Scale. This scale is a combination of the adjective checklist with an interval scale, classically the horizontal numerical scale. (See Figure 4.20.)

School-Grade Scale. If simplifying the respondent's task of conceptualizing the scale is a concern, then the school grade scale should be considered. This is a five-point scale of *A, B, C, D,* and *F.* You need to provide verbal anchors for each point, such as "*A* is exceptional performance. *B* is above average performance. *C* is average performance. *D* is barely acceptable performance. *F* is unacceptable performance." Most people understand this scale, even if their schools used a different grading system. (See Figure 4.21.)

Fixed-Sum Scale. This is an extremely useful scale, but it is also prone to data submission errors. (See Figure 4.22.) With this scale, you give the respondent a block of points and ask them to assign points among a list of items. (Sometimes, it's stated that the respondent has $100 to "spend" on a group of items.) For example, you might present a list of attributes of service delivery and ask the respondent to identify the relative importance of each by allocating 100 points among the items, or you might respondents to identify the relative importance of actions that your group is considering for next year. The power of this scale is that it combines the benefits of a ranking scale with an interval scale. Respondents have to make clear choices and trade-off as in a ranking scale, but the numerical responses present relative relationships as with an interval scale that can manipulated mathematically.

As stated, this scale is prone to one critical error. The block of

Figure 4.15
Likert-Type Scale
Identify Opinion or Level of Agreement

Listed below are several statements. Please indicate your level of agreement with each by selecting a number from 1 to 5, where 1 represents Strongly Disagree and 5 represents Strongly Agree.

	Strongly Disagree				Strongly Agree
I was on hold for a short time	1	2	3	4	5
The service agent was courteous	1	2	3	4	5
The service agent was competent	1	2	3	4	5

Figure 4.16
Verbal Frequency Scale
Use When Frequency of an Action, not the Absolute Number is Needed.

Listed below are different means of submitting a request for service. Please choose a number to indicate the frequency with which you use each, where 1 represents Never and 5 represents Always.

	Never				Always
Telephone call	1	2	3	4	5
Email submission	1	2	3	4	5
Fax	1	2	3	4	5
Electronic Bulletin Board	1	2	3	4	5

Figure 4.17
Comparative Scale
Use When Concern is for Comparisons to Some Standard or Benchmark

You likely have had experiences with customer service from many organizations. **Compared to the best support organization you have experienced**, please rate our support services on a scale of 1 to 5, where 1 represents very inferior and 5 represents very superior.

	Very Inferior				Very Superior
The speed of problem resolution	1	2	3	4	5
The courtesy of our support reps	1	2	3	4	5
Ease of doing business	1	2	3	4	5

Figures 4.18
Horizontal Numerical
Use When Evaluations Are All to Be Made on a Single Dimension

How important to you is each of the following factors? Pick the number from the scale that is appropriate and write it next to the item.

Extremely Unimportant	1	2	3	4	5	Extremely Important

The technical competence of the staff ____

The courtesy of the staff ____

The speed with which the phone is answered ____

Talking to a technical representative first ____

Figure 4.19
Semantic Differential
Use to Identify the Image of a Person or Organization.

Circle the number to indicate your opinion about the service you received over the past year.

Slow	1	2	3	4	5	Fast
Accurate	1	2	3	4	5	Sloppy
Consistent	1	2	3	4	5	Unpredictable
Cheap	1	2	3	4	5	Expensive
Thorough	1	2	3	4	5	Cursory
Punctual	1	2	3	4	5	Frequently late

Figure 4.20
Stapel
Combines Semantic Differential and Adjective Checklist: Interval Data.

How important to you is each of the following factors about your job? Pick the appropriate number from the scale and write it next to the item.

Extremely Disadvantageous	1	2	3	4	5	Extremely Advantageous

____ Amount of Work   ____ Riskiness

____ Control   ____ Personal Thanks

____ Challenging   ____ Stepping Stone

____ Visibility   ____ Learning Opportunity

Figure 4.21
School Grade Scale
Use when you want a readily understandable scale.
Presented as in a telephone script.

We'd like to know how well we're doing in various areas of our service. Please grade our performance using letter grades like a school report card, where
 A means exceptionally good,
 B means very good,
 C means acceptable,
 D means poor,
And F means totally unacceptable.

1.   How would you grade the service agent on his or her courtesy?

2.   What grade would you give the resolution to your issue?

3.   The service agent probably gave you some information. How would you grade the accuracy of that information?

4.   How would you grade how clearly the service agent explained how your issue would be handled?

Figure 4.22
Fixed Sum
Creates a Ranking of Items Indicating Relative Relationships or
Identifies the Proportion With Which Different Items Are Encountered.

Listed below are five summary attributes of the service delivery by the Information Technology Services (ITS) group. We would like you to indicate which are most important in your evaluation of the performance of ITS. Please allot 100 points among the attributes as you feel appropriate. Allot more points to those attributes that are more important, and fewer to those of lesser importance. You may allot zero points to any attribute. The allotted scores across all attributes **must** total 100.

_____ Responsiveness in resolving my service requests

_____ Technical quality of the work performed

_____ Professional conduct of the service agents

_____ Concern shown for my problems by the service agents

_____ Quality of communications by service agent

_____ TOTAL

points to allot is typically 100 since most people are comfortable thinking in percentages, but will the allotted scores add to 100? If they don't, then you can reapportion them, but that is time consuming. (The section in Chapter 6 on data cleansing covers this in more detail.) To minimize error, don't have more than 10 items, and in the instructions, state what an equal weighting would be. For example, if there were eight items and 100 points, say, "If you feel that every item is of equal importance, then assign a score of 12.5 to each item." Ideally, you should have four, five, or 10 items because those divide evenly into 100.

This scale is most amenable to use with a web-form survey — assuming the survey software supports the question type. Why? Because the web form can display a running total as people enter their responses and tab to the next entry box. Fixed-sum scales are least amenable to telephone surveys. This is a lot for the respondent to process in his head.

There are several *critical design considerations* when constructing interval-rating scales. These considerations address four major areas: simplifying questionnaire development, reducing respondent confusion, generating true interval data, and promoting a dispersion of results.

- **Advantages of grouping by type.** If you must use more than one scale type, then group your questions by scale type. This may force a compromise for the normal sequencing of questions by some logical order, such as the chronology of a service call. If the survey is done by telephone, this is essential because the respondent has no visual aid.

- **Which step first, developing the scale or writing questions?** When developing a questionnaire you need to write the questions and you need to decide on scales. Which do you do first? You need to write some questions to decide on the scale you want, but you need to know the scale to write the questions to match it. Once again we're confronted with a chicken-or-the-egg question. Early in the question-writing process, try to identify the scale or scales you plan to use. You will then need to write the questions to fit the dimension measured by the scale. Exercise 2 will give you some practice with this. (A discussion of Exercise 2 is in the Appendix.)

- **The importance of anchor choices.** Consider what you want to learn about the phenomenon, and consider how the potential respondents think about the items for which you want information. Is it value, importance, extent of expectations met, extent of use, or something else that best gets to what you want to understand *and* best describes the respondent's view? Be sure that the dimension expressed in the anchors is something that everyone will understand, and be sure the anchors all express the same dimension. Since it is best to use one or two scale types throughout a survey instrument, the choice of anchors is very important. See Figure 4.14 for ideas for dimensions and anchors.

◆ **Scale direction.** Our society is duplicitous about which is better, a higher or lower number. At any sporting event you'll hear, "We're Number 1," yet Bo Derek was a "10" in her movie by

---

Exercise 2
Developing Scales

Take some attribute of service delivery, perhaps from Exercise 1. Develop a set of anchors to measure a respondent's feelings about the attribute. Do this for:

- A 5-point scale where you anchor the end points and the midpoint

- A fully anchored, 5-point verbal scale. That is, create a verbal anchor for all five points.

Try developing a scale specific to the attribute before you attempt to use a more generic scale. As you develop your scale, think about using the scale on a written instrument and in a telephone survey. Are there potential shortcomings?

---

that name. Have the higher number represent more of a dimension. When plotting data on bar charts, larger bars visually imply more or better. To have shorter bars, for example, representing greater satisfaction, will confuse readers of your report.

◆ **Interval equality.** This is a *critical* consideration when constructing verbal frequency scales. At the analytical phase of the survey project, you probably will be calculating averages of the data, if not some higher level statistical analysis. For this to be valid, the respondent has to view that there is an *equal difference* *or interval* between each ordered pair of verbal statements. We've said this before, but this point is critical.

An example of a poor set of anchors is: *Extremely Poor — Poor — Fair — Good — Excellent.* Research shows that people perceive the difference between *Poor* and *Fair* as greater than the difference between *Fair* and *Good.* That is, *Fair* is closer to *Good* than it is to *Poor.* Thus, this scale would have a downward bias because more respondents will choose *Fair* than they otherwise would if the scale were truly interval. Those additional *Fair* responses would otherwise be *Good.*

Another example of a bad scale *is Not At All Satisfied — Satisfied — Very Satisfied — Extremely Satisfied.* It's an example of a *truncated scale.* The difference between the first two points (*Not At All Satisfied — Satisfied*) is likely to be far greater than the other intervals. This scale is certainly ordinal, but claiming interval properties takes a leap of faith. Inserting *Somewhat Satisfied* would improve its interval properties.

♦ **Anchor balancing.** As a general rule, the anchor words on the two extremes of the scale should be polar opposites, for example, *Extremely Dissatisfied* and *Extremely Satisfied.* If they are not balanced, then you may have a biased scale. Truncated scales just mentioned are an example of unbalanced anchors. Some dimensions really only go in one direction while others are clearly bidirectional. Let's take the *satisfaction* dimension just used. We would all probably agree that there are degrees of satisfaction **and** degrees of dissatisfaction. So, *Not Satisfied At All* may not be the same as *Extremely Dissatisfied.* Now let's take the *importance* dimension. Are there degrees of unimportance? Perhaps, but it probably sheds little light to know the degree of unimportance. So, *Not Important At All* for most purposes is an acceptable endpoint anchor.

♦ **Even versus odd-numbered scales.** A frequent question is whether to have an odd-numbered scale (for example, 1 to 7) or an even-numbered scale (for example, 1 to 6). The answer is: it depends. Is it perfectly acceptable for someone to straddle the fence and express a neutral opinion? If so, then an odd-numbered scale is fine. If you want to force the respondent to commit to one side or the other, then an even-numbered scale is appropriate.

Even-numbered scales[5] ease the task of designing verbal scales. Developing verbal descriptors for midpoints is a real challenge! Let's say you're using an ease-of-use scale. *Very Easy* and *Very Difficult* are the endpoints. What's the midpoint? Here are your choices: *Neutral, Indifferent, Okay,* or *Neither Easy Nor Difficult.* None of those is very good. With an even-numbered scale, the two verbal descriptors around the center could be: *Somewhat Easy* and *Somewhat Difficult.*

◆ **Number of points on the scale.** As a rule of thumb, the more points the better, since abundance allows more precision in measuring respondents' feelings. From the perspective of formatting the instrument visually, however, the longer the scale the more difficult the task. Once you go beyond perhaps 7 points, or certainly 10 points, it is very difficult to display the entire scale. You may need to ask the respondent to enter a number or use a pull-down box rather than circle a number or click on a specific radio button. Also, more points require the respondent to think about the differentiation along the extended scale. This increases response burden. In a recent experiment in a telephone survey with a number of different scale types, the author found that respondents were able to answer questions more quickly on a 1-to-5 scale than on a 1-to-10 scale.

You must have at least five points on the scale, since fewer than five points will not generate normally distributed data necessary for the data to be truly interval in nature. Seven-point and 10-point scales are most common, but answer this quickly: What's the midpoint of a 10-point scale? If you said five, you're wrong! Since a 10-point scale is an even-numbered scale, the midpoint is 5.5. Yet people will choose five as a neutral position, giving this scale a downward bias. As the number of points in the scale gets larger, the midpoint issue just discussed becomes moot.

◆ **Presenting the scale low-to-high or high-to-low.** Some research has shown that people tend to pick the first or the last choices presented to them, the primacy and recency effects. Further, the primacy effect tends to be stronger, especially for written surveys (and presumably web-form surveys). Presenting the scale from low to high seems to make more sense since we read from

---

[5] Just to be clear, we're discussing scales with an even number of points, not a scale that uses only even numbers.

left to right, but this may lead to a slight downward bias because more respondents will choose the lower ratings. The author tested this effect in a telephone survey experiment just mentioned. The scale was verbally presented in one of the two directions for different respondents. We found no statistically significant differences in the responses.

♦ **Use of multiple scale types creates confusion.** Elsewhere we have talked about creating a "mental set" for the respondent. This extends to the use of scales. For example, if we get the respondent thinking along an expectations scale — service received compared to expectations — then we switch to an importance scale and later an extent-of-use scale, the respondent can get confused — and annoyed. Try to phrase as many of your questions, if not all of them, using one scale type. This is where generic scales, such as Likert-type, satisfaction, extent-of-expectations-met, and school grade scales, have a real advantage. Most phenomena can be expressed in a question item that fits those scales.

♦ **Avoiding response ruts.** One problem with using an interval scale for a long list of questions is that respondents can fall into a *response rut*. They may stop listening to the precise wording of the question and mechanically give the same response to every question. On a telephone survey you may hear respondents say, *"Just give them a 10 for all these questions."* *Reverse-coded questions* combat this. Here, an occasional question is phrased in the negative. For example, instead of posing "My question was answered quickly," you could reverse it and say, "It took a long time to get my question answered." By using one of these early in a list of questions, you tell respondents they need to listen carefully. When you get to the coding phase of the survey project, you should reverse the coded response to these questions. Otherwise, the reader of your report will get confused when you present the results. Some survey automation software packages may specifically support reverse-coded questions, simplifying this process.

♦ **Dispersion of results.** In our data we want variability. That may sound odd since we want our organization to get high scores. But the point of doing data collection for quality improvement is to identify "the critical few from the trivial many," which is the goal of Pareto Analysis, a key tool in Total Quality Management. Properly designed scales promote a dispersion of responses across the scale. For example, if you asked about the *importance* of service attributes on a 1-to-5 scale, you will likely find that everyone thinks that everything is fairly important! The author saw a recent study where the importance of 35 attributes were all rated between 3.5 and 4.5 on a 5-point scale. With those results, where would you focus your efforts? For the statisticians among you, if you were to do statistical analysis, you would likely get weak findings.

Another cause of poor dispersion is inappropriate truncation. Here the anchors are not extreme enough. If we have endpoint anchors of *Poor* — *Good*, then responses of *Excellent* would be included in the *Good* rating, but the fact that some people thought the service was excellent would be invisible to the analyst. As mentioned, a scale with *Not At All Satisfied* as an endpoint, is an example of truncation on one end of the scale. Thus, in addition to being balanced, anchors typically should also be *extreme* to properly differentiate among respondents' feelings.

When shouldn't the anchors be extreme? If most respondents have lukewarm feelings towards the service, then you will need more differentiation around the midpoint of the scale. In this case, an endpoint of *Very* as opposed to *Extremely* may be more appropriate.

As mentioned earlier, you have a choice between verbal or numeric scales. It boils down to the question of having anchors for every point on the scale or only on the endpoints, and perhaps the midpoint. Research has found that telephone surveys lead to higher responses, especially when using numeric scales. Telephone respondents tend to gravitate toward the endpoints because that's what they hear. For a client recently, the author conducted an experiment using different scales. Applying statistical tests, we found that verbal scales, that is, presenting a verbal description for each of the five scale points, led to responses more centered on the midpoint and with a greater dispersion of results. The downside of this scale type is that it takes longer to administer by phone. Plus, verbal scales are more likely to compromise the interval properties of the scale.

> **Research has shown that people tend to pick the first or the last choices presented to them, the primacy and recency effects.**

A good midpoint anchor can also promote broader dispersion of results, and research has shown that expectations-based scales provide good dispersion. Here the midpoint is where perception of service received matches expectations. You might even use a numeric scale whose midpoint is zero and exceeding expectations is represented by positive numbers, and not meeting expectations is represented by negative numbers. For example, a 7-point scale would range from -3 to +3. This reinforces the range in the respondent's mental frame and anchors the midpoint as a neutral position.

Ratio Scales

Fractionation Scale. This scale has been used for years in certain academic fields[6]. It is an open-ended scale, in that there is no upper end point. For example, you ask the respondent, "If 0 represents expectations completely unmet for <a certain attribute> and 30 represents expectations just barely being met, what score would you assign..." The benefits of this scale are two-fold. First, it has greater precision because it has a greater number of points in the scale. Second, because it has no upper limit, the scale can measure changes over time. (See Figure 4.23.)

Guidelines for Questionnaire Design

As we design our questionnaire and specific questions, we are torn between two, somewhat competing objectives:
1. Maximizing the information we receive
2. Minimizing respondent burden.

Respondent burden is the term used to describe the amount of work the surveyor is asking the respondent to do. The fundamental goal of a questionnaire design effort is to minimize respondent burden, consistent with the objectives of the survey. As the respondent burden increases, the response rate will likely fall. So the challenge is to extract the greatest amount of information, while alienating the fewest respondents. Many means of achieving these goals have been presented. Here we restate some of the most critical considerations and add some other ways to manage that difficult balancing act.

♦ **Don't ask meaningless questions.** Respondents will analyze your instrument, consciously or unconsciously, and respondents

---

[6] See for example, Barnett et al., 1982.

Figure 4.23
Ratio Scale
Use to measure changes in some phenomenon over time

The questions in this section of the survey use the following scale:

0	30	60	90	120
None	Average	Twice Average	Three Times Average	Four Times Average

For each question, 0 represents none of the item described in the question and 30 represents an average amount. If you experienced less than an average amount, then choose a score between 0 and 30. If you experienced more than an average amount, then choose a score greater than 30. Enter your score in the space provided.

Responsiveness to my issue   _____

Technical quality of the resolution _____

Concern shown for my situation   _____

---

don't want their time wasted with questions that seem pointless. This includes questions for which respondents feel you should already know the answers. For example, if you're conducting a transaction-driven survey and the introductory note includes the log number and brief description of the transaction, then the survey is not anonymous. The respondent will be puzzled if you ask demographic questions, such as the number of calls the respondent has placed in the past three months. "You should know that," is what they will be thinking.

- **Keep the instrument focused.** Perhaps the greatest temptation is to add a few extra questions "while we have our customers' attention." Resist this temptation. It will lengthen the survey and these questions are unlikely to jibe with the purpose stated in the introduction. Remember: the respondents are customers. Don't overburden and annoy at the same time.

◆ **A survey is not a test.** The respondent should not have to work to figure out what it is you want them to do. Be sure the instructions are clear, especially if you are posing complex questions, such as fixed-sum questions.

◆ **Be concerned about the visual impact of the questionnaire design.** As a survey designer you are a graphic artist in part. The layout of the instrument should be pleasing to the eye and guide the respondent through the survey.

◆ **Keep wording and grammar simple**. Short declarative sentence structure is more readily intelligible to readers.

◆ **Be creative in question design.** As you develop your questionnaire, seriously ask yourself what you want to learn from the respondent. Are there ways to get more or richer information, with little increase in respondent burden? Consider the following example.

The phenomenon under study is the communication of information from customer support groups to product development organizations. (This example comes from a research study by the author.) An open-ended question could be posed to learn how the respondent handles this business issue. (See Figure 4.24.) That has a high respondent burden. Alternatively, a multiple-choice question could be posed that asked which mechanisms were *used*. Note that the response is binary: yes or no. While the use or non-use of a mechanism is of interest, the *importance* of each mechanism really gets to the heart of understanding the phenomenon, helping us to compare the mechanisms. A rating scale uncovers this factor. We can include a *not applicable* or *not used* response on the scale.

> The respondent should not have to work to figure out what it is you want them to do.

How much incremental information is gained from the latter question design compared to the early versions? How much added effort is being asked of the respondent? Certainly, the small, added effort is worth the wealth of richer information. Of course, the open-ended question might reveal some interesting, unexpected information. You might consider a follow-on open-ended question that is entirely optional for the respondent.

Pilot Testing

Showing the survey questionnaire to a project team inside the company could be termed the Alpha or System Test — to use terminology from new product development processes. Once the product passes that test and problems are corrected, the next stage is to test it with live customers. That's the Beta Test or Field Test stage. A survey questionnaire *is* a new product and should be treated that way. You need to do a Field Test with actual respondents. In survey design jargon, this is known as a *Pilot Test*.

The purpose of the pilot is to catch the last few — hopefully — mistakes that are in the instrument, mistakes that only those in the target respondent group will catch. You and your project team will get so close to the questionnaire that you will operate with certain blinders on. Respondents will see things that are beyond your peripheral vision.

Don't underestimate the importance of pilot testing! It's a relatively quick step, and it is critical to developing a clean survey instrument. Yet most people will want to skip this step as unnecessary. *Don't skip it!*

Pilot testing is not complicated, but there are some conventions that should be followed in order to gain maximum advantage from the exercise. These are covered in the answers to frequently asked questions provided below.

How do I conduct the pilot tests? The pilot tests should be conducted as a series of one-on-one, personal administrations of the survey instrument. (You might consider bringing a colleague who can take notes, but it's not essential.) The reason for conducting pilot tests in person is to catch the visual clues to problems in the questionnaire found in respondent's reactions to questions.

To start the pilot, explain to the person the reason you have asked them for their input. If your survey is to be administered by postal mail, electronic mail, or a web form, then give the respondent the introductory note(s) and the questionnaire. Make it as realistic as possible. If you are using a web form or electronic mail, having them see the questionnaire on a computer screen is ideal, but giving the respondent a paper copy is a reasonable compromise. If you plan to administer the survey by telephone, then you need to read the survey script. In other words, pretend this were the actual way you would be administering the questionnaire.

What should I be looking for? Look at their expression as they read or hear the introduction. Walk through the questionnaire one question at a time, asking the respondents to actually complete the questionnaire. Encourage them to verbalize their thinking processes. You may ask them to restate the question in their own words. Think about how Regis Philbin gets contestants to think out load when they're stumped on a question on *Who Wants to be a Millionaire*. Without that audible thinking, the respondent may say the question is perfectly clear, but they may have interpreted it totally differently than you intended, which would indicate a lack of question validity. If they furrow their brow or use other body language, ask them if something is unclear or disturbs them.

The purpose of the pilot test is to test the instrument at both the micro and macro levels. At the micro level, we want to know if the questions conveyed the intended meaning, if the questions were too difficult to answer, if we have the proper response choices for multiple choice questions, and if we are getting a good dispersion of responses. At the macro level, we want to test the flow of the questionnaire (that is, did we engage the respondent), the length of the survey, the clarity of any branching conditions, and whether the respondents felt all their relevant issues were covered.

> The reason for conducting pilot tests in person is to catch the visual clues to problems in the questionnaire found in respondent's reactions to questions.

If you find some awkward wording, ask the respondent to help you out. Explain what it is you're trying to measure. What change in phrasing would make the question clearer? Say you found a question that posed problems for the first two pilot tests. Then on subsequent pilots try out the revised wording the interviewees have helped you develop. This may eliminate the need for another iteration of pilot testing. Of course, this assumes the problems were minor!

Whom should I recruit to pilot test the survey? As with the selection of people for the interviews or focus groups, you should select people who cover the range of customers you want to survey. Ideally, you should not use people who were part of that initial research. They will have a bias when they read the questionnaire. The author encountered a situation where the dynamics of the focus group led the attendees to take "ownership" of the survey in-

Figure 4.24
Improving Question Design

Notice that these three questions all address the same phenomenon, but each increase in information gained causes little extra respondent burden.

Free-Form

What techniques do you use to communicate feedback from the support organization to product development?

_____

_____

Multiple Choice

Which of the following means of conveying information from customer support to product development do you use? (Check all that apply.)

____ Hard copy report
____ Electronic report
____ Data base accessible by other groups
____ Liaison communication at team meetings
____ Direct contact between ...

Scaled Response

Please rate the importance of the following means of conveying information from customer support to product development. (Circle the appropriate number.)

	Low				High
Hard copy report	1	2	3	4	5
Electronic report	1	2	3	4	5
Data base accessible to development	1	2	3	4	5
Liaison communication	1	2	3	4	5
Direct contact between personnel	1	2	3	4	5

strument. In a case like this, you may need to use some of the focus group attendees for the pilot for political reasons, but also conduct a pilot with some other people.

How many pilot tests should be done? As we have said in regard to initial research and focus groups, you've done enough when you're not getting any new answers. A minimum of four or five pilots should be done. A longer instrument should need more pilots. These pilots do cost time and money since you should travel to a place convenient to the respondent.

Can these pilot tests be done by phone? The first pilots should definitely be done face-to-face. Later ones could be done by phone if you need to cover some segment of the respondent pool that is geographically distant and your budget prohibits such travel. Pilots by phone should supplement the other pilot administrations.

Summary

In this chapter we've covered a lot of territory on the trail map! But this is the heart of the survey process. First, we presented techniques for identifying the questions to pose on the survey instrument, emphasizing the need for customer input for this process. Next, the elements of a well-designed questionnaire were presented, followed by issues caused by the sequencing of questions. Question formats was the next point on the trail. There are a great many formats, each with specific strengths and weaknesses. The interval-scale formats present the additional challenge of constructing scales, which create dangerous footing for the survey designer. The chapter ended with the last step in the questionnaire design process, the pilot test, which is the opportunity to catch the last few mistakes in the instrument. By applying the lessons from the chapter, you should minimize the instrumentation biases presented in Chapter 2. Now, to see the impression the trail has made, turn to Exercise 3 on page 114 and 115. (A discussion of Exercise 3 is in the Appendix.)

CБCБCБ

Exercise 3
Analyzing Instrumentation Bias

The survey instrument below contain a compilation of survey examples. Examine the questions and see if you can spot what's wrong with them. Some of the questions have multiple errors. The answers are in Discussion of Exercises in the back of the book.

_____

Please answer the following questions. Thank you for your time.

1. Your name and title are: _____

2. Please rate the service you received for each support event in the past year.

Very Invaluable		Poor	Fair	Good	Extremely Valuable
1		2	3	4	5

3. _Please rate your satisfaction with the availability of Customer Care._

Very Dissatisfied	Somewhat Dissatisfied	Neither Satisfied Nor Dissatisfied	Somewhat Satisfied	Very Satisfied
1	2	3	4	5

4. How important is the following? Please use the following scale:

Not Important	Important	Somewhat Important	Very Important	Extremely Important
1	2	3	4	5

Courtesy & Friendliness: _____
Competence & Speed: _____
Thoroughness & Accuracy: _____

5. Please check the services below that you believe the Association offers members and then rate your satisfaction with each

		Not Satisfied		OK		Very Satisfied	
Affinity credit card ❑	1	2	3	4	5	6
Travel services ❑	1	2	3	4	5	6

6. Do you attend local chapter meetings?

__ Yes __ No __ Sometimes

7. When using your Platinum Training Membership, what factors influence your decision about which courses to attend? (Please rank, with a 5 being the most significant and a 1 being the least.)

__ Training Services Representative   __ Skills Assessment

__ Training Services Catalog   __ Self

__ Certification Learning Plan   __ Manager or Supervisor

__ Other_____

8. You recently contacted Frozen Systems' Technical Support Help Desk. In an effort to continually improve our service to you, our valued customer, we would appreciate it if you answer the following short survey. Please rate the following questions using the following scale.

Completely Satisfied	Very Satisfied	Fairly Well Satisfied	Somewhat Satisfied	Somewhat Dissatisfied	Very Dissatisfied
1	2	3	4	5	6

Your call was answered in a timely manner ____

The analyst was able to answer your questions in the initial call ____

If a follow-up expectation was set, it was met ____

The analyst assisted in ultimately resolving your problem ____

The analyst was courteous and professional ____

5 Administering the Survey

By the end of this chapter, you will learn:
- The different methods of administering a survey
- The criteria for evaluating these methods
- The advantages and disadvantages of each method
- How to generate a sample
- What sample size is needed for a certain level of confidence
- How to increase response rate
- The tasks required for each administration method

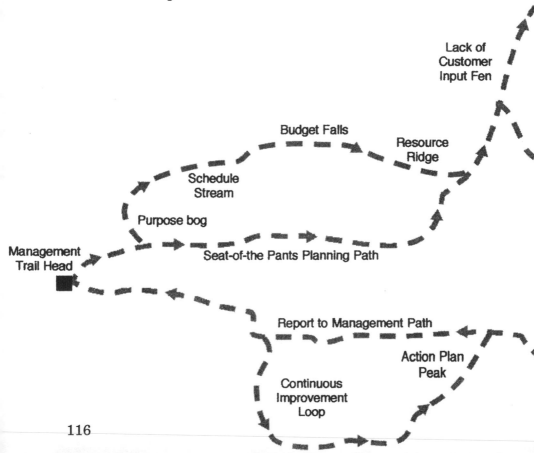

Lack of Customer Input Fen

Budget Falls

Resource Ridge

Schedule Stream

Purpose bog

Management Trail Head

Seat-of-the Pants Planning Path

Report to Management Path

Action Plan Peak

Continuous Improvement Loop

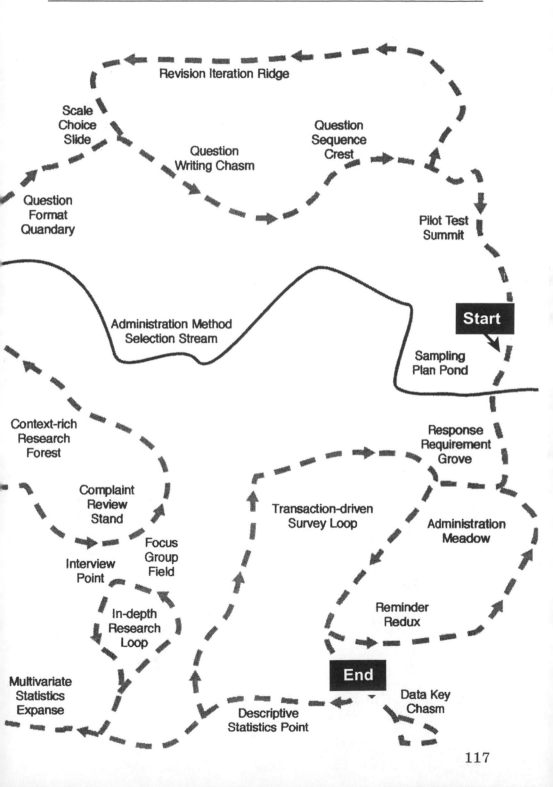

This chapter will address the options and tasks involved in administering the survey instrument you've developed. Chapter 2 outlined the different sources of *administration bias* that can compromise the accuracy of administration. We recommend that you review those as you consider each administration method as an option for your survey project. Briefly, the six sources of concern are:

- ◆ Bias through the administration process.
- ◆ Bias through the administration method.
- ◆ Bias from targeting the wrong population.
- ◆ Bias in the sample generation.
- ◆ Bias in the respondent group.
- ◆ Statistical strength of the generalizations from the sample to the population.

Survey administration entails many steps, primarily generating the sample, sending the surveys, and keying in the responses. These will be described later, but one of your first decisions will be the choice of administration methods. So, we'll describe the various administration methods and compare their advantages and disadvantages.

Choosing an Administration Method

Which administration method to choose is a major question in a survey project. From a project management standpoint, *when* that choice is made is also a critical issue. As presented at the end of Chapter 2, the questionnaire design, especially the question formats selected, set requirements for the administration method, but the administration method sets constraints for the questionnaire design. You should make the choice of an administration method when the questionnaire is taking form and the strategy for this research effort is well understood. While the questionnaire design work is being completed, you can be setting up the logistics of administering the survey, either doing it all yourself or hiring a vendor.

There are six ways that a survey can be administered:

1. Hard copy by postal mail or interdepartmental mail
2. Telephone interviews
3. Electronic mail using ASCII text or an attachment
4. Web-form
5. Survey "by disk"

6. Interactive Voice Response (IVR)

Perfect solutions are rare. Trade-offs among competing alternatives are more common, and that's the case here. For simplicity's sake, you will probably choose one administration method, but there are situations where you may want to use a second method for the same instrument, and then merge the data into one data file. The possibility exists that the administration method will affect the nature of the responses, so you should check for differences. If anything, using multiple methods will offset the differences.

Criteria for Evaluating Administration Methods

Before describing the relative merits of each administration method, let's outline the criteria for selecting an administration method. These criteria are not listed in any particular order, and your project team will need to decide what criteria are most important.

- **Response rate.** Response rate is important because it determines the statistical accuracy of a survey's results, which will be discussed in detail later. Response rates will vary across administration methods perhaps by a factor of two to one. More expensive methods tend to have a higher response rate. Response rates will also be different for every customer group, so it's hard to come up with benchmarks for response. If your customers have a strong affinity with your organization — and you've done an excellent job designing and marketing the survey — response rates will be higher. Response rates overall have fallen recently, probably due to the proliferation of surveying. Many practices that can improve response rate are covered later in this chapter, but the administration method sets a baseline.

- **Speed of administration.** We all want everything yesterday. That goes for survey results as well. It's more than just a matter of patience, however, if we are performing the surveying for quality improvement initiatives and to identify the need for service recovery efforts for specific customers. Here, speed is essential to achieving the purposes of the research effort. If you are conducting transaction-driven surveys, customers may raise issues that demand an immediate response, and we want to correct structural problems quickly so that no other customers experience the problem.

- **Cost per completed survey and cost per attempted survey.** Is there any service organization that isn't concerned about the cost of doing a survey? Of course, cost is an issue. There are many elements in costing out a method, but it's important to examine which costs are one-time investment or set-up costs, which costs vary with the volume of surveys sent, and which costs are incurred every time you conduct a survey. Notice that the cost is expressed in terms of *completed surveys* as well as cost per surveys *attempted*. This is an important distinction, especially if you are contracting for surveying services, since cost per completed survey should be a key element in the contract alongside cost per attempt. Including both metrics puts the onus on you to provide the vendor with a clean list of customer contact information, and puts the onus on the vendor to truly attempt to complete the surveys.

- **Scalability.** Just as with information technologies, the scalability of a method should be a selection consideration since it helps determine effort and cost. An administration method may be perfectly suitable for a target population of 25, but may not be suitable if you're surveying 500 or 5,000 potential respondents. Costs scale at different rates across administration methods due to the mix of set-up versus variable costs.

- **Ability to clarify questions.** If the survey instrument is flawed, then the ability to compensate for the flaws during the administration is a valuable trait. Some administration methods are more amenable to providing help to a respondent. Hopefully, the pilot test has caught all the flaws, but some may still exist.

- **Ability of the respondent to provide feedback on the instrument**. If your instrument has flaws, they will become evident to the respondent during the administration. But can the respondent readily make those flaws evident to you? Certain administration methods allow respondents to provide feedback to the surveyor; whereas, others do not. For a novice survey designer, this is an important consideration because with some administration methods you may never learn that your instrument is invalid.

- **Complexity of questions.** As you become more creative in using surveys to gather research, you may move beyond simple scales and multiple-choice questions. Balancing the opposing goals of maximizing information gain while minimizing respondent burden may lead you to design more complex question structures. For example, what if you wanted to pose a series of questions with the same set of categorical (as opposed to numerical) response choices. In this case, a matrix or spreadsheet-like format might be the most efficient way to pose the question. Some administration methods better support complex question formats.

◆ **Administration control.** When the respondent takes the survey, who controls the flow of the questionnaire, the respondent or

---

Figure 5.1
Comparison of Survey Administration Methods

	Telephone	Mail	Electronic
Response Rate	High	Low	High
Speed^	Fast	Slow	Very Fast
Cost per Completed Survey	High	Low	Lowest
Scalability	Linear	Some	Very High
Ability to Clarify	High.	None	None
Instrument Feedback	Yes	Some	None
Question Complexity	Very Low	Highest	Low/High*
Administration Control	Interviewer	Respondent	Low/High
Administration Bias	Interviewer Bias	Limited	Sample Bias
Anonymity	None	Yes	Questionable
Comments	Spontaneous	Low	Contemplative

^ IVR is faster than telephone, mail, or electronic.

* "Low" refers to the email survey method. "High" refers to the web-form survey method.

---

the surveyor? This is an important consideration if you plan to use conditional branching or customize the survey in other ways for specific respondent subgroups.

◆ **Administration bias.** Some administration methods are more prone to biasing respondents' answers. This, of course, can give us false readings. The bias may come during the sample generation process or during the actual administration of the survey.

◆ **Anonymity.** Respondents are more likely to be forthcoming, if their answers will be confidential and their identities are

121

unknown. Some administration methods support anonymous surveying better than others.

◆ **Willingness to provide comments and the nature of those comments.** Virtually all surveys will have at least one open-ended question, perhaps more. When you deliver your report, the first thing to which most readers will turn is the appendix with the comments from open-ended questions. The administration method will affect the willingness of respondents to provide any comment. Further, the form of administration will affect the type of comments provided.

Administration Methods

In this section we'll review each of the administration methods listed at the start of the chapter with more emphasis on the four major types: hardcopy, telephone, email, and web form. For each method, we'll apply the criteria just defined. See Figure 5.1 for a summary.

Hard Copy Surveys, Postal Mail, and Interdepartmental Mail

Sending out printed surveys by postal mail is the oldest means of conducting scientific surveys. It entails mailing the survey instrument to respondents, along with an introductory letter and a return envelope with postage affixed. If your survey population is employees within your company, then the printed survey may be sent though interdepartmental mail. A pre-administration letter may also be sent, and follow-up notices may be sent to those who have not yet responded after some period of time, say three weeks.

Invest in a high-quality look for a postal survey. It shows you're serious. If you cut corners and the survey looks cheap, then respondents will ask themselves why should they bother to give you time when you weren't willing to put the time in to design a good looking survey. Use moderate-weight paper, and if the survey is more than two pages, consider formatting it as a pamphlet with saddle stitching. A good, clean layout is also important to guiding the respondent's eyes through the instrument.

If you are sending the survey to an international audience, acquiring return postage is an additional task. International postage is available through postal services. Friends, relatives, and business associates around the world can also buy postage locally and send it to you. Be sure to weigh the return letter in units of measure (grams or ounces) from which the returned survey will be sent. Don't recreate NASA's mistake on the recent Mars probe when scientists forgot to convert English to metric measures!

Because of the logistics of generating mailing labels, mailing the surveys, and keying the responses into a database, this method does require some dedicated staff for the surveying period. If the survey is long or if a large number of responses is expected, then consider using a questionnaire form that can be scanned. Of course, the entire survey administration can also be outsourced or the mailing portions to a mailing house.

Surveys by postal mail have several major *advantages.*

♦ **Cost per completed survey and cost per attempted survey.** This is an inexpensive means of surveying. In addition to copying costs, the material costs for a mail survey will run about $1.00 for each survey mailed. Add about $.50 each for a pre-administration announcement and for follow-up notes. Add to this the cost of executing the mailings and keying in the data. Cost per completed survey is found by dividing the sum of these costs by the number of properly completed responses.

> Cost per completed survey is determined by dividing the sum of costs by the number of properly completed responses.

♦ **Administration bias.** Since the interaction with every respondent is identical and you most certainly have mailing addresses for all customers, administering surveys by mail cannot bias the respondent.

♦ **Anonymity.** Respondents can be relatively certain about promises of anonymity since they can look for any "secret codes" on the survey or the return envelope.

♦ **Complexity of questions.** Perhaps the greatest strength of postal mail as an administrative method for surveys is the flexibility it provides in designing the questionnaire. The only limitation on the formatting is your imagination — or the word processing or publishing software you use.

♦ **Ability of the respondent to provide feedback on the instrument**. Expect to find notes written in the margins on questions the respondent found hard to complete for whatever reason. (The author is known to do this on surveys he takes!) If a large number of people do this, then the question may lack validity and/or reliability, and the question should be dropped from the analysis. While the feedback will not help the current survey, it will help future administrations of the same survey and future questionnaire design efforts. Feedback is all part of the learning process.

There are several considerable *disadvantages* to the postal survey method.

- **Speed of administration.** This is the slowest means of survey administration, along with "survey by disk." You need to allow one week for the survey to arrive at the respondent's address, a week for it to be completed, and a week for its return. Thus, from the time of survey mailing, you need to allow three weeks before sending out follow-up notices and at least five weeks before starting the analysis. Even then, a few last responses may straggle in as respondents find the survey when going through their less urgent mail. Of course, keying the responses can begin as soon as they arrive. What if you don't get the number of responses needed for statistically valid responses? You may need to send surveys to another sample, further slowing down the effort.

- **Scalability.** The effort and cost of hardcopy mail surveys rises in direct proportion to the number of surveys sent out. Using a form that can be scanned provides scalability for the data keying process. If this is a large surveying effort, then use of a mailing house makes sense as they have the equipment to provide scalability. There will probably be a one-time fee plus a per-mailing charge. Ask people in your marketing department whom they use for mailings.

- **Ability to clarify questions.** Questions cannot be clarified with a mail survey and the responses given cannot be corrected with any knowledge of the respondent's intent.

- **Administration control.** When respondents take a hard copy survey, they are in control of the administration process. This makes the use of conditional branching more problematic, and the instrument's visual design requires good, clear formatting. Truly customized instruments, say for each stratum, can only be done by creating variations of the original instrument. You will need to identify the instruments variations to ensure they are coded properly. Different colored paper is the simplest technique, but don't use garish colors.

◆ **Response rate.** Response rate for mail surveys is generally low, somewhere in the 15% to 25% range, depending upon how well you have motivated the respondent.

◆ **Willingness to provide comments and the nature of those comments.** Respondent burden is very high for open-ended questions on hardcopy surveys. People are unlikely to write much of a response and the type of information will be short, direct comments.

Telephone Surveys

Telephone surveying entails even greater logistics than mail surveys, but the rewards can be great due to the higher response rate and personal interaction. Announcement letters should still be sent out a couple of weeks in advance, and you might consider including the questionnaire in the letter, especially if it is at all complex. This allows respondents to have a visual reference in front of them when the telephone interviewer calls to administer the survey.

Administering a survey by phone is not a casual activity. Interviewers must be well trained and provided with a good script to follow. The interviewing can be contracted out or can be done by your staff. In fact, conducting surveys may be a good task to balance someone's workload. However, the people conducting the survey should not be people directly involved in service delivery. Since service agent names may be given, there are serious personnel considerations here.

With telephone surveys, you must develop more than just the questionnaire. You must develop an entire *script* for the interviewer to follow, anticipating all the various paths the interaction could follow. For example, if interviewers encounter a very unhappy customer, the script should direct them to transfer the person to the appropriate customer service desk, preferably as a "hot" transfer, that is, with the interviewers making initial contact with the customer service agents. Be sure respondents are asked if they would prefer to be called at a different time. Keep a log for telephone surveys for scheduling callbacks.

Interviewers must be properly trained, and you must decide how much discretion to give them. In the example above, how upset must the customer be for the interviewer to not even attempt to conduct the survey before transferring the call? You must set guidelines, and the interviewers must knowledgeably apply them. What if a person responds to a question with "I'm not really sure." How much prompting do you want the interviewers to perform before they record a blank answer? Be sure to listen to calls as a quality control check.

Automation software can guide the interview and is especially valuable to manage branching. If you have multiple interviewers sharing the same calling list, then the tracking and control task is more complicated, and some automation software becomes a necessity.

Keying the data should be done concurrently with the administration. The personal interaction may allow additional data beyond the survey responses to be captured. However, this type of interviewing requires more highly trained interviewers who know how to probe for information. Beware that the telephone survey administration does not turn into an interview — if you want to develop scientifically valid data. If each survey becomes a unique interview, then bias has been introduced into the results.

> Interviewers must be properly trained, and you must decide how much discretion to give them.

The areas where telephone surveying has *advantages* are:

- **Speed of administration.** Compared to postal surveys, gathering data by telephone surveys is faster. Speed is dictated by the size of the sample, length of the survey instrument, and the number of interviewers you have. Once you get the number of responses you want, you can also terminate the calling.

- **Ability to clarify questions.** Shortcomings in the questionnaire can be mitigated by the interviewer if the respondent does not understand a question. The interviewer can also prompt the respondent to answer questions in a correct fashion. Of course, this interaction presents the possibility of introducing bias.

- **Administration control.** Customizing the survey delivery is very easy for telephone surveys because the interviewer is in control of the administration, not the respondent. If a great many conditional branches are designed into the instrument, then administration software becomes important. Otherwise, the interviewer may get confused.

- **Ability of the respondent to provide feedback on the instrument design.** When certain questions repeatedly need clarification, this is a signal those questions are flawed. Train the interviewers to capture this information. It's also a good idea to debrief the interviewers (in a focus group of sorts) after the survey effort is completed. These folks have lived with the survey more than anyone and will have opinions about how well some questions worked. They will also be flattered with this job enrichment!

- **Response rate.** Telephone surveys tend to have higher response rates because the interviewers are actively soliciting participation. Response rates should be in the 50% range, but could be much higher. The author had a 90% response rate on a project where the respondent group had a strong affinity with the surveying company. Also, that respondent group is seldom surveyed. This situation is a rarity.

  For telephone surveys, response rate has to be measured more finely than with other methods. There are respondents who decline to participate, those who cannot be reached, and those who are reached but who can't be understood for any number of reasons. Those who decline create a "refusal rate," which is perhaps the most telling measure of success, but all these measures should be tracked.

- **Willingness to provide comments and the nature of those comments.** Because respondents only have to verbalize responses, they are usually willing — sometimes overly willing! — to provide comments to open-ended questions. Many times the interviewer is confronted with a running monologue in response to every structured question. Some respondents, though, will feel pressured to provide a response to open-ended questions, and they may just make something up. Recognize also that those comments will be spontaneous. That's not necessarily bad, but it is different than the nature of the comments garnered through other administration methods.

The areas where telephone surveys are at a *disadvantage* are:

- **Cost per completed survey and cost per attempted survey.** Telephone surveying is the most expensive method. Even though the time to conduct each survey may be short, most interviewer time will be spent trying to get respondents on the phone — unless computer generated dialing is used. For even a short questionnaire, three to four completed surveys per hour per interviewer is an accomplishment. With computer-generating dialing, each interviewer might be able to complete eight to 12 interviews, depending on the survey length. Obviously, long distance telephone costs can also be significant. Set-up costs, including training, can be substantial.

- **Administration bias.** This is a major issue with telephone surveys. Each interviewer *must* deliver the script identically to each respondent, otherwise the responses may be affected. Even intonations and off-hand comments can be enough to compromise the scientific nature of the surveying effort. This is why it is important to develop a script that anticipates respondents' comments and provides interviewers with good rebuttals. Depending on the degree of deviation from the script, customer research goals may still be accomplished, but there is a definite risk to data reliability without solid interviewer training.

- **Scalability.** The effort required to perform telephone surveys increases proportionately with the number of surveys performed. Automation software and computer-generated dialing offer some scalability, but these tools are out of the reach for a do-it-yourself effort.

- **Anonymity.** Obviously, anonymity is not possible in a telephone survey. Hiring an outside agency to perform the surveys will increase the forthrightness of respondents, but if respondents are truly concerned about confidentiality, then even that step won't fully ameliorate the issue.

- **Complexity of questions.** Because of the nature of the interaction, telephone surveys have to be structured very simply, and only one scale type should be used. If you add variations, respondents will get confused among the mass of words being thrown at them. You might consider faxing a copy of the instrument to people if they get confused, or as suggested previously, mailing a copy with the announcement letter.

Electronic Mail Surveys

There are three means of conducting surveys electronically: electronic mail (email), web form, and survey "by disk." Because the characteristics of each are very distinct, we will address them separately here, starting with email. (Chapter 8 is devoted to an extended discussion of survey automation tools.)

Surveying by electronic mail entails sending out the survey instrument as part of an email message. The questionnaire can be done entirely in ASCII text, or it can be attached as a separate document, perhaps using a Microsoft Word form or HTML. Survey software packages, which create the survey in ASCII text or HTML, can automate the tasks, specifically loading the responses into a data file. An email survey created by a software tool in ASCII text uses special characters (such as "::" or ">>") to isolate the respondent's answer from the question text. Because respondents may delete these characters, this type of email survey is prone to error. Email surveys obviously can also be done without a survey automation package, but then you will have to manually key the data. Under either scenario email addresses are a must.

It is probably best to send the pre-administration announcement by postal mail rather than by email, but you certainly can opt to send it by email. A postal letter formalizes the survey process, and using a second medium may increase the visibility to the respondent. Before sending out a blast of emails, do talk with your IT department. It is probably best to send these out as a scheduled task in the wee hours of the morning. After the email containing the survey instrument is sent, monitor the rate of responses. Plan to send out a follow-up notice when responses drop off, which should be about three to four days after the initial emailing. This follow-up notice will lead to a small flurry of additional responses within the next few days. Some survey automation tools will track the responses coming in, so that the follow-up notice is sent only to those who have not responded. This is a very nice feature, especially if you plan to engage in a continuous survey process. Remember, the point of the survey is not to annoy your customers.

The areas where email surveys have *advantages* are:

◆ **Cost per completed survey and cost per attempted survey.** A real appeal of email surveys is the cost, especially if a survey automation package is used. Once the system is set up, including the distribution lists, there is very little incremental cost to survey administration. In fact, the major cost may lie in the time needed to learn to use the software. If no automation package is used, then the data keying effort is similar to a postal mail survey.

◆ **Speed of administration.** As with web-form surveys, the time from sending out the surveys to getting the data back is quite short. Think about how you handle email messages. You read and respond to the email almost immediately or you delete it. This also applies to email surveys. Respondents will answer the email within three days, or they won't at all. If you send follow-up notices, then in little more than a week, data analysis can begin.

129

◆ **Scalability.** The power of email makes scalability a real strength of this method. Sending the survey to one or 10,000 respondents takes the same effort. With a survey automation package, the effort to load the data into a data file does vary a little with the number of responses. Also note that many vendors of survey software tools price their products based upon the number of responses that can be loaded. So, scalability may come at a price.

◆ **Willingness to provide comments and the nature of those comments.** You might think that the willingness of a respondent to provide comments on an email survey is about the same as for a hardcopy survey. Because so many of us have become adept at typing, the willingness to provide comments on an email survey is actually much higher than for a hardcopy survey. Do consider how many characters you want to allow for open-ended comments. In contrast to a telephone survey where the responses are spontaneous, responses here will be more thoughtful.

The areas where email surveys are at a *disadvantage* are:

◆ **Administration bias.** There is a potential bias in email administration, but it is different from the bias in telephone administration. Look at the percentage of your customers for whom you have email addresses. If it's well under 100%, then using email will introduce a *sampling bias*. You must ask a serious question. Is that subset of customers for whom you have email addresses different in any substantive way from the customers for whom you do not have email addresses? For example, are they customers with whom you transact less business or are they smaller customers? If there is a difference, then you will introduce a sampling bias, and you must consider using a second administration method for the non-email group.

> You don't want to ignore a block of customers consistently in a surveying effort.

Note that the data from different administrative methods can all be loaded into the same data set, but you should include a field that identifies the administrative method. With that, you can check if the responses do differ. This will guide future customer survey efforts. Using multiple administrative methods is especially important if your surveying effort is as much for customer relationship management as it is for customer attitude profiling. You don't want to ignore a block of customers consistently in a surveying effort.

You may decide that the bias is acceptable. For example, if you've only recently been collecting email addresses from clients, then your sample will be biased toward customers with whom you have recently conducted business. You may consider the other customers "lost" and not care about their opinions. Go back to your Statement of Purpose in the project plan. Does this bias compromise your objective? If it's acceptable, be sure to report this in the methodology section of your final report.

- **Anonymity.** Anonymity is an issue with email surveys. Some survey automation software have methods for stripping off identification numbers so that the respondent is anonymous, but how many respondents will truly believe that their answers are anonymous, especially since the returned email must contain an identification number sent with their responses?

- **Complexity of questions.** An instrument formatted in ASCII is, frankly, ugly. Very ugly. You must keep the questionnaire simple because you can't apply visual design techniques. If on the other hand, you are attaching a word-processed document, such as a Microsoft Word form or HTML form, your formatting options are as good as with a hardcopy instrument.

- **Ability to clarify questions.** During the administration itself, respondents' questions about the instrument cannot be clarified, nor can errors be corrected, but respondents might take advantage of email to pose a clarification question. Be careful not to bias the respondent with any clarification provided, much as a telephone interview must exhibit similar caution.

- **Administration control.** Much like a hardcopy survey, the respondent controls the flow of the administration. Branching is especially difficult in ASCII text surveys. If you are using automation software, then you cannot even customize surveys by sending out slightly different instruments as one can do for postal mail surveys. With survey software packages, one instrument is tied to the returned survey data file. You could create a work-around, but it would be cumbersome.

- **Ability of the respondent to provide feedback on the instrument.** Unlike postal mail surveys or telephone surveys, feedback on shortcomings in the instrument will be sparse.

Providing feedback requires an extra step of writing an email instead of scribbling comments on a hardcopy instrument right in front of you. The pilot of the instrument is thus *very* important.

♦ **Response rate.** Email surveys are still relatively new, so there is not much history here. There is likely to be a "novelty effect" with an email survey that will lead to higher initial response rates. We do not yet have solid research on response rates for electronic media, and rates are likely to fluctuate. Do note that response rates will be lower if you are administering the survey through a file attached to the email. This increases the response burden for the respondent, and there is a legitimate concern about viruses hiding in the file.

Web-Form Surveys

A second electronic method of surveying is through the use of a web form. Here, a survey is constructed using HTML and posted on a web page, the respondent accesses it, makes entries on the web form, and submits it. Most survey automation software packages will generate the HTML web form. You may want to enhance the HTML by hiring a web designer to customize the web page. Be sure the web designer works with the vendor of the automation software to ensure the coding to capture responses is not corrupted. Also be sure that response scales are shown with equal intervals. (See Chapter 4 issues on scale design.) HTML tables will be used to generate the response scale with radio buttons. If only the endpoints are anchored, then the spacing may not be equal.

A key issue with web surveys is *how* the customer gets to the web-form survey. If the survey is just posted on some web page and responses are taken from people who stumble upon it, then this is *not* a scientific survey. For a scientific administration, we need to actively solicit responses from a sample that is generated to reflect the population of interest, similar to hardcopy and telephone administration.

Typically, active web-form administration involves sending an email message to the sample with a link to the web page containing the instrument. Ideally, an authentication code should be used to prevent people outside of the sample from accessing the survey. These codes, which are embedded by the survey automation tool, also prevent multiple submissions. Sending follow-up notices for web-form surveys is the same as for email surveys.

The areas where web-form surveys have *advantages* are:

- **Cost per completed survey and cost per attempted survey.** The cost structure here is virtually the same as for email surveys. After the initial investment is made in the survey design and a survey automation software package, the administration cost is minimal.

- **Speed of administration.** As with email surveys, results probably can be tallied in a little over one week after the email announcement is mailed out.

- **Scalability.** Scalability is as strong a suit for web-form survey administration as it is for email surveys.

- **Complexity of questions.** HTML provides for strong formatting capabilities, similar to a printed survey questionnaire. This is a major advantage over an email survey using ASCII text. Web forms make fixed-sum questions less troublesome since the entries can be subtotaled as each entry is made. This reduces respondent burden and increases the likelihood of entries that add properly.

- **Willingness to provide comments and the nature of those comments.** As with email surveys, many respondents feel comfortable typing in an extended answer. These comments will be more contemplative than the spontaneous comments from a telephone survey.

- **Administration control.** Two years ago, this factor would have been listed under the disadvantages. A "standard" web-form survey is much like a hard copy survey. The respondent controls the administration, and conditional branching is very cumbersome. But that has changed. Now, respondents' answers can be processed in real time for multi-screen survey instruments as screens are submitted. Administration control is in the hands of the surveyor much as it is with a telephone survey, making branching much simpler. Note that after any branching or filtering question, the web form must be submitted and processed.

  Also, the software can be programmed to ensure answers are entered correctly. Do be thoughtful about how the respondent is told their entry is incorrect. Some error messages can be annoying or insulting, leading the respondent to quit the survey.

- **Ability to clarify questions.** Similar to administration control, this factor has changed through new technologies. It is now possible to clarify questions through hover text or pop-up windows. Be careful that these are not cumbersome and annoying.

◆ **Response rate.** The novelty of web-form surveys may lead to high response rates initially, but expect a drop off.

The areas where web-form surveys are at a *disadvantage* are:

◆ **Administration bias.** Since everyone experiences the identical survey, there is little chance to bias a respondent in the administration of the instrument. However, sample bias is a genuine concern. The issues are the same as those outlined above in the discussion of email surveys, but the risk of sampling bias here is even greater. Links to a web form from an email message are most useful for respondents with high-speed internet access, which is common in most corporations. However, some companies block certain employees' access to the internet. More importantly, consumers working on low-speed modems with dial-up access will be less willing to link to the web form. With multi-screen instruments needed to effect branching, this becomes a real issue because of the time to process and load each screen. Track the number of surveys started but not completed if possible. You must strongly consider sampling bias by examining the characteristics of your respondent pool.

> Be thoughtful about how respondents are told their entry is incorrect. Some error messages can be annoying or insulting, leading the respondent to quit the survey.

◆ **Anonymity.** Many respondents may not believe any guarantees of anonymity because of the "cookie" scares. The author used one of these tools to gather mid-semester feedback from university students. The response rate was low. Even after showing them how the responses came back with no identification tags, they remained skeptical about the anonymity of the process.

◆ **Ability of the respondent to provide you feedback on flaws in the instrument design.** Respondents can't write marginal notes on the survey form to give you feedback. Again, pilot the instrument. While you will get responses, the validity of the instrument may make them meaningless — or worse — misleading.

Surveying "by Disk"

Surveying by disk is a technique for electronic administration that precedes widespread use of the internet. Survey automation software tools would generate an executable file that was mailed to the respondent. Prior to the advent of email, the executable file was sent by floppy disk, but it can now be sent as an attachment to an email message or placed on an intranet server.

If floppy disks are being sent out, then surveying by disk resembles a postal mail survey in its cost structure and other characteristics. Material and postage mailing costs will be slightly higher because of the floppy disks. If the executable file is being sent as an email attachment, then it resembles a web-form survey in most of its facets.

For two of the criteria we have outlined, surveying by disk is sufficiently different to merit mention in these areas:

♦ **Complexity of questions.** Working with an executable file provides greater flexibility in questionnaire construction. Branching can be executed that is transparent to the respondent, as it would be for a telephone survey. In essence, the interviewer is in control of the survey. Edit controls can be created to assure that respondents don't make illegitimate entries. This could be important for a fixed-sum question format.

♦ **Response rate.** Because the survey is sent as an executable file, however, response rates will be much lower. If sent as an attached file, respondent burden is higher, and many people are legitimately leery of downloading executable files because of viruses. If this is an executable file on an intranet server, then the concerns are lessened.

Interactive Voice Response (IVR)

This is a new surveying technique, which takes advantage of telecommunications technologies, especially private branch exchanges (PBX), commonly used in call centers. An IVR survey system can also be used to administer a periodic survey by directing respondents to the IVR survey through an introductory letter or email. However, IVR surveys' real strength lies in transaction-driven surveying. Such a survey is conducted as follows.

When customers call for service, they are asked by the IVR system if they would be willing to participate in a survey at the end of the service call. When the call is completed, those respondents are automatically forwarded to the IVR survey system, which then delivers the survey instrument much as a telephone interviewer might. Responses are entered on the telephone keypad or by voice recognition. Responses are processed in real time. Business rules establish whether a response should be forwarded to a specific manager to initiate service recovery actions. The ability to address a service issue literally moments after the service is delivered is the key strength of IVR surveys, along with its scalability.

However, also consider *when* the survey is being administered in the overall service transaction. Is the entire service transaction complete when the phone interaction ends? If not, then an IVR survey cannot measure all aspects of the service transaction, only those from the telephone interaction. (This issue is true for all administration methods, but it stands out most here.) Further, people's opinions and attitudes will be strongest just at the completion of the service interaction. Do you want people's feelings at that point or after they have had a chance to reflect? With telephone surveys we mentioned the spontaneity of comments. With IVR surveys, everything is spontaneous. This is not necessarily bad; just know what you're getting and use it appropriately.

Sampling bias must be addressed here. How the respondent is chosen to complete an IVR survey will determine whether a sampling bias is created. If respondents are randomly chosen to participate in the survey before service begins, then there is no sampling bias. However, if customers can elect to take a survey after the service is completed, then we will have a bias toward people holding extreme views. Also, the service agent should never know which calls will have the follow-up survey, otherwise we have created a sampling bias.

Targeting the Population and Selecting the Sample

At this point in the project, you've developed the questionnaire and chosen an administrative method. Now the question is: whom do we sample? There are several means of generating a sample. The ones most applicable to customer satisfaction surveys are described here. The goal in selecting the sample is to be sure that the results reflect the population we want to understand, that is, that the process of generating the sample is not introducing some bias into the results.

Before we can generate a sample, we have to identify the population from which we will draw the sample. (See Figure 5.2) This may sound obvious, "It's my customers." But what customers? Is it people who tangibly receive service? Is it people who handle invoices and bill payments? It is new customers? Is it customers who are on trial memberships? Is it your most active customers? Is it customers who have defected? Look to your Statement of Purpose that guided the development of your questionnaire. That should point you to the definition of the target population, which may well be a subset of your overall population. Now, you can select a sample following the principles below.

Figure 5.2
Targeting the Wrong Population

Population Used for Sampling

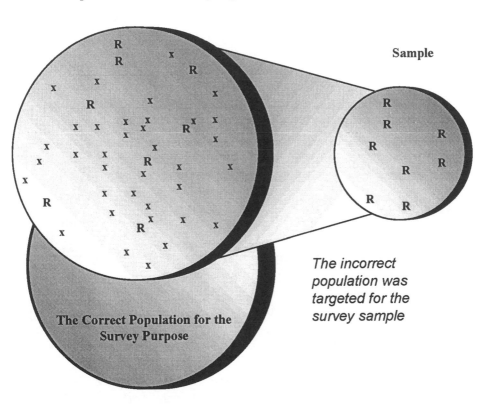

Sample

The Correct Population for the Survey Purpose

The incorrect population was targeted for the survey sample

Taking a Census —
The Impact of Electronic Survey Techniques

A *census* occurs when everyone is surveyed. Thus, the sample equals the population. The scalability of electronic survey tools makes attempting to take a census a real possibility. If you're conducting a transaction-driven survey in part to get customers to voice their complaints, then a census may make sense. However, customers may get tired of being surveyed constantly and thus will complete a survey only when they have a complaint. This results in a *non-response bias*. Ask your customers how often they would be willing to be surveyed.

Random Samples

When surveying a sample, the best means of selecting respondents is to select them randomly from the population as a whole. *Random selection* helps ensure that there is not a bias in the sample, meaning that the sample properly represents the population as a whole. Many of the survey automation packages will generate a random sample if you import a customer list.

Perhaps the simplest means of generating a random sample yourself is to use a spreadsheet, such as Excel. Place your customer names on separate rows in one column and in the next column use the function, RAND, to generate a random number between 0 and 1 for each customer. Sort the two columns by the random number, and create your sample from the entries. If you determine you need 50 customers in your sample, select the first 50 entries after the sorting.

Stratified Samples

In most survey projects, we will want to examine different groups or strata in the returned data. For example, we may want to examine the data by customers, by customer type, by industry type, or by product type. We may want to have reasonable confidence in our data for each stratum. In this case, we first sort our customer list along the stratum, and then generate random samples for each stratum. Without this step, we may — by chance — end up with a small number of potential respondents in the overall sample for a stratum. Our statistical confidence in the results for that stratum could be quite low. Do recognize that confidence levels in each stratum will be less than for the sample as a whole, and the confidence for each stratum will differ according to the formulas to be presented shortly.

One stratum that may be overlooked is time period. If you're performing transaction-driven surveys, then you probably want to examine the results by week, by month, and so on — in addition to segmenting by service agent and other pertinent characteristics.

Determining the Sample Size and the Sample Distribution Size

The very first axiom about determining the appropriate sample size is: don't listen to marketing. The author frequently hears service managers say, "Marketing tells me that if I get a five to 10% response rate, I should be ecstatic." This is not an apples-to-apples comparison. It's an apples-to-kumquat comparison. Marketing is talking about the response to a direct mail campaign. We're talking about the sample size needed to get a statistically viable result. The author has also heard people say there is some magic number, e.g., 30 or 50 responses, to make the results valid. This is a serious oversimplification. Most people focus on the *response rate* — as we did earlier in this chapter in comparing administration methods — but a "good" response rate has to be considered in the context of other factors, especially the population size as we shall see.

To determine the sample size we have to employ statistics, and many people get a cold chill down their spine at the very term. A college stat professor who talked in theoretical concepts probably is to blame. We'll try to make statistics real here. For a more in-depth treatment, pick up a statistics text. There's usually some "numbers person" in the office whom you should have on your project team just for this task. We'll explain the factors that determine sample size and the calculus involved, but then we'll simplify matters with a chart. To understand the chart properly, though, you need the background provided in the next few pages. Bear with us.

First of all, many statistics texts confuse sample size discussions. The equations they present for sample size really represent the *sample response size*. That is, the sample size they describe is for the number of responses received, not a determination of the number of surveys that must be sent out. So, we'll distinguish the sample response size from the *sample distribution size*.

Determining the sample distribution size is a simple process. The sample distribution size is affected by two factors: the *number of responses needed* and the *expected response rate*. Figure 5.3 shows the equation. The number of responses needed is the hard part. We'll turn to that after addressing the expected response rate.

The expected response rate is the percentage of respondents who will likely complete a survey. Preferably it's based upon some past surveying experiences with your customer base. No "national average" for a response rate exists. The response rate will be affected by your administration technique, the relationship you have with

Figure 5.3
Determining the Sample Distribution Size

$$\text{Sample Distribution Size} = \frac{\text{\# Responses Needed}}{\text{Expected Response Rate}}$$

Expected Response Rate

• Based on historical experience preferably

Number of Responses Needed

• Decide on the accuracy desired

• Determine size of relevant population

your customer base, any incentive you've offered, and the quality of your questionnaire — a point we cannot stress too strongly! If you have no past survey history, then use a conservative estimate, such as 25% for web-based surveys and 15% for postal mail surveys.

The sample distribution size is found simply by dividing the number of responses needed by the expected response rate. So, if you expect a 25% response rate and need 100 responses to achieve the desired confidence, then you will have to attempt to survey 400 people (100 / 0.25 = 400).

Now let's turn to the hard part: the number of responses needed. There are two equations that determine the number of responses needed depending upon whether the key questions in the survey instrument produce numeric data (from interval-scaled questions) or proportions (from categorical questions).

Numeric

$$n = \frac{Z^2 \sigma_{\bar{x}}^2}{e^2}$$

Proportions

$$n = \frac{Z^2 p(1-p)}{e^2}$$

Where:

n = number of responses needed (this is typically called "sample size")

Z = the number of standard deviations that describes the precision of your desired results

e = accuracy or error of the results

$\sigma_{\bar{x}}$ = standard error of the estimate (pronounced as "sigma sub x bar" or "sigma x bar")

p = expected sample proportion

All of those terms need explanation. Let's say your most important questions are interval-scaled questions using a 10-point scale, and you want your answers to be fairly accurate, say within 0.2 of the "real answers." Note that by "real answers" we mean the ratings that would be found if we conducted a census, getting responses from everyone.[1] So, if your survey got a rating of 7 on these questions, the real answer would range between 6.8 and 7.2. That 0.2 represents the *accuracy* or error of the results, represented by the term *e* in the above equation. (*e* is sometimes called *tolerable error.*)

What if your critical question was an ordinal question where you asked respondents how satisfied they were with the service, presenting them with five categories to choose from. Let's say you want the percentages for each category to be accurate within 5%. So, if the *Extremely Satisfied* category received a sample mean percentage of 35%, the real answer would range between 30% to 40%. No doubt you have heard public opinion polls described as having an "accuracy of plus or minus 5%." That's the *e* or error term in the equation we've just described.

---

[1] For those of you who are statistically inclined, the distinction here is between the *sample mean* and the *population mean*.

Now let's turn to the Z term in the equations. Z represents the *precision* of the results. Likely, you're asking, "Precision and accuracy? Aren't those the same thing?" Not to a statistician. Accuracy depicts the band within which the real answer should lie based upon the sample data. (This band is known as the *confidence interval.*) Precision depicts how likely the real answer is to fall within the confidence interval. By convention, Z is set at a 95% probability, which translates to 1.96 standard deviations for the purposes of the above equation. (Rounding to 2 standard deviations is acceptable.) Because a convention is followed, the precision is typically not disclosed. If those public opinion pollsters told you everything, they would report that the results of the poll are "95% certain of being within plus or minus 5%."

There is the fear that the pollsters — or any surveyor — could lie with statistics.[2] Perhaps the survey received a low response rate, and they want to make the survey seem more valid than it really is. The surveyor could still claim an accuracy of plus or minus 5%, but the precision might be only 90% or lower. To be consistent with accepted practice, you should adhere to the 95% convention for precision.

Before turning to the last two variables, let's address the critical question for the surveyor: *What accuracy is right?* The number of responses you get will determine your accuracy, but you should enter the survey process with an idea of the accuracy you want in order to set a target response level. (Note that the above equations — and the ones that follow — can be used to determine the accuracy of results given the number of responses received. Just rearrange the equation solving for *e*.)

To set your required accuracy level, think about the amount of error that you can tolerate. Using the above example, pretend you were going to compare individual service agents using the survey data. The organization as a whole received a 7.0, one agent got a 6.9, and another agent received a 7.2. What conclusions could you draw? Answer: None. You could not say definitively that one agent is better than the other, because both scores fall within the confidence interval. Similarly, if you were trending data from one period to the next, you could not definitely say that an improvement or decline had occurred if the averages fall within the confidence

---

[2] To repeat the oft-quoted line attributed to both Mark Twain and Benjamin Disraeli, "There are three types of lies: lies, damn lies, and statistics."

interval. Going back to the public opinion polls, you may have heard the term *statistical dead heat* when one candidate polls 35% and another 31% for a survey with a plus or minus 5% error. This is the same situation. If you're using these data for performance evaluations, then you probably can tolerate less error.

We left two variables in the equations until the end. Both $\sigma_{\bar{x}}$' and p describe the expected variation among the respondents' answers. The variation is important for determining the necessary sample sizes. This may not seem obvious at first, but let's consider the classic example used in statistics class. Say you were blindfolded in a kitchen, and two pots of soup were put before you. You were asked to describe the soups, naming as many ingredients as possible. One soup is a bisque where everything has been pureed, and the other is a stew. The second spoonful of the bisque will yield little new information beyond the first spoonful, but you might have to take several spoonfuls of the stew before you have sampled all the ingredients in it. Why? Because there is more variation in the stew than in the bisque. The analogy applies to surveying. The greater the variability, the larger the number of responses needed to achieve the same degree of accuracy.

Determining $\sigma_{\bar{x}}$ presents a real dilemma. We can only know the variance in the data after we have collected it, but we need to estimate the variance in order to know how big a sample to take! (Those of you who have taken a statistics class may recall such delightful paradoxes.) There are four ways we can take proceed.

1. If we have done previous surveying of that population, then we can estimate the variance based upon that data.

2. If we have not surveyed that population before, we can just do our survey and intentionally sample a large number. Then we can generate the standard error from that data, and do future surveys more efficiently.

3. We can use a conservative estimate. In statistics, we learn that 3σ (three standard deviations) to the left of the mean and 3σ to the right of the mean (for a total of 6σ) describes virtually the entire area under a normal distribution curve. Let's say we are using a 10-point scale to gather our responses and assume that the responses will be found that span across the entire 10-point scale. Thus, one standard deviation, σ, = 10/6 = 1.67, and the variance, σ^2, = 2.78. That is a conservative estimate, meaning that the variance is probably much smaller. If you believe that

your responses will range between 3 and 10 on the 10-point scale, then $\sigma = (10\text{-}3)/6 = 7/6 = 1.16$, and $\sigma^2 = 1.36$.

4. As a compromise to the above options, we can calculate n using the conservative assumption, and distribute the survey to a sample that we hope can generate say half the needed responses for a conservative estimate. With that data received, we can calculate our sample variance and use that in the above equation applying the approach in option 1. Then we sample additional people to get the number of responses needed.

With proportional data, determining p is a bit easier since we are calculating the term $p(1\text{-}p)$. Note first of all that a proportion can only range between 0 and 1. Thus, the highest that calculated term can be is found with $p = 0.5$, yielding 0.25 for the term[3]. Like the determination of $\sigma_{\bar{x}}$ in the third option above, this is the most conservative estimate for a proportion. Of course, we can use past history, which is the best option by far.

Does all this sound complicated? Unfortunately, we have to add another very important complication. The two equations above incorporated an assumption: that the size of the population — in our case, the customer base — is very large. If the population is very large, then population size does not affect our calculations above. But when the population is small, it *does* matter. The sample size equations below add the variable of population size, N.

<table>
<tr><td align="center"><u>**Numeric**</u></td><td align="center"><u>**Proportions**</u></td></tr>
<tr><td align="center">$$n = \frac{\sigma_{\bar{x}}^2}{\frac{e^2}{z^2} + \frac{\sigma_{\bar{x}}^2}{N}}$$</td><td align="center">$$n = \frac{p(1-p)}{\frac{e^2}{z^2} + \frac{p(1-p)}{N}}$$</td></tr>
</table>

Where: N   = population size

All other variables defined as above. [4]

Notice that as N gets large, that term in the denominator approaches zero, and the equations become the same as the ones presented earlier. Once the population of customers gets large enough, say around 2,000, these adjustments become unnecessary, but when

---

[3] Try substituting other numbers for p in the term $p(1\text{-}p)$ and you will find the result to be less than 0.25.

[4] You may see a slightly different equation in some texts. This is Hamburg, 1977.

we plan to analyze the data for various strata, then the population of each stratum might be small enough to require this adjustment. For example, if you were planning to analyze the data at a service agent level or regional service center level, then you would need to apply the equation to those strata.

Also, what if you are conducting transaction-driven surveys. What is the population? Option 1: the total number of customers. Option 2: the number of customers with whom you had a closed transaction in the period for which you're calculating results. You probably guessed from the presentation that option 2 is the answer. This can dramatically change the sample size requirements for a given level of accuracy desired!

Now let's simplify matters a bit. Nearby is Figure 5.4 which applies the sample size calculations for a survey using the proportions equation. The most conservative assumption for p has been applied to the calculations. We chose to show a chart for proportions for two reasons. First, any scaled question can also be interpreted as using proportions. For example, the proportion responding with a 10 on a 1-to-10 scale. Second, the most conservative assumption for a proportion is fixed. For a numerical scale, the most conservative assumption varies with the length of the scale. *Use this chart as a guideline.*

Notice the two axes are the size of the population and the percentage of the population responding, which is the sample response size divided by the population. There are 7 curves on the chart, one for each of 7 accuracy levels. Notice that we've applied the 95% precision convention to all but one of them. The "curve" at the top of the chart is actually a line. It represents the accuracy of taking a census. In that case, we are 100% certain that the population mean *is* the sample mean. There's no error. The next six curves show decreasing accuracy ranging from +/-1% to +/-20%.

What does this chart tell us? First, higher accuracy requires responses from a larger percentage of the population. That's obvious! Second, and less obvious, notice the impact of population size. As the population gets larger, the curves start to converge, but at smaller population sizes, the response percentage ranges dramatically with accuracy levels. For a population of 500, accuracy of +/-10% requires about 18% of the population to respond equal to 90 responses. An accuracy of +/-3% would require about 70% of the population to respond equal to 350 responses! The conclusion: surveys of small populations require larger response percentages for higher levels of accuracy. Remember: this chart applies the most conservative estimate of the variance in the responses.

Budget concerns may also affect sample sizes. Larger sampling may increase cost. However, electronic administration methods mitigate that effect. Still, though, we do not recommend attempting a census, even for a one-time, as-needed survey. Your survey

Figure 5.4
Statistical Accuracy of a Survey

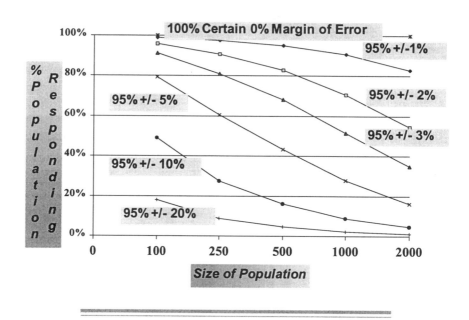

will likely pose new questions you want answered. By surveying only a sample, you now have customers for a follow-up survey, reducing the likelihood of "survey burn-out." For transaction-driven surveys, survey burn-out is a real concern. If people are constantly surveyed, they just stop completing the survey unless they have a gripe. That means we have introduced a non-response bias to our sampling! We'll turn to that issue later.

Determining the Confidence of the Results

The previous section described how to determine the sample size needed for an accuracy level. That was based upon an estimate of the variance in the data collected. After you have conducted the survey, the same equation can be used to identify the confidence that results from the number of responses actually received. In this case, n and N are known, the variance of the responses, p or $\sigma_{\bar{x}}$ can be calculated, and you will solve for e, holding Z at 95%.

Pre-administration Notification

You've established the administration method for your survey and chosen the sample you intend to survey. Now you begin the actual administration process, and *every step is vital for getting a large and unbiased response.* Before sending the survey, consider sending a note to the sample, or perhaps to the entire population of customers, announcing the survey program. (See Figure 5.5) If this is an on-going customer research program with recurring surveying, then be sure to communicate this to the entire customer base. Be sure to state whether everyone will get the survey or just a random sample.

This is your first chance to motivate the respondents. Tell the respondents why you're doing the survey. (Hint: look at the Statement of Purpose in your project planning documents.) Tell your customers how completing the survey will benefit them, in terms of the action plans that the survey will prompt. Also, state how you will communicate the results to your customers if you plan to. As you might imagine, a promise of communicating results back to customers should increase the response rate.

This notification usually takes the form of a hardcopy letter sent through postal or interdepartmental mail, but notification could also be made through an article in a regular customer newsletter or through email — if you have email address for all your customers.

Sending the Survey

The administration technique chosen obviously drives the medium in which the survey is delivered. Also consider how quickly you administer to the sample. For hardcopy mail, web-form, and email surveys, you could send out the survey to the entire sample at once or in waves. There are two reasons for the "wave" method, particularly for an initial survey effort. As the first wave of responses comes back, you now get the first historical data for measuring the variance, which is used to determine sample size requirements.

Second, the first wave also allows assessing response rates. If you are offering incentives for respondents, this will help you keep to your budget for those gifts. (We'll cover incentives a bit later.) With telephone surveys, there's not a wave, but rather a constant stream of responses that can be used for the above measurements.

Regardless of how quickly you send out the surveys, don't underestimate the logistical efforts involved in the actual administration of a survey. Plan this phase well. Survey automation software will simplify, but not eliminate, the logistical issues. Create a log to track surveys sent and received. As noted earlier, this log is most critical for telephone surveys. Below are specific tasks that must be accomplished for each type of survey administration.

Figure 5.5.
Sample Pre-Administration Note

Dear <customer>:

We at Acme Manufacturing recognize that in order to retain your business we have to strive constantly to meet your needs. Toward that end, we are instituting a customer surveying program for our support organization. The goal of the survey is to identify where our services have fallen short of your expectations in order to correct our shortcomings. We also want to identify where we excel to reinforce those aspects of our service delivery.

Each week we will survey a group of customers who called our support center. This survey will be conducted by telephone, so occasionally you may receive one of these calls.

We trust that you will see a steady improvement in our service delivery, and at the next users group meeting we will let you know how your feedback has helped us serve you better.

Thank you in advance for your assistance.

Sincerely,

Mary Forni
Vice President, Customer Service

Postal Mail Surveys

- Print copies of the instrument and other correspondence.
- Produce mailing labels or envelopes printed with customer addresses.
- Generate return envelopes with postage.
- Stuff the envelopes.
- Create a log for returned surveys.
- Produce mailing labels and note cards for follow-up notes.
- Print follow-up notes.

Telephone Surveys

- Develop the interview script, including rebuttals to likely responses and transfer options for unhappy customers.
- Create a work area with necessary office technology, including phones with head sets.
- Hire and train the interviewers.
- Buy or build a data entry system — a spreadsheet can work, although this method is prone to data entry error.

Email Surveys

- Purchase survey automation software or write your own.
- Generate questionnaire in electronic tool.
- Develop data entry system for returned surveys (only necessary if you have not purchased survey automation software).
- Notify your system administrator before you hit the send key. You may be sending out hundreds—or even thousands—of emails. While the size of the message is likely to be small, the volume may cause problems with the mail server. Better to be safe than to incur the ire of your system administrator.

Web-Form Surveys

- Purchase survey automation software, or develop your own web form and system for loading responses from returned surveys into a data file.
- Generate questionnaire in HTML. You can enhance the HTML from survey automation survey, if desired.
- Notify your system administrator before you hit the send key if you are administering the survey through an email with a link

to the web page. The same potential for overload of the mail server exists here as it would for an email survey. Capacity for the server on which the web form sits should also be considered.

Increasing Response Rates and Reducing Non-response Bias

"How can I increase my response rate?" is a frequent question. The concern about response rates is well-founded, but the concern should not be just about the accuracy gained from more responses. Perhaps more important is that the *responses from the sample properly reflect the sample*. (See Figure 5.6) Remember, you randomly chose a sample from the population to guard against a sampling bias, but now within that sample, some people may be more motivated to respond than others. As you might imagine, the people with extreme views, positive or negative, are more self-motivated. The "middle of the road" people need extra motivation, and you need them in order to obtain an accurate, unbiased profile of the population. The goal is to reduce any *non-response bias*, which has been mentioned several times previously.

For any survey, there are five critical steps to a response. You have to get the survey *noticed, opened, read, completed,* and *returned*. *Read* and *completed* relate to the introduction and questionnaire design, which are common across administrative methods. For each administrative method, the means for getting it *noticed* and *opened* will differ. Whatever method is used, however, the pre-administrative notification is an essential tool to gain notice from prospective respondents. A key goal across all methods is to get the announcement and survey instrument beyond any "gatekeeper" and to the respondent.

With postal surveys, getting the survey mailing *noticed* and *opened* means making it stand out. Use a real stamp, not a postage meter. Using bulk rate postage will almost guarantee that the envelope winds up in the trash unopened. Handwritten envelopes will also attract notice. Good handwriting is essential! There are some type fonts that mimic handwriting. Those might backfire, however, if the respondent recognizes the attempt at deception.

Getting the survey *read, completed,* and *returned* will be affected by the quality of the instrument design, including its formatting. With a telephone survey, *noticed* and *opened* means getting the respondents to the telephone and convincing them to give you some time. This is one instance where the script and training of the interviewers are critical. For web and email surveys, getting *noticed* means having a compelling subject line. The sender's name may also help get it noticed. Novelty and ease of survey completion hopefully will get it *opened* and *completed*.

Figure 5.6
Non-Response Bias

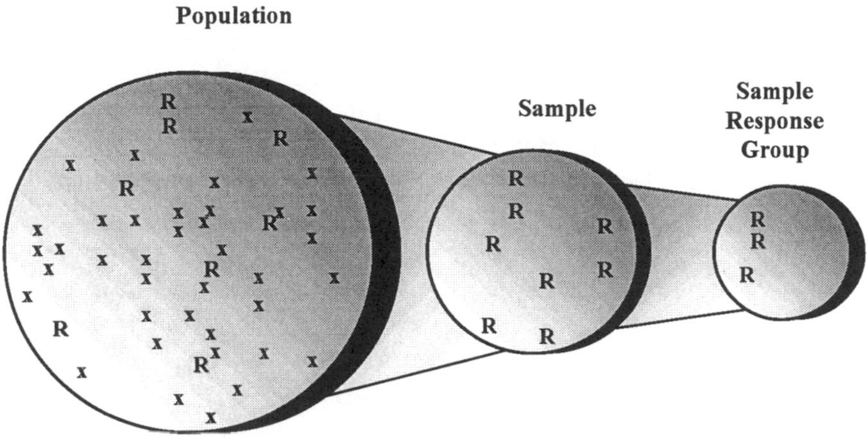

Population

The Sample was drawn randomly from the Population, but the Response Group is not representative of the Sample.

There are two techniques commonly used to reduce non-response bias while increasing response rates. They are the use of reminder notes and the use of gifts. Another option is to use a third-party vendor.

Follow-up Reminder Notes

You've sent out the survey by mail or email, and the results are coming in. You may think the administration is complete, except perhaps for the data keying. However, you should now send out reminder notes. Why? They're an inexpensive way of increasing responses, but more importantly, they reduce non-response bias.

To minimize this task, send the notes only to those who have not responded. Many survey automation packages will track who has responded and only send reminders out to those who haven't responded. This is true even for anonymous electronic surveys. The invitation sent out by the survey automation tool can contain a unique code (every vendor uses a different term for this code) to identify the respondent to the system even though the names are not reported to the data set. The reminder note should be sent once the responses tail off, which should be three to four business days from the initial electronic mailing.

With a hard copy mail survey, anonymity poses more problems for reminder notes. You have to send the reminder note to everyone, which may annoy some people. Typically, the reminder is a post card with a short message. Include a phone number, preferably toll free, for the person to call if they have misplaced the survey form. Note: you'll get better results if you send another survey instrument out with a stamped return envelope. But this increases the logistical effort and the cost. You also run the risk of multiple submissions from the same person. Post card reminders are the normal technique. The time until the reminders are sent depends upon the geographic dispersion of the responses and thus the anticipated mail delivery times. Wait at least two weeks from initial mailing before sending the reminders.

If the survey is not anonymous, then you can target the non-respondents with notes or a new survey. In lieu of post cards, consider making quick phone calls. Even if you don't reach the individual, you can leave a voice mail message offering to send or fax another instrument. With telephone and postage rates moving in opposite directions, telephone calls may prove cheaper and more effective. Obviously, reminders are not an issue for telephone survey administration. The fact that reminders are not necessary to reduce non-response bias is a real strength of telephone survey administration.

Thank You Gifts

Many people turn immediately to gifts to improve response rates, not realizing that gifts should also reduce non-response bias. Before turning to gimmicks like gifts, be sure you have handled the survey fundamentals properly. A good response rate from an unbiased response group should result from the steps laid out in this guide — pre-administration notification, a good introduction, a well-designed questionnaire, low respondent burden for completing and returning the questionnaire, and follow-up notices.

The gift can either be given in *anticipation* of completing the survey or as a *reward* for actually completing it. Mention the gift in your pre-administration notification and the cover note sent with the survey. Be sure to stress to the respondent that the gift is truly a *token* and is not meant to compensate fully for the time the respondent has given you.

- **Anticipation gift.** The idea behind the anticipation gift is to get the respondent to complete the survey by thanking them in advance with the token gift. A more cynical view is that you're trying to make the person feel guilty if they just keep the gift. Think about what would likely motivate your respondent group — or activate their guilty conscience. Are they likely to already have a drawer full of those gifts? Notice also that the cost of this technique is based upon the number of surveys *sent*, not received.

  Money is a frequently used gift, and two-dollar bills are commonly used since they are novel. Consider putting money in the pre-administration letter. This may get people to notice and open the upcoming survey envelope. Time is so precious for most people, however, that the guilt associated with keeping an unearned dollar or two is low. Do an informal survey of your colleagues or customers and ask them what gift dollar amount would make them feel guilty if they didn't complete the survey.

  Anticipation gifts are most appropriate for hardcopy mail surveys. You could use one for telephone surveys if you're sending out a pre-announcement letter. For electronic surveys you could set up a gift certificate with an authorization code. But in both cases, you're probably better off using a reward gift.

- **Reward gift.** With a reward gift you do something for respondents when they return completed surveys. You may send respondents some gift or enter them in a contest for some larger prize — or both. The advantages of a reward over anticipation gifts lie in the level of incentive for a given budget. Say you have a 25% response rate. For the same budget you can give a reward worth four times an anticipation gift. The motivation to respond should be far greater. Using a wave method of sending out the surveys will allow you to more easily limit the number of responses — and thus gifts — to your budgeted amount. The shortcoming of reward gifts is that anonymity is compromised or more difficult to achieve. You really need a third party to handle the gift fulfillment process. For electronic surveys, it's common to provide an electronic gift certificate to an on-line retailer.

Here's a variation of the reward gift. *Consider appealing to the respondent's altruism.* Agree to make a donation, say $10, to some charity for each completed survey. At the end of the survey, give a short list of charities and ask the person to check one. This maintains an air of professionalism; whereas, entering a respondent's name into a raffle can give the process a carnival feel. Choose a range of charities, but don't include anything that might be controversial or political. Few people would take umbrage at the International Red Cross, Boys and Girls Clubs, or American Cancer Society as charity options. If you have an international audience, be sure to include international charities. With a charitable donation as a "reward" gift, anonymity is preserved, and the world will be a little better place. The author has used this technique successfully in his academic research work.

Use of Third-Party Vendors

We've stressed throughout this book that you can do a surveying program yourself, but there are times where outsourcing makes sense for reasons beyond time, money, and unique expertise. If you have a respondent population whom you fear will not respond to a survey request or not respond forthrightly and honestly, then using a third party may be the route to follow. This concern is greatest for company-internal surveys, for example, an employee satisfaction survey or a survey of help desk customers. There's the fear — even with an anonymous survey — that somehow, "they" will find out the bad things you said and hold it against you. What will happen the next time you call the help desk?

> There are times where outsourcing a survey makes sense for reasons beyond time, money, and unique expertise.

In this case, consider using some vendor to administer the survey. People are more likely to communicate honestly to an independent party. You could still do the data analysis.

Collecting the Results

The results have poured in — hopefully. If you are using an automation tool, follow the instructions to load the responses into a data file. If you're performing a telephone survey, the results should have been keyed into a data file via the scripting software or via a spreadsheet as the calls were made. If you conducted a hardcopy mail survey on a non-scanable form or manual email survey, then you have to key in all the data. Create a coding example for those performing the data entry to reduce the possibility of data entry error. Keying data manually is like preparing a complex tax return. Do it once, and you'll be incredibly motivated to find a better technique next time! Consider hiring a temp agency to key the data. Be sure to perform a quality check by randomly pulling a few responses and visually scanning the data. Look for values that don't match the question. For example, a question with a 1-to-5 scale should not have an entry of 7.

When creating the record definition for the survey data file, include a field for the date of data entry. You should also consider adding data from your customer data base into these data records — assuming this is not an anonymous survey. These data may be useful for demographic segmentation or other analysis.

For multiple-choice questions that create nominal data, you have two choices on how to key in the data. One choice is to have one field and assign a number to each choice. Alternatively, you can have a field for each choice in the question. Enter a 0 if the respondent did not select the choice. Enter a 1 if the respondent did select the choice. This method can make the analysis easier.

Once your data set's complete, you're ready for data analysis.

Summary

In this chapter, we've covered major considerations for administration of a survey. Done properly, administration biases should be minimized.

- Reduce *bias from the administration process* by guaranteeing anonymity if necessary or by using a third party to conduct the survey.
- Reduce *bias through the administration method* by implementing the technique properly, for example, by training telephone interviewers, and by insuring the method doesn't lead to a biased sample.

- Reduce *bias from targeting the wrong population* by ensuring that the questionnaire is appropriate for the population of names from which you've drawn your sample.

- Reduce *bias in the sample generation* by randomly selecting respondents from each stratum of interest.

- Reduce bias *in the respondent group* by designing good questionnaires, sending out reminders, and providing a gift.

- Have the *necessary statistical strength* by calculating the response size needed for the accuracy desired.

Let's turn to Exercise 4 as a chance to exercise our new-found skills.

∽∽∽

Exercise 4
Instrumentation and Administration Bias

The following polling results were reported in the *Wall Street Journal*, August 9, 2001. Both surveys were administered in January 2001. Notice how divergent the results are. Can you speculate what biases may have led to the differences in the findings? See the Appendix for a discussion.

Poll conducted for the US Sentencing Commission, January 2001.

Question: "In general, would you say criminals who commit nonviolent crimes in the US are not punished enough, are adequately punished, or are punished too harshly?

Results:

Not punished enough:	52%
Adequately punished:	28%
Punished too harshly:	12%
Don't Know:	7%

Poll conducted by Beiden Russonello & Stewart Research and Communication for the American Civil Liberties Union, January 2001.

Question: "Please tell me if you agree or disagree with the following statement: We need to change the laws so that fewer non-violent crimes are punishable by prison terms."

Results:

Strongly Agree:	30%
Somewhat Agree:	32%
Somewhat Disagree:	17%
Strongly Disagree:	16%
Don't Know:	5%

6 Analyzing Survey Data and Presenting the Results

By the end of this chapter, you will know:

- The types of statistical analysis best suited for customer surveys
- The analysis that can be performed for different data types
- How to analyze a data set using Excel®
- The charting tools that best display different data types
- The contents of a final report

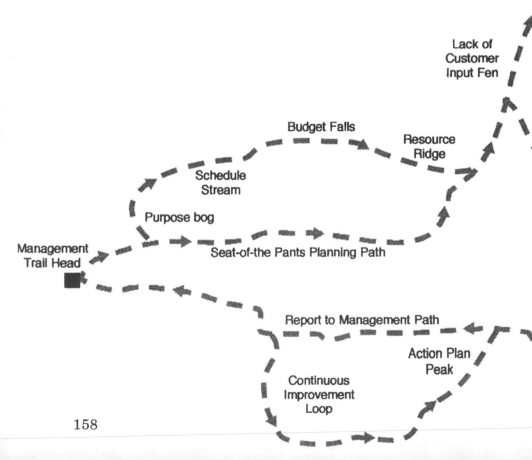

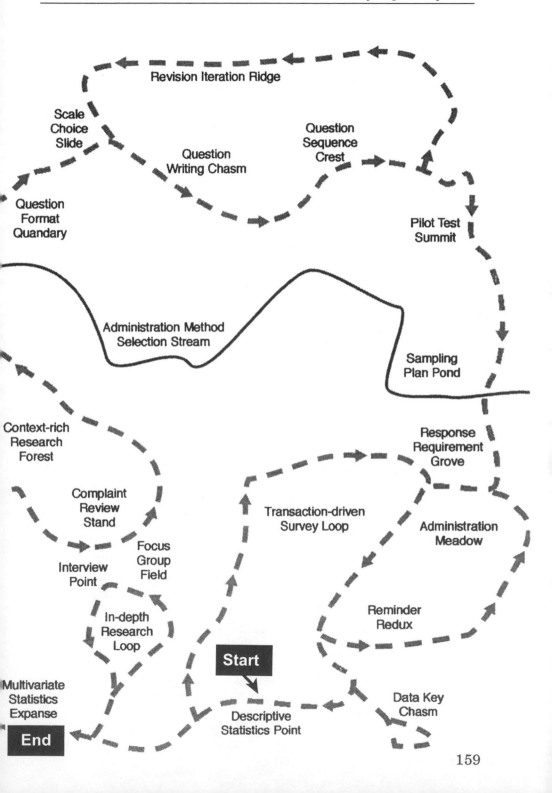

Revision Iteration Ridge

Scale
Choice
Slide

Question
Sequence
Crest

Question
Writing Chasm

Question
Format
Quandary

Pilot Test
Summit

Administration Method
Selection Stream

Sampling
Plan Pond

Context-rich
Research
Forest

Response
Requirement
Grove

Complaint
Review
Stand

Transaction-driven
Survey Loop

Administration
Meadow

Focus
Group
Field

Interview
Point

In-depth
Research
Loop

Reminder
Redux

Start

Multivariate
Statistics
Expanse

Data Key
Chasm

End

Descriptive
Statistics Point

You've planned your project. Designed your instrument. Administered it. Received responses. Created a database. Now the whole project comes to fruition with the analysis of all that data, followed by the presentation of the results to business colleagues who will formulate action plans based upon the results. This may seem like a formality at this point in the project since you've been living with the project for so long. Remember the purpose of the analysis and presentation stage: *Give voice to the data.* The data have a message. You need to translate that into written words and charts so that others can hear the message.

> Remember the purpose of the analysis and presentation stage: Give voice to the data.

As you analyze the data, you will almost certainly think to yourself — or say loud enough for your cubicle neighbor to hear — "Darn, I wish I asked this *one* other question!" Or, "I wish I had changed the way I worded that question." If you experience this, you're in good company. *Every* survey designer/analyst has these moments of angst.

This angst is good! It means you're developing insight into the proper design of a survey instrument for the next survey project or the next round of surveying with a revised instrument. Early in this book we mentioned the "start from the end" concept in designing the survey instrument. Now that you're at the end of the process, the logic of that concept will be starkly evident. You're maturing as a researcher.

This chapter will walk you through the steps for data analysis and report writing. We'll show how to analyze a sample set of survey data using an Excel spreadsheet. While you may use a different analysis package, for example, if you have purchased a survey automation tool, the type of analysis will be the same. Excel has become a common language, and you can do the analysis very readily in a spreadsheet. If you're facile with the charting tools in Excel, this may be the fastest route to take.

Plan of Analysis

The start of the analysis phase is analogous to the start of the entire project: planning. Before attacking the data, develop a plan for what you intend to do. After you begin analyzing the data, you may change your plans as unexpected results emerge, but you should still have a plan. Otherwise you might expend too much time on an area of marginal value, and you may have to redo some analysis. Further, the analysis stage is preparation for writing the report, including creation of charts and data tables. How you structure your data analysis will affect the time needed for subsequent steps. For example, if you lay out the data on your spreadsheet properly, you may be able to cut and paste it directly into the report. Figure 6.1 contains some ideas for laying out the spreadsheet.

As part of the planning process, you also have to make some decisions about how to handle data issues. These are described below. Do include in your report's methodology section how you have handled these issues, if any.

Handling Missing Data. One critical element of the plan is deciding what you will do with incomplete surveys. Unfortunately, you can count on some number of surveys not being completed in full. Perhaps the survey was too long, the respondent didn't understand a question, some questions didn't pertain to the respondent's area of knowledge, or the respondent for some other reason chose not to answer some questions.

While telephone surveys are the least prone to this problem, even they are not immune. Sometimes respondents balk part way through a survey interview or the interviewer realizes that the seriousness of the service issue requires transferring the respondent to the customer service desk immediately. Forcing the person to complete the survey may only exacerbate the dissatisfaction. In a paper survey, a respondent might accidentally miss an entire page, or section, if the branching logic wasn't presented clearly or there were no instructions to turn the page over. Some question types also lead to errors by the respondent, most notably ordinal scale and fixed-sum question formats. If a large percentage of surveys weren't completed in full or completed properly, this is important feedback for the next survey design project or the next administration of this survey.

Regardless of the reasons, you are confronted with a dilemma. What will you do with these surveys? Your options are: discard the respondent's entire survey, discard the questions that are not answered or answered incorrectly, or "correct" the mistakes and omissions. Discarding the compromised surveys is the cleanest approach. However, this lowers the confidence of the remaining results. After all that hard work, any researcher is reluctant to discard data. Discarding only the questions that are not completed or completed incorrectly may cause confusion. First of all, the number of responses across the questions will differ, which may confuse readers. More importantly, multivariate analysis looks for relationships among the responses on each survey, and blank cells are not allowable for most multivariate procedures.

The third option, correcting answers, is problematic. Some corrections may be very legitimate, if you find an obvious error. But what if the nature of the error is not obvious? One possible solution for correcting or completing answers is to calculate where that respondent fits in the overall distribution based on his other responses, and then complete missing questions with answers that match that position in the distribution. This can take considerable work and the validity is questionable! It's probably best to follow the second option and just ignore improperly completed questions on individual surveys. If the respondent has only completed half or less of the survey, then you should probably follow the first option and discard the entire survey from those respondents.

What shouldn't you do? Do *not* zero-fill responses or fill with a neutral value, for example, a "3" on a 1-to-5 interval-scale question. If the entry is blank, then it won't be included in the calculations of descriptive statistics[1]. By making some entry, you're distorting data. There is one exception to this rule, and it relates to fixed-sum questions.

Correcting Fixed-Sum Question Entries. Fixed-sum questions ask the respondent to allot a number of points, say 100, across a series of options. (See Chapter 4 for a more complete description of this question format.) What if someone chooses to allot no points to an item? They could enter a zero, but more likely they will leave the entry for that item blank. You *must* zero fill these blanks.[2] If you don't, then the average scores for all the items in the question will sum to more than 100 (assuming you gave 100 points to allocate). Clearly, that is illogical. Those blanks are truly zeros, and the software tool you're using, if any, should perform this task for you. If it doesn't, then import the file into Excel and execute a global find and replace command (Control-H) for those affected cells *only*. You will then find the sum of the average scores equaling 100.

---

[1] A 0 (zero) is different from a blank. Excel excludes blank cells when it calculates averages and other statistics. Do verify that the analysis tool you are using follows this convention.

[2] The author had a long argument with a survey software vendor over this point. The vendor argued that zero-filling fixed-sum responses was assuming an answer on the part of the respondent. It's not!

Fixed-sum questions are also prone to data entry error since respondents' entries may not total to the specified number, again let's say 100 points. Maybe your survey tool doesn't provide a running total or enforce a correct entry. What to do then? If you do nothing, then the sum of the average scores will not total to 100. Here's how to find the offending surveys. Insert a column in your spreadsheet after the last item for the question and sum the entries for each response. Sort the data set on that summed column and you will have grouped together all the surveys with totals less than — and more than — 100.

If the total for a survey is not even close to 100, say anything under 80 or over 120, then discard the response by blanking out the entries. (Don't zero fill!) Some respondents start answering these questions, then find they're too much work and move to the next question leaving entries that may total to something like 35. Clearly, those responses should be excluded from the final analysis of the fixed-sum question.

If the entries sum close to 100 so that it indicates an addition error, say 95, then you can correct the entries to add to 100. The simple way is to add or subtract points across the entries. This technique may be fine. To be fully proper, divide each entry by the current summary total. For example, if a respondent's entries sum to 95, then divide each entry for that respondent by 95. The adjusted entries will sum to 100. This technique is actually faster than eyeballing corrections.

You now may be scared off from using fixed-sum questions. Don't be. They provide very rich data. The author's experience, using software that provides a running total of the entries, is that fewer than 5% of the respondents' surveys will need correction. One last concern must be noted if you're using fixed-sum questions and a survey software tool. The tool may not bound respondent's entries between 0 and 100. The author found one respondent on a survey for an internal help desk who was attempting sabotage. He found the survey tool would take negative numbers. His entries summed to 100, but the entries ranged from -491 to 516. I excluded his entire survey from the analysis. How did I find this? I did a visual scan of data file. Some of the statistics described below can also help catch such sabotage.

Accounting for "Not Applicable" Responses. If you have created questions with *Not Applicable* or *Don't Know* as response options, you must consider how that has been coded before you crunch any numbers. In most circumstances it is best to have these entered as blank responses. Say you have a 1-to-10 interval-scale question and you code *Not Applicable* responses as 0s (zeros). Those zeros would distort calculations. Another option is to code these as some text, such as *X* , *N/A,* or *DK.* As text entries they would be excluded from any analysis, and you could then count them with commands outlined below. Remember, a blank due to branching is different than a *Don't Know* response.

Cleaning Textual Data. You will almost certainly have open-ended comments in your survey data. Unfortunately, language skills are not what they could be. Some respondents will be rushing through this process and will purposefully write in a cryptic style. Others simply don't know rules of grammar, punctuation, and spelling. You must decide right away whether you are going to take them as is or correct them. *Do not underestimate the time sink correcting these mistakes can be!* Aside from being tedious, relieved by an occasional humorous written faux pas, this will take hours if not days. By default, it is probably best to leave them as is, unless you find a truly vulgar and offensive comment.

Cleaning "Other" Responses. For some nominal or categorical questions, you may have included an *Other* category and asked the person to explain in an open-ended text box. You need to review those comments to see if they really represent one of the response categories. Many times respondents will be confused, check *Other,* and enter a quick response. If this is a Single-Choice nominal question, respondents may select *Other* because they want to make a statement, and that's their only way. If this is a Multiple-Choice nominal question, respondents may select a response but also select *Other* to use the text box to amplify a statement. To shorten the time to deliver a telephone survey, you may chose to not have the response list read to the respondent but instead rely upon the interviewer to categorize the free-form response. The interviewer may be confused (or lazy) and just check *Other.* Regardless of the reason, these *Other* comments need to be reviewed and re-categorized if need be. Otherwise, the frequency distributions will be distorted. A second benefit of this practice is that it identifies updates for the next administration of the survey instrument.

Segmenting and Filtering Data. You will likely be looking at your data for both the entire response group and for particular segments or strata, such as customer type, geography, product type, or service agent. To do this, sort your data into the segments and perform the statistical analysis upon the subset of data. If you are using a spreadsheet to analyze your data, it's advisable to create a separate worksheet for each stratum of data. This will avoid confusion. Some survey automation software is designed to support this type of analysis with *filters*. (Excel does something similar using pivot tables.) Filtering capabilities may be an important factor in decid-

Figure 6.1
Laying out the Spreadsheet

When preparing your spreadsheet for data analysis, a few simple additions can save time in the long run. Good column headers will help direct you as you get mired in the detailed analysis and save time when you chart data.

First, insert a row at the very top of the spreadsheet that describes the question type, such as "multi choice 6," "interval 1-10," and "open end (weeks)." This tells you there were six choices for the multiple choice question, that interval question was on a 1-to-10 scale, and the open-ended question asked for a response in weeks. In the last case you might otherwise think the data were from an interval scale. You'll likely develop your own shorthand.

Second, you have these long survey questions that won't fit in the spreadsheet, nor will they fit on any chart. Develop *short names* for each survey question, such as, "Response Time" and "Met Commitments" and put these as the column labels directly above the raw data. There's a reason for putting them directly above the data rather than in the first row, as we shall see in the discussion on pivot tables.

Third, put the question number before the short name, such as, "1. Response Time." When you graph the data, you can apply these cells for short names as labels and you have now also communicated the question number in the chart.

Fourth, after all the rows with the survey data — each row will be an individual survey response — then create a row for each calculation. Lay out the calculations in the order in which you intend to present it in the written report. This will simplify transcribing or copying the data to the Word document.

This added work up front will prevent you from having to search the survey instrument to find this information as you're doing the analysis. In some figures in this chapter you will see examples of this type of layout.

ing which software to purchase. Why? Analysis along each segment is not complicated, but can be very time consuming.

Let's say you want to analyze data for three customer types, four product types, four geographic regions, and 10 service agents. You would be doing analysis for 3+4+4+10 = 21 data sets! If you want to analyze responses for product types *within* customer types, then we would have 3 X 4 = 12 data sets, just for those two combinations! Software-supplied filters help considerably, but the real lesson is to carefully consider what analysis is important to do, before you collect data that you might not use. This is the "start from the end" approach to the questionnaire design. A reasonable compromise is to perform in-depth analysis on the data set as a whole, and perform a more cursory, high-level analysis for the strata. For example, you might calculate only arithmetic means for the strata but also calculate frequency distributions for the entire data set.

You may also want to filter the data beyond just the demographic segments mentioned. Perhaps you want to look at the responses for people who rated overall satisfaction as very high or very low. In a spreadsheet you can do this by sorting the data. But again, it is important to realize that this kind of analysis will be time consuming.

Incorporating Other Data. If your survey is not anonymous, then you could append your survey with data from your customer database. Basic demographic information, such as product and geographic location, should be among the data selected. Beyond that, the data you chose should be driven by the reasons for the survey. For example, if the survey was about order and fulfillment processes, then you may want to include data about the more recent order or order history. These data may prove to be useful segmentation variables.

Statistical Analysis

The desktop software you use will determine how you analyze the data, create the charts, and present the data. Most survey software packages have some basic analytical and graphing capabilities. Those are important features to examine before buying a software package. You might pay more for a package with high quality analysis and graphing tools, but the investment could save you several days' work.

If you aren't using a survey software package or don't like the graphing tools your package supplies, then you will probably import the data set into a spreadsheet (e.g., Excel or Lotus 1-2-3) or a statistical package (e.g., SAS, Minitab, or SPSS). The discussion that follows is built, in part, around features in Excel. The Excel function names are shown in parentheses at the beginning of each section describing a statistical operation, and Figure 6.2 contains a list of the functions described in this chapter using examples from a spreadsheet also shown in figures in this chapter.

There are three broad types of analysis that we will cover:

◆ Univariate or descriptive statistics

◆ Bivariate statistics

◆ Multivariate statistics

The difference across the three analysis types lies in the number of variables (meaning survey questions) being analyzed at any one time in the statistical procedure: one, two, or many variables, respectively.

Univariate or Descriptive Statistics

The term *descriptive statistics* may sound intimidating, but it really means just what it says. These are statistics that describe (or "are descriptive of") a set of data, which in this case is all the responses for an individual survey question. Descriptive statistics are also called *univariate statistics* since you are analyzing one (*uni*) variable (*variate*) at a time. You've probably been working with descriptive statistics in other analyses without even knowing it.

You can think of descriptive statistics as summary data. Their purpose is to paint a broad profile of *what* the response group thinks. In contrast, bivariate and multivariate statistics, try to uncover *why* the response group thinks that way, by examining relationships among the data across variables.

Descriptive statistics portray two aspects about the data for a survey question. First, these statistics describe the *typical response*. This is done by determining an average, which may be the mean, mode, or median. Second, these statistics describe the *dispersion* (or *range*) *of responses*. The type of analysis you can do for a survey question depends upon the *data type* generated by the question. (See Chapter 4 for a discussion of the data types.) Figure 6.3 provides a summary of the types of analysis that can be done for each data type. After describing each statistic and showing how to use them in Excel, we'll show a quick way to produce these statistics.

Before we turn to those statistics, there are two basic descriptive statistics to cover — counts of responses and blanks.

Figure 6.2
Summary of Excel Commands Useful
for Analyzing Survey Data

Function	Format	Example
Count	=Count(RangeStart:RangeEnd)[1]	=Count(B3:B153)
Blanks	=CountBlank(RangeStart:RangeEnd)	=CountBlank(B3:B153)
Mean	=Average(RangeStart:RangeEnd)	=Average(B3:B153)
Median	=Median(RangeStart:RangeEnd)	=Median(B3:B153)
Mode	=Mode(RangeStart:RangeEnd)	=Mode(B3:B153)
Frequency	=CountIf(RangeStart:RangeEnd, "criteria")[2]	=CountIf(F3:F153, "4")
Cumulative Frequency	=CountIf(RangeStart:RangeEnd, "<=criteria")	=CountIf(F3:F153, "<=4")
	=CountIf(RangeStart:RangeEnd, ">=criteria")	=CountIf(F3:F153, ">=1")
Maximum	= Max(RangeStart:RangeEnd)	=Max(B3:B153)
Minimum	=Min(RangeStart:RangeEnd)	=Min(B3:B153)
Standard Deviation	=StDev(RangeStart:RangeEnd)	=StDev(B3:B153)
Confidence Interval	=Confidence(alpha, Standard Deviation, Count)	=Confidence(.05,B162, B155) where those cell references contain those statistics
Skewness	=Skew(RangeStart:RangeEnd)	=Skew(B3:B153)
Kurtosis	=Kurt(RangeStart:RangeEnd)	=Kurt(B3:B153)

[1] Note that we've presented the format of the calculation using a range of cells. These commands do not require a range. You can specify individual cells, but for our purposes, using ranges makes the most sense.

[2] Note that the "criteria" can be a text string, number, or date. The quotation signs must be included.

Figure 6.3
Summary of Analysis and Presentation by Data Type

Data Type	Analysis	How to Display	Advanced Analysis
Nominal	Frequency Distributions	Histograms Pie Charts	Chi-square tests
Ordinal	Frequency Distributions Cumulative Frequency Dist.	Histograms Stacked Bar Charts	Chi-square tests
Interval	Frequency Distributions Cumulative Frequency Dist. Descriptive Statistics	Histograms Stacked Bar Charts Scatter Plots	ANOVA t-tests Correlations Regressions
Ratio	Frequency Distributions Cumulative Frequency Dist. Descriptive Statististics	Histograms Stacked Bar Charts Scatter Plots	ANOVA t-tests Correlations Regressions
Textual	Coding the data into frequency distributions	Histograms	

Count (COUNT). It's likely that not every question will be completed by every respondent. This may be because a respondent skipped a question or because of branching logic. Although the *count* of responses doesn't have any meaning by itself, it can be useful to know. It is also used in the calculation of the confidence interval. The command simply counts the number of cells in the specified range that have non-blank entries.

Blanks (COUNTBLANK). Just as with the count of responses, the *number of blanks* has little direct meaning. Although, a high count of blanks, excluding blanks due to branching, may indicate a poorly worded or confusing question. The command simply counts the number of cells in the specified range that have no entry. Note: if the count and blanks don't add up to the total number of surveys, then you have a problem. That's the other purpose of these very basic statistics — they serve as a sanity check. If you have coded non-responses in some fashion other than blank or null entries, for example with *N/A*, then you can use the CountIf statement described below to count these entries.

Determining the Typical Response

There are three mathematical terms that are called averages: *mean, median,* and *mode.* The intent behind the average is to describe the typical response. For that reason statistics books call these *measures of central tendency.* Each type of average may be most appropriate in certain situations. With all of them you must consider what to do with blank answers or "not applicable" answers in the data set. Note that Excel excludes blank cells when it performs these calculations, which is why you should not zero fill blanks, except for fixed-sum questions as noted above.

Mean (AVERAGE). Most people think of the *arithmetic mean* as the average. In fact, the Excel function name "average" refers to the mean. We're all familiar with the concept. The mean is found by adding all the values in a data string and dividing by the count of values. In other words, for one survey question, you add all the responses and divide by the number of surveys with that question completed. Mathematically, the mean, $\bar{x}$, is:

$$\bar{x} = \frac{\sum x}{n}$$

where x = each value in the data string (that is, each response for the survey question)

n = the number or count of values in the data string

The mean is the best overall descriptor of a typical response. It is used in part because everyone understands it. Means can only be calculated when we have true numerical data, and only interval and ratio survey data are truly numerical. You may be tempted to take the mean of ordinal data, but that is not legitimate. As has been noted, a poorly written interval scale may actually produce only ordinal data, though you won't necessarily know this.

In the discussion of data types, we noted that sometimes we request ratio data in a multiple-choice format to ease respondent burden or to reduce fears of disclosing confidential information. For example, we may ask how many service agents an organization has by providing a list of choices, each of which is a range (e.g.,

1-10, 11-20, 21-50, 51-100, etc.). Since this is truly continuous or ratio data captured in a multiple-choice format, we can legitimately take a weighted mean by using the midpoint of the range for each choice as the response. The result is not perfect, but the trade-off to get the respondent to complete the question is well worth the compromise.

When isn't the mean the best descriptor of the typical response? The mean statistic is vulnerable to *outliers* in the data set, that is, extreme values that may be legitimate or may be due to data entry mistakes. In surveys, outliers are really only an issue if you are asking for a free-form numerical answer from the respondent. For example, let's say you asked respondents what would be an acceptable response time to a request for service. If most responses range from two to 16 business hours but one response is 1,612 hours, which most certainly is a data entry error, that data point would distort the mean as a typical response. In this case, either eliminate the outliers or rely upon the median as the descriptor of a typical response.

One technique for handling outliers is to calculate the mean eliminating 5% or 10% of values at *both* ends of the distribution. That is, sort the data and exclude from the calculation the 10% of responses at the high end and low end.[3] Be cautious about exercising your pre-emptive judgment and simply excluding some extreme value, however. That value may truly express the customer's feelings. If you eliminate outliers, you should note that action in the methodology section of your report and in a footnote in the chart presenting the data that has been massaged.

Many companies will use the mean as a goal or standard for all employees or operating units to achieve. Remember that the calculation of the mean makes it impossible for *all* the component data to be greater than the mean. The author did work for a company where the goal of each region in the US was to exceed the US average, which was composed of the eight regions' data! A basic example of the mechanics of calculating a mean was necessary to convince these senior level managers of the folly of their goal-setting

---

[3] Amateur sports statisticians know all about eliminating outliers. You may have heard someone argue over the water cooler, "Except for the game when the pitcher was shelled for seven runs in the first inning, he'd have a great earned run average," or "Take out those two games where the offensive line was hurt, and the running back had the best yards per game in the league." Notice they only want to eliminate the outliers for *their* team — and only the *bad* outliers. Any data massaging should be applied uniformly.

process. Only in Garrison Keillor's fictional Lake Wobegon can all the students be better than average.

Median (MEDIAN). The *median* is the *response in the center or heart of a data string*. If you take all the responses for a survey question and sort them in order, the median is the value found at the midpoint. This is also known as the value at the 50th percentile of the frequency distribution. The median is a good descriptor of the typical response when the data set is skewed toward one end of the distribution. It is also very useful when there are extreme outliers in the data set, as described in the section on the mean, since these outliers don't "pull" the median as they do the mean. Finally, the median can be used to describe the typical response for ordinal data.

Mode (MODE). The *mode* is the most commonly found value in a data string. If you sort your data into a frequency table, the mode is the *value with the most number of responses*. The concept of the mode is most important when analyzing nominal data since the mode will tell us which response was most common. The mode can also be applied to textual data from open-ended questions that you have coded. With textual data you want to present the predominant themes found and that will be determined by the finding the most common responses. If you are conducting a small-sample research project, the mode may be the best descriptor of a typical response. The mode is not commonly used to describe a data set when analyzing numerical data from a survey, though technically it certainly can be calculated.

If the data for a question are normally distributed, then the mode, mean, and median should be approximately the same. The mode is a useful statistic for data sets that are *bimodal* or even *trimodal*. For example, if you asked respondents how quickly they expected a response to a service request, you might see a large cluster of responses around two hours and another large cluster around eight hours with few responses between those points. This distribution would be bimodal. The mean would not represent a typical response since there are actually two typical responses for two apparently different segments. If you find a bimodal distribution, look for some underlying characteristic of the respondents that explains the bimodality.

Describing the Range of Responses

There's an old statistician's joke that says if you have your head in the oven and your feet in the refrigerator, on average the temperature is fine. (Statistician humor is an oxymoron.) That bimodal distribution described in the joke is why we need to know more than just the typical, average response. We also need to know how the responses are distributed. After all, each response came from a customer, so don't we want to know how extreme customers' feel-

Figure 6.4
Calculated Descriptive Statistics —
Spreadsheet Example

	A	B	C	D	E	F
	Question Type	Interval -3+3	Interval -3+3	Mult choice (1-6)	Interval -3+3	Mult choice (1- Mu
2	Short Name	1. Response Time	2. Meets Commitments	7. Problem Notification	11. Overall Service Quality	12. Expertise Level 13
3	1	2	2	3	1	3
151	149	-1	0	3	2	4
152	150	0	0	2	-1	2
153	151	1	2	3	2	2
154						
155	Count	150	150	151	149	149
156	blanks	1	1	0	2	2
157	Mean	0.55	0.80		0.56	
158	Median	1	1	3	1	3
159	Mode	0	2	3	0	3
160	Maximum	3	3	5	3	4
161	Minimum	-3	-3	1	-3	1
162	Standard Deviation	1.29	1.39		1.26	
163	Skewness	-0.37	0.82		-0.63	
164	Kurtosis	-0.23	0.45		0.75	
165	Confidence Interval	0.21	0.22		0.20	
166						
167	Count 6			0		
168	5			1		
169	4			0		22
170	3	6	9	90	5	73
171	2	32	44	6	30	51
172	1	40	44	54	44	3
173	0	47	30	0	49	
174	-1	11	12		12	
175	-2	13	6		4	
176	-3	1	5		5	

Desc Stat / Data2 \ Data / Pivot Table / Sample Chart /

ings are? Don't we want to know how many people have their heads in the oven and feet in the fridge? To portray the entire distribution we create frequency distribution tables and we calculate statistics such as range, standard deviation, variance, and skewness, and kurtosis.

Range, Maximum Value (MAX), Minimum Value (MIN). The simplest way of describing the breadth of responses for a survey question is to state the *range*. The range is quite simply the difference between the highest value and lowest value in a data string. *Maximum* and *minimum* values are self-explanatory. The next time you watch a weather forecast, notice the meteorologist will give the high and low temperature for the day. There's the range.

Reporting all three — range, maximum, and minimum values — tells us something about the spread of responses for a survey question, but since the range uses only two data points, that is, the values from two surveys, it disregards almost all the data. Further, for scaled questions, you'll almost certainly get people who will rate a survey question at the highest and lowest points in the scale. How useful is that information? That is why we typically use frequency distributions and the standard deviation to describe the dispersion of responses.

For an open-ended numerical response, such as the number of weeks for a shipment to be received, these calculations have more meaning. We've shown maximum and minimum on the nearby spreadsheets although later we do not include them in the management report.

Frequency Distribution Tables. (COUNTIF) In surveys we typically have nominal or categorical data from multiple choice questions. We can't take an average, because we don't have numerical, interval data. Instead, we have to analyze our responses looking at the frequency with which respondents chose each response category. We create a *frequency distribution table* by calculating how often each response category is chosen. These frequencies should be expressed as the count of responses for each category and also as a percentage. [4]

Excel does have a function for generating frequency distributions, and we'll show that below. We can also calculate frequency distributions using the CountIf function. In the nearby screenshot of a spreadsheet (See Figure 6.4.) we have a survey question, "Problem Notification," that asked how clients would prefer to be notified about system outages. Six options were presented to respondents, and the responses were keyed as 1 through 6. The CountIf statement is used in six rows to identify the number of people who

---

[4] If you included an "Other" category as a response option, these need to be reviewed for possible re-categorization prior to the creation of any frequency tables. See the planning section at the start of this chapter for more information.

chose each option. As shown in Figure 6.5, we can then express this as a percent by dividing by the Count, using that cell reference[5]. Note that the CountIf command can be used on text strings if the responses are keyed as text rather than numbers.

We may have ordinal data from some survey questions. For these, too, frequency distribution tables are a good means for portraying the information — since we cannot calculate means. With ordinal data, we can also go one step further because of the scaled

Figure 6.5
Calculated Frequency Distributions

Short Name	1. Response Time	2. Meets Commitments	7. Problem Notification	11. Overall Service Quality	12. Expertise Level	13
1	2	2	3	1	3	
Percent 6			0%			
5			1%			
4			0%		15%	
3	4%	6%	60%	3%	49%	
2	21%	29%	4%	20%	34%	
1	27%	29%	36%	30%	2%	
0	31%	20%		33%		
-1	7%	8%		8%		
-2	9%	4%		3%		
-3	1%	3%		3%		
Ascending % 4					100%	
3	100%	100%		100%	85%	
2	96%	94%		97%	36%	
1	75%	65%		77%	2%	
0	48%	35%		47%		
-1	17%	15%		14%		
-2	9%	7%		6%		
-3	1%	3%		3%		
Descending % 4					15%	
3	4%	6%		3%	64%	
2	25%	35%		23%	98%	
1	52%	65%		53%	100%	
0	83%	85%		86%		
-1	91%	93%		94%		
-2	99%	97%		97%		
-3	100%	100%		100%		

nature of the data. We can report the *cumulative frequency*. Say we asked the respondents to tell us how they viewed our service organization. They had to choose among five answers that ranged in

---

[5] Here's the reason for calculating the Count and using that cell reference. If you were to divide the values found with the CountIf statements by the number of survey responses, you would be including blank responses.

175

order, from *Unconcerned about my business issues* to *A true business partner.* We would be interested in knowing the percent that reported each answer, but we could also report the cumulative percentage that reported the first and second options, the first through third options, etc.

We likely will want to report these cumulative frequencies in *both directions,* that is, the percentage reporting that answer or below and the percentage that answer or higher. These cumulative

Figure 6.6
Descriptive Statistics Formulas

	A	E	F	
1	Question Type	Interval -3+3	Mult choice (1-4)	Mult
2	Short Name	11. Overall Service Quality	12. Expertise Level	
3	1	1	3	2
4	2	-1	2	3
152	150	-1	2	2
153	151	2	2	4
154				
155	Count	=COUNT(E3:E153)	=COUNT(F3:F153)	=COU
156	blanks	=COUNTIF(E3:E153,"")	=COUNTIF(F3:F153,"")	=COU
157	Mean	=AVERAGE(E3:E153)		=AVE
158	Median	=MEDIAN(E3:E153)	=MEDIAN(F3:F153)	=MEI
159	Mode	=MODE(E3:E153)	=MODE(F3:F153)	=MO:
160	Maximum	=MAX(E3:E153)	=MAX(F3:F153)	=MA:
161	Minimum	=MIN(E3:E153)	=MIN(F3:F153)	=MIN
162	Standard Deviation	=STDEV(E3:E153)		=STD
163	Skewness	=SKEW(E3:E153)		
164	Kurtosis	=KURT(E3:E153)		
165	Confidence Interval	=CONFIDENCE(0.05,E162,E155)		=CON
166				
167	Count 6			
168	5			=COU
169	4		=COUNTIF(F3:F153, "4")	=COU
170	3	=COUNTIF(E3:E153, "3")	=COUNTIF(F3:F153, "3")	=COU
171	2	=COUNTIF(E3:E153, "2")	=COUNTIF(F3:F153, "2")	=COU
172	1	=COUNTIF(E3:E153, "1")	=COUNTIF(F3:F153, "1")	=COU
173	0	=COUNTIF(E3:E153, "0")		=COU
174	-1	=COUNTIF(E3:E153, "-1")		
175	-2	=COUNTIF(E3:E153, "-2")		
176	-3	=COUNTIF(E3:E153, "-3")		
177				

frequencies describe the ends of the distribution, and management can learn, for example, the percentage that report the two "best" choices as well as the two "worst" choices. This conveys tremendous information about how well we are meeting the needs of the entire breadth of customers.

In the sample spreadsheets in Figures 6.5 and 6.6 we have a demographic question, "Expertise Level," where respondents were asked to self-assess their level of expertise from *Novice* through *Expert*. These were keyed as 1 through 4. Notice that this question is ordinal. So, in addition to calculating counts and percents for each option, we can calculate the cumulative frequencies, both ascending and descending. There are different ways to perform these calculations. We can add the percentages for each option, we can add the counts for each option and divide by the overall count, or we use the CountIf statement on the survey data using the "less than or equal to" and "greater than or equal to" arguments. Those arguments can only be used when the keyed data are numbers. They cannot be used if the data are keyed as text strings. We've shown both ways.

Frequency distribution tables are also useful for interval and ratio data. If we have a question where we solicited responses on a 1-to-10 scale, we certainly would want to know the percent that chose each point on the scale. Again, for interval data, bi-directional cumulative frequencies are very useful for painting the entire picture. These cumulative frequencies are also what you will want to highlight in your written analysis because they are more readily interpreted by the reader or audience. Compare the following two statements.

♦ "Customers' satisfaction with Overall Service Quality received a mean score of 0.56 on the –3 to +3 Met Expectations scale."

♦ "86% of customers said their expectations for Overall Service Quality were met or exceeded."

Both statements are derived from the same data shown on the nearby spreadsheets. How readily can the reader of the report interpret the mean ratings? This survey used a scale than ranged from -3 to +3 asking the respondent the degree to which their expectations were met. Zero represented expectations being met. The scale had good dispersal properties, but the mean scores are harder to interpret. The cumulative frequency of 86% represents the percent of respondents who gave a rating of 0 through 3. That is very easy to understand.

When questions solicit a free-form numerical response, creating a frequency distribution table requires an intervening step. First, we must create categories into which all the responses will fall. How many categories — or "bins" as Excel calls them — to create will depend upon the data, but the number should range from five to no more than 10 categories. Ideally, the categories should be of equal size, to avoid reader confusion, but either the top and/or bottom categories may reasonably cover a broader range if there are few responses in either tail of the distribution.

Figure 6.7
Descriptive Statistics Formulas (cont.)

	A	E	F	
2	Short Name	11. Overall Service Quality	12. Expertise Level	
3	1	1	3	2
178	Percent 6			
179	5			
180	4		=F169/F155	=G16...
181	3	=E170/E155	=F170/F155	=G16...
182	2	=E171/E155	=F171/F155	=G17...
183	1	=E172/E155	=F172/F155	=G17...
184	0	=E173/E155		=G17...
185	-1	=E174/E155		=G17...
186	-2	=E175/E155		
187	-3	=E176/E155		
188				
189	Ascending % 4		=COUNTIF($F$3:$F$153,"<=4")/$F$155	
190	3	=(E176+E175+E174+E173+E172+E171+E170)/E155	=COUNTIF($F$3:$F$153,"<=3")/$F$155	
191	2	=(E176+E175+E174+E173+E172+E171)/E155	=COUNTIF($F$3:$F$153,"<=2")/$F$155	
192	1	=(E176+E175+E174+E173+E172)/E155	=COUNTIF($F$3:$F$153,"<=1")/$F$155	=(G1...
193	0	=(E176+E175+E174+E173)/E155		=(G1...
194	-1	=(E176+E175+E174)/E155		=(G1...
195	-2	=(E176+E175)/E155		=(G1...
196	-3	=E176/E155		=(G1...
197				
198	Descending % 4		=F169/F155	=(G1...
199	3	=(E170)/E155	=(F170+F169)/F155	=(G1...
200	2	=(E171+E170)/E155	=(F171+F170+F169)/F155	=(G1...
201	1	=(E172+E171+E170)/E155	=(F172+F171+F170+F169)/F155	
202	0	=(E173+E172+E171+E170)/E155		
203	-1	=(E174+E173+E172+E171+E170)/E155		
204	-2	=(E175+E174+E173+E172+E171+E170)/E155		
205	-3	=(E176+E175+E174+E173+E172+E171+E170)/E155		=(#RE...

Standard Deviation (STDEV). This statistic describes the variation found in the data for a particular variable. The Greek letter sigma, σ, is used to denote *standard deviation*. This can only be calculated for numeric data. Statistically, the standard deviation is the square root of the *variance* (VAR). We calculate the standard deviation by calculating the difference between each value in the data string and mean of the data string, squaring the difference, summing all those squared values, dividing that sum by the number of

Figure 6.8
Sample Data Sets with Different Variances

	Low 1	2	3	4	High 5	Count	Mean	Standard Deviation
Data Set 1	15	0	5	0	15	35	3.0	1.88
Data Set 2	2	5	21	5	2	35	3.0	0.87

values in the data string minus one, then taking the square root of the result.

$$\sigma = \sqrt{\frac{\sum (x_i - \bar{x})^2}{n-1}}$$

where x_i = each value in the data string

$\bar{x}$ = the mean of the data string

n = number of values in the data string

The standard deviation describes the *dispersion of results*. It tells us how tightly clustered the responses lie around the mean. You may have seen the standard deviation given in a study and wondered how you would use that information. Let's take an example. Imagine we have a question asking overall satisfaction on a 5-point scale. We administer it to two groups each with 35 responses. In Figure 6.8 we give the two sets with their means and standard deviations.

The mean for both data sets is the same, 3.0, but if you were the manager whose organization delivered this performance, how would you interpret these results? Does the mean tell you how a typical respondent feels in the first data set? No, it doesn't, because in that first data set we have a bimodal distribution with a large number of responses in the extremes as indicated by the high standard deviation. The frequency distribution table shows us this, but the standard deviation is a single statistic that gives us this information. A high standard deviation would tell us to be more cautious about interpreting the mean as a true indicator of the typical response.

Skewness (SKEW). The *skewness* statistic characterizes the degree of asymmetry of a distribution of values around its mean. It gives us information about the shape of the distribution of survey responses for a question. Positive skewness indicates a distribution with a tail of values extending toward more higher values. Negative skewness indicates a distribution with a tail of values extending toward more lower values. With a skewed distribution the mean and median will be different.

Kurtosis (KURT). *Kurtosis* gives us different information about the shape of the distribution of survey responses for a question. It describes how peaked or flat a distribution is, compared with the normal distribution. Positive kurtosis indicates a relatively peaked distribution. Negative kurtosis indicates a relatively flat distribution.

Both the skewness and kurtosis statistics are more for advanced readers of a report. While they are typically part of most statistical packages included with survey software, they are seldom included in management reports. If among the readers of your report you have some statistically-inclined folks, consider including these statistics.

Confidence Interval (CONFIDENCE). Our last statistic is not truly a description of the range of responses, but instead tells us the confidence we can have in the accuracy of results for each question. Remember the discussion in Chapter 5 about the determination of sample sizes and the impact of knowledge about the distribution of responses? We now have the distribution of responses in the standard deviation. So, we can calculate the accuracy, or *confidence interval*, of the data.

To calculate the confidence interval, we have to know the count of values[6] and the standard deviation, both of which we've calculated. We also have to assign an *alpha* in the command. Remember we talked about the conventional use of 95% as the confidence we have that true answers (that is, the population mean) lies in a band

---

[6] Excel inexplicably uses the term *size* in its definition of the confidence interval. *Size* means the *count* of values in the calculation.

defined by the accuracy? The same applies here — except that alpha is the flip side of the coin. Alpha is the probability we're willing to accept that we're wrong and that the true answer lies outside the confidence interval. Thus, by convention, alpha equals 5%, or 0.05, as it must be entered in the command.

To understand how to interpret the confidence interval, turn to Figure 6.9. We've graphed the results from the nearby spreadsheet

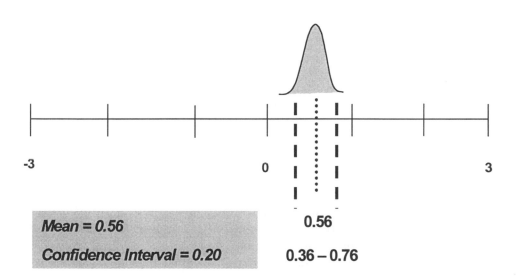

Figure 6.9
Interpreting the Confidence Interval —
Using "Overall Service Quality" Survey Question

Mean = 0.56

Confidence Interval = 0.20

0.56

0.36 – 0.76

for the Overall Service Question. We assume a normal distribution of values around the mean rating of 0.56. The confidence interval is 0.20. This tells us that we are 95% certain that the true mean score lies in a band +/- 0.20 around the mean, or within the range from 0.36 to 0.76. Obviously the tighter the confidence interval, the tighter the responses are clustered around the mean and the greater confidence in the sample results as reflecting the underlying population.

Descriptive Statistics — The Easy Way

We've just walked you through a whole slew of statistics with lots of formulas, and you may be envisioning a few days in front of a spreadsheet. True, you can set up the equations for one survey question and paste the formulas to other cells — with a good quality control check on those pasted formulas! But there's another way to get descriptive statistics using Excel. First, with the spreadsheet

Figure 6.10
Descriptive Statistics Dialogue Box

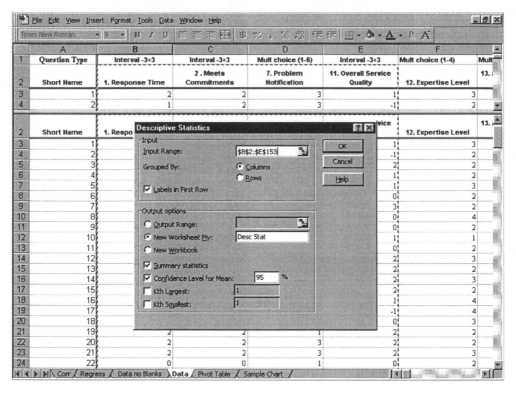

open, go to the Tools menu. You may see "Data Analysis…" as an option. If not, then you need to click on "Add-ins…" on the "Tools" menu. In the dialogue box that appears, place a check next to "Analysis Toolpak." Exit Excel and reopen it, and you should see the "Data Analysis…" option in the "Tools" menu.

Click on "Data Analysis..." and a dialogue box will appear with a list of analytical procedures, some of which we'll discuss later. Right now, click on "Descriptive Statistics" and select OK. Another dialogue box will appear. First, you have to enter the range of data for which you want descriptive statistics. This is the raw survey data. Notice in the screen shot in Figure 6.10 that the range selected covers multiple survey questions. (This is indicated by the dashed line around a range of data cells.) With one execution you can generate descriptive statistics for many survey questions. Include the row with the column labels in that range and check the box that says "Labels in First Row." Earlier we said you should put the labels directly above the data. Here's why. Those labels will be carried to the output.

Next, decide where you want the output. Placing it in a new worksheet minimizes confusion. Then, check the boxes for "Summary Statistics" and for "Confidence Level for Mean" using the 95% convention entry. That sets alpha for the confidence interval at 0.05. That's it. Check OK. The new worksheet contains all of the above statistics (except for the count of blanks). The order of the calculated data may not be ideal, but it's a quick way to the answers. Excel repeats the statistical labels for each survey question as you can see from Figure 6.11, but that can be cleaned up quickly.

Now let's turn to frequency distributions. Go back to your initial worksheet and select "Data Analysis..." again from the "Tools" Menu. This time click on "Histograms" and select OK. First, you have to enter the "Input Range" which is the raw data for a single survey question. (If you select more than one column of data, one frequency distribution will be produced for all the selected data.) If your range includes the column label, check the "Label" box. Figure 6.12 shows a sample dialogue box.

Next, there's an optional "Bin Range" field. This sets up the groupings or "bins" into which the responses will be grouped. You need to set up a range of spreadsheet cells that defines the bins. For interval data or multiple choice data keyed as numbers, this is simple: create cells each with one number from your scale, for example, -3, -2, -1, etc. Figure 6.12 shows this bin range. For data with a broader range, say an open-ended question asking Reasonable Fulfillment Time in weeks, you might create five cells with entries of 2, 4, 6, 10, and 15. That would create six bins — the sixth bin would be greater than 15. A value in the data string is assigned to a bin if it is less than or equal to the bin designator and greater than the next lower bin designator. So, the bin labeled "6" would count values greater than 4 and less than or equal to 6.

Next, you tell Excel where to put the output, and finally there are three optional boxes. Checking "Pareto" will put the bin with the largest frequency first and then present each bin in descending order. It is unlikely you would use this option with survey data. Checking "Cumulative Percent" creates a cumulative frequency table, and checking "Chart Output" produces a chart in addition to the table. In our example both these latter options were selected and the result is shown in Figure 6.13.

Figure 6.11
Descriptive Statistics Output

	A	B	C	D	E	F	G	H
1	1. Response Time		2. Meets Commitments		7. Problem Notification		11. Overall Service Quality	
2								
3	Mean	0.546666667	Mean	0.8	Mean	2.258278146	Mean	0.563758389
4	Standard Error	0.105587381	Standard Error	0.113121265	Standard Error	0.079437079	Standard Error	0.103152797
5	Median	1	Median	1	Median	3	Median	1
6	Mode	0	Mode	2	Mode	3	Mode	0
7	Standard Deviati	1.293176032	Standard Deviati	1.385446891	Standard Deviati	0.976139171	Standard Deviati	1.259140353
8	Sample Variance	1.672304251	Sample Variance	1.919463087	Sample Variance	0.952847682	Sample Variance	1.585434428
9	Kurtosis	-0.228143545	Kurtosis	0.450423729	Kurtosis	-1.38620675	Kurtosis	0.749171773
10	Skewness	-0.368477365	Skewness	-0.816463005	Skewness	-0.365707	Skewness	-0.629691645
11	Range	6	Range	6	Range	4	Range	6
12	Minimum	-3	Minimum	-3	Minimum	1	Minimum	-3
13	Maximum	3	Maximum	3	Maximum	5	Maximum	3
14	Sum	82	Sum	120	Sum	341	Sum	84
15	Count	150	Count	150	Count	151	Count	149
16	Confidence Leve	0.208642107	Confidence Leve	0.223529165	Confidence Leve	0.156960084	Confidence Leve	0.203842594

Minor formatting done to improve readability.

The title of this section said this was the "easy way" to get descriptive statistics. You may be challenging that assertion right now. As with many desktop "productivity tools," there's a learning curve you must go down before you reap the benefits. This is a case in point, but in the long run it is faster.

Bivariate and Multivariate Statistics

Describing a data set can be just the beginning of the information extraction process. Further analyses can be performed to uncover meaningful interactions, such as cause-and-effect relationships, captured by the data. This is the role of *bivariate* and *multivariate statistics*, which is the analysis of "two variables" and "multiple variables." We're going to present a quick overview of a few techniques here. For more detail, please refer to a statistics text. Bob E. Hayes' book, *Measuring Customer Satisfaction*, also does a very good job explaining some of these techniques in the context of analyzing survey data.

To perform any of these analyses there is one critical data quality issue: the techniques cannot accept blank cells in the data. With univariate statistics, blank cells can be ignored, but with these advanced statistics the relationship from one survey question to another is being analyzed. Blank cells are unacceptable.

What to do? First, create a copy of the worksheet with the raw survey data, probably in a new workbook. Now, you have two choices. You can either fill in blanks with some answer using the techniques discussed earlier in the chapter or you can delete the rows that have blanks. Before you do this realize that blank cells are critical only for those survey questions you intend to use for advanced analysis. Find the blank cells by sorting the data for each column in succession.

Correlation Analysis (CORREL). If you want to understand how closely the responses for two survey questions correspond, then you examine the *correlation* between the data strings. This is a very common bivariate analytical technique. Analysts commonly construct a table showing the correlation between each survey question and every other question. The important correlations will be those between survey questions about service performance and questions that address overall service evaluation. Now you have statistics to show you which performance attributes are most strongly associated with overall satisfaction.

The *coefficient of correlation* as it is technically known, ranges from -1 to +1. A +1 correlation means that two variables are perfectly correlated, that is, there is a very strong positive relationship between the two. For example, a correlation of 0.99 between Response

Time and Overall Service Quality (See Figure 6.15) indicates that individual respondents tended to give the same rating to both those measures. This indicates that responsiveness is a very important element in determining overall satisfaction.

A -1 correlation means there is a strong relationship between two variables, but it is negative. That is, when respondents rate one

Figure 6.12
Histogram Dialogue Box

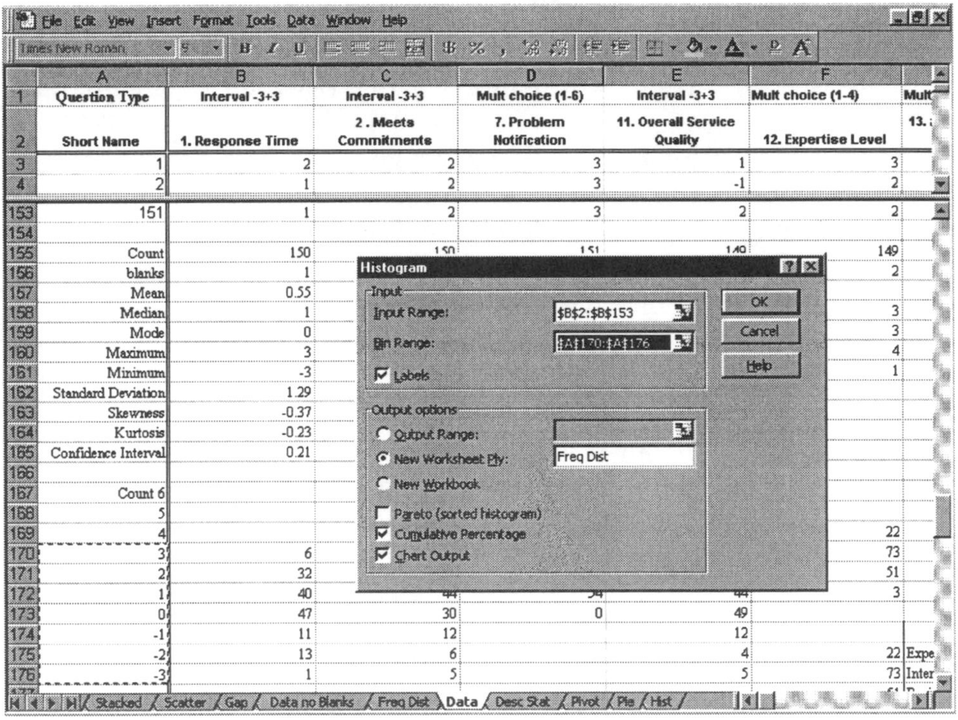

question high, they rate the other question low. For example, if we found a -0.63 correlation between Willingness to Escalate a Problem to Management and Overall Service Quality, it would indicate customers are unhappy with the escalation procedures. Note that the way a question is phrased may determine whether a correlation is positive or negative. A correlation near 0 (zero) means there is no statistical relationship between the variables.

You might want to perform correlation analysis on segments of your data set. Let's say your help desk supports both Macintosh users and PC users. You might want to know if the two groups think alike, regarding your services, and correlation analysis could be used here.

To execute correlation analysis we return to the "Tools" menu and select "Data Analysis…" again. This time select "Correlation," which will lead to a dialogue box. Once again you have to provide an "Input Range." This could be for just two columns of survey data or for many columns. It's best to include the column labels in the range and check the "Labels in First Row" box. Next, tell Excel where to put the output, and you're done. The result is a half a matrix — a half pyramid of sorts — that shows the correlation coefficients for all the survey questions you specified. Notice the 1s down the diagonal. That's the variable correlated with itself.

A way to visually display the correlation between two variables is through scatter plots, which are covered in the section on displaying data with charts.

Regression Analysis (LINEST). Your survey will likely ask questions about individual attributes of service delivery, as well as asking an overall evaluation of service quality or other attitudinal questions. Our assumption is that the overall evaluation is dependent upon the level of service delivered along those different attributes. There are a couple of ways of analyzing these data in combination. You could look at the correlation between each individual attribute and the overall evaluation as described above, or you could run a *regression analysis*.

Regression analysis finds the association between an outcome or *dependent variable*, which in this case is the Overall Service Quality, and the causal or *independent variables*, which here are the various measures of service performance. Technically, regression analysis performs what is known as a "least squares estimation procedure." It fits a line through all the data points for the independent variables that best explains the relationship of those variables to the dependent variable. It fits this line by minimizing the sum of the squared difference between all the independent variable data points and the dependent variable across all respondents.

The output of a regression is the equation of a line as follows:

$$y = a + B_1 x_1 + B_2 x_2 + B_3 x_3 + B_4 x_4 + ... + error$$

where y = dependent variable (summary or attitudinal survey question)

a = y-intercept

B = coefficient

x = independent variables (service performance survey questions)

Figure 6.13
Histogram Output

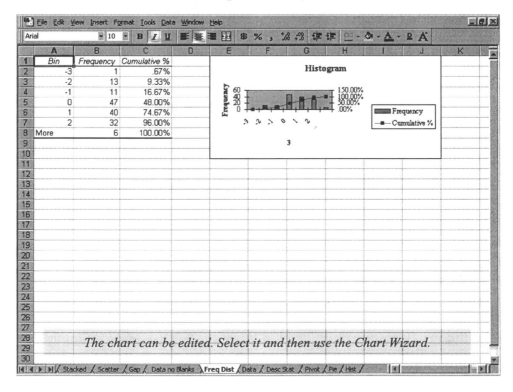

Why run a regression? Regression analysis will tell you which individual performance attributes are most closely associated with the Overall Service Quality score. In fact, it will tell you the *relative* association of a number of attributes (independent variables) to an overall score (dependent variable). Regression analysis also has pre-

188

dictive capabilities. The equation for the regression line indicates the potential impact of a change in the overall service quality score (the dependent variable) if the performance attribute score (the independent variable score) were changed. This is indicated by the coefficients for each independent variable in the regression line. Thus, regression analysis can indicate the importance of service attributes to overall satisfaction.

Notice the use of the term *association*. Technically, regression analysis cannot make ironclad statements about cause-and-effect relationships. It can only tell you the *strength of association* found in the data. It is up to you, the analyst, to decide whether there is a true cause-and-effect relationship. The classic example of a spurious association with no cause-and-effect relationship is that the stock market tends to go up if the NFC team wins the Super Bowl in January and down if an AFC team wins.

Elsewhere in this guide we have discussed the problems that can arise when you ask respondents to rate the importance of service attributes. The reliability of responses is questionable since respondents usually list everything as important, and the importance question likely is tainted by the nearby question on service performance for that attribute. The best way to determine importance is through regression analysis. This is sometimes called *derived importance* measures since we are not explicitly asking importance but rather deriving it from the data.

You may have more than one attitudinal variable in your survey instrument. Which one should you use as the dependent variable? You can run many multiple regressions each with a different dependent variable.[7] If there's a strong correlation among the dependent variables, the results should be very similar. Alternatively, you could also average those dependent variables into one dependent variable and run one regression analysis.

The mechanics of executing regression analysis are simplest for interval and ratio data, because those provide numeric data. Nominal and ordinal data require the creation of "dummy variables" because of the limitations of those data types. This type of regression study requires an analyst with experience. The example we'll show here just uses interval data.

---

[7] There are techniques that accommodate more than one dependent variable, but that discussion is beyond the scope of this book.

Executing a regression is very similar to executing a correlation. (See Figure 6.16.) Go to "Data Analysis…" on the "Tools" menu and select "Regression." (Again, you should first make sure there are no blank cells in the survey questions you intend to use.) Now you need to provide two input ranges, one for the "Y" variable and one for "X" variables. See the definitions in the equation above. Check the box for "Labels" if the first row in the ranges contain column labels, and specify a place for the output. What follows are a number of options that require a level of understanding that is beyond the scope of this book. You can leave those blank.

Figure 6.14
Correlation Dialogue Box

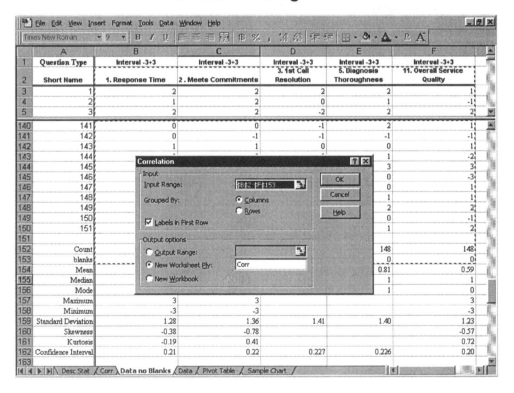

A screenshot of the output is shown on Figure 6.17. There's a lot of information here! We'll focus on a few key pieces of information. In the lower left in the column marked "Coefficients" are the elements to fill in the equation given above. Here is the y-intercept and the coefficients for each of the independent variables.

Overall Service Quality =   -0.04 y-intercept
+ 0.29 (Response Time)[8]
+ 0.20 (Meets Commitments)
+ 0.18 (1st Call Resolution)
+ 0.25 (Diagnostic Thoroughness)

With the equation completed, how do we interpret it? Let's use the sample survey data shown in Figure 6.4. The mean rating for Response Time in our sample data set is 0.55. If operational improvement led to a 1.0 increase in the rating for Response Time to 1.55, then Overall Service Quality, the dependent variable, should increase by 0.29 from 0.56 to 0.85. Why 0.29? That's the coefficient of the Response Time variable. (Note: coefficients can be negative.) Look across the coefficients. Response Time has the largest coefficient. That indicates that Response Time is the most important of those variables in determining Overall Service Quality, followed by Diagnostic Thoroughness, Meets Commitments, and 1st Call Resolution.

We've said the regression output is an equation that explains variation in the dependent variable. But how good is the explanation? The "R-Squared" in the upper left corner of the output screen shows this. This ranges between 0 and 1, and the sample output says that about 67% of Overall Service Quality is explained by the four service performance attribute variables. That's a healthy percentage. The significance of the F statistic shows the strength of the regression equation overall. The smaller the number here the better. (Note the scientific notation. E-33 is a very small number! It means there are 33 zeros to the right of the decimal point.)

So, the equation is good but do all the independent variables included in the equation have good explanatory power? (That's statistician jargon.) The p-value answers this question. As a rule, if the p-value is less than 0.05, then that independent variable is statistically significant. What if the p-value is greater than that threshold? You should re-run the regression removing that variable from the

---

[8] Note that Response Time refers to the rating found in the survey, not an actual measure of response time.

Input X Range. With a small number of variables they are all likely to be significant, but if you include six or more variables, some will likely prove to be insignificant. Why? Because the impact of the variable is probably explained by some other variable with which it is highly correlated. Look at the correlation matrix, and you'll likely find which variable is showing the impact. Removing vari-

Figure 6.15
Correlation Output

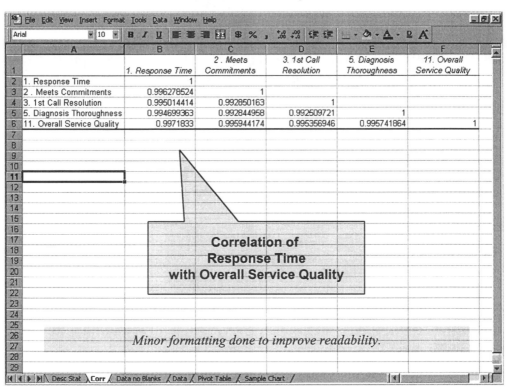

ables can prove tedious. You can never predict what one change in the equation will produce. The *stepwise regression* technique adds independent variables to the equation in order of their importance. However, Excel does not support the stepwise function.

Other Statistical Tests

Some of these tests may more accurately be called univariate, but since they can be applied in different scenarios, they are treated here.

Tests of Independence. Let's say you have two major customer segments for your help desk, Macinstosh and PC users or two major segments for your catalog operation, businesses and consumers. You have surveyed both segments in one survey, and you want to know if their ratings of your service differ. Obviously, you can look at the means developed by your survey responses. But because you obtained data from a sample and not from the entire population, there is some possibility that a difference between those means will be the result of sampling error and not actual differences in the way those groups view your services. What we want to understand is whether those two groups are really part of one larger group, that is, that there is no difference in how they view your service quality, or whether there are unique, independent groups who view your service quality differently.

The *t* test (TTEST) is the statistical test used to validate the likelihood that groups are the same or different. When performing a *t* test, a statistical package will tell you the *level of significance*. This means the likelihood that the differences between the groups are due to chance in the sampling process, versus true differences. By convention, a 95% significance level is chosen as the threshold point where we feel confident in saying the differences are due to real differences between the groups rather than sampling error. At this level, there is only a 5% chance we are wrong and that the apparent differences are due to chance in the sample we drew.

The *t* test is used if we have numerical data and are comparing only two groups. If we want to compare multiple groups, then we must perform ANOVA, or ANalysis Of VAriance, which you will find under the "Data Analysis…" function. This test will tell whether the various pairs of groups are statistically different by giving us the *t* tests for all the pairs of groups, and it will give us an F value to test whether all the groups are statistically different from each other. If we have nominal data and thus have proportions, then we must perform a χ^2 (Chi squared) test (CHITEST).

A discussion of these procedures in more detail is beyond the intended scope of this book. There are also a great number of other statistical techniques that might be valuable, such as factor analysis, cluster analysis, multidimensional scaling, MANOVA, and discriminant analysis. Statistics books present these concepts and Terry G. Vavra's book, *Improving Your Measurement of Customer Satisfaction*, and Hayes' book, *Measuring Customer Satisfaction*, present a discussion of some of these tools in a surveying context.

Since customer surveying falls into the domain of quality management and improvement, look to the tools used in Total Quality Management programs. Pareto analysis, fishbone or Ishakawa dia-

Figure 6.16
Regression Dialogue Box

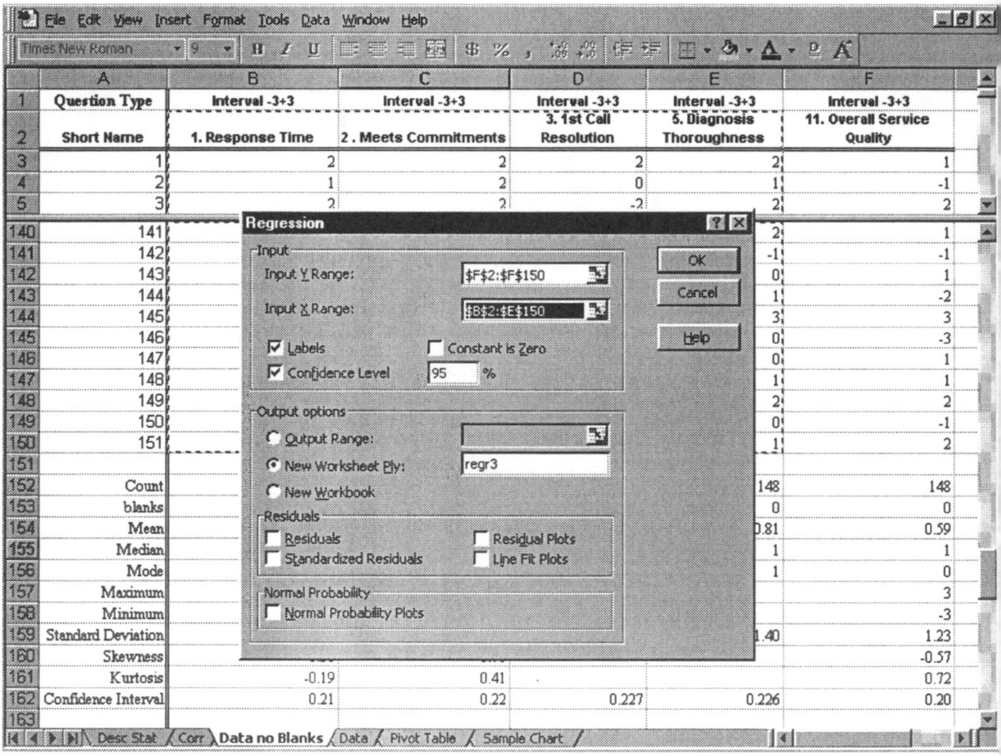

grams, and other TQM tools may be quite appropriate for the analysis of your data. If your organization has developed TQM disciplines, then those tools will be readily comprehended and accepted.

Pivot Tables

The analysis we've presented thus far has been very structured, but what if you want to do more ad hoc analysis and drill down to those specific responses that fit some criteria? *Pivot tables* provide a means to perform this type of analysis. (Pivot tables are very similar to the *cross tabs* function in other statistical packages.) Unfortunately, using pivot tables is not intuitive. Unless you use them very frequently, you will have to relearn much of how to use them each time. Our purpose here is to provide you with a quick overview of their potential. We recommend purchasing a book on using Excel for more detailed information.

Pivot tables are very handy for analysis of different strata of the survey responses. You could calculate the descriptive statistics without pivot tables by sorting the data set along the segmentation variable and applying the descriptive statistics function for each stratum. This is a bit tedious and prone to error, but it's certainly possible. Unless you create a separate worksheet or workbook for each segmentation, you will lose your results when you do the next sort. What if you have another issue to explore? Pivot tables can provide many descriptive statistics and are flexible enough to do other analysis.

To create a pivot table, go to the "Data" menu in Excel and select "Pivot Table Report..." At this point the software will walk you through a four-step wizard. In the first step, select "Microsoft Excel list or database," which should be the default. In the second step, shown in Figure 6.18, you specify the range of data for the pivot table. While you can create multiple pivot tables, it's simplest to create one pivot table with all the raw survey data. When you create a pivot table, you are creating a duplication of what ever data you select in this step. So, file sizes can increase greatly with multiple pivot tables. If you're working with a large survey, you may find you hit a memory constraint on your computer.

The third step is the heart of the process. Here's where you set up the pivot table. (See Figure 6.19.) To the right are all the variables (survey questions) you selected in the previous step. In the center are four areas—Data, Row, Column, and Page. You set up the table by dragging and dropping the variables into the appropriate places. Place the segmentation variables in the Page area, except for one that should be placed in the Row area. (Don't worry — you can easily change all these assignments later.) Drag one of the service performance variables into the Data area. Notice that it will say "Count of ..." Double click on that. You now have a dialogue box, shown in the upper right of Figure 6.19, that allows you to set what calculation to apply to the Data variable. "Average" was selected in our example. You can drag one or more of the variables into the Data area. The last step is to specify the location of the output.

Figure 6.20 shows the output from the pivot table just created. Some rearranging was performed by dragging the Data variables into the left-hand column. Experiment with drag-and-drop. You may stumble upon a very useful formatting of the data. In this screen we see the mean scores for the service performance variables for

Figure 6.17
Regression Output

		Standard			Lower	Upper	Lower	Upper
SUMMARY OUTPUT								
Regression Statistics								
Multiple R	0.820193967							
R Square	0.672718144							
Adjusted R Square	0.663563407							
Standard Error	0.712575028							
Observations	148							
ANOVA								
	df	SS	MS	F	Significance F			
Regression	4	149.248	37.31199	73.48306	1.02E-33			
Residual	143	72.61013	0.507763					
Total	147	221.8581						
	Coefficients	Standard Error	t Stat	P-value	Lower 95%	Upper 95%	Lower 95.0%	Upper 95.0%
Intercept	-0.044168462	0.072034	-0.61316	0.540745	-0.18656	0.098221	-0.18656	0.098221
1. Response Time	0.285925479	0.073922	3.86792	0.000166	0.139804	0.432047	0.139804	0.432047
2. Meets Commitment	0.199477483	0.059725	3.339925	0.001069	0.081419	0.317536	0.081419	0.317536
3. 1st Call Resolution	0.184221704	0.052521	3.507612	0.000605	0.080405	0.288039	0.080405	0.288039
5. Diagnosis Thorough	0.247569301	0.051663	4.79198	4.09E-06	0.145447	0.349692	0.145447	0.349692

one of the demographic variables, in this case, the Expertise Level of the respondent. There were four options for that demographic variable, Novice to Expert, but the data were keyed as numbers. Now, on that screen, you can swap the Page variables (which are the demographic variables) by using drag-and-drop and get the mean scores for all the different strata. Do you want to see which surveys gave the responses you see in a cell? Double click on the cell. You'll see the raw survey data that led to the results displayed in that cell.

If you want to save the data for inclusion in the management report as a table, you cannot select the individual cells. However, you can select the rows and paste them into another worksheet where they will be stored as values. That is, they won't change as you alter the pivot table. This is a quick way to create tables for your written report and avoid transcription errors. You will be doing a lot of mouse work formatting the tables.

In summary, pivot tables have a lot of power for ad hoc analysis, but you do need to play with the tool to learn all its capabilities. We've just scratched the surface here.

Analyzing Textual Data

There are three sources of textual data in a survey project, and we'll touch on each briefly. Prior to any of the analysis below, you must decide whether to clean the free-format data as discussed at the start of this chapter.

"Other" Responses. For some nominal or categorical questions, you may have included an "Other" category and asked the person to explain in an open-ended text box. As covered earlier, you need to review those comments to see if they really represent one of the response categories. You also need to review these to see if you should include additional response options or revise one of them for future administrations of the instrument.

Open-Ended Questions. You most likely will have some open-ended questions on your survey. Early in this guide, we stated that having too many open-ended questions was a bad idea, in part because they are messy to analyze. Here's where you'll pay the piper if you did not heed that advice. If you have only a few verbatim comments, the task is relatively simple, but if you have a lot of written responses to a lot of open-ended questions, you will spend more time — by far — analyzing and reporting these data than the numerical data.

The good news, though, is that these quotes will bring the numerical data to life. One cogent statement from a customer may reinforce and explain the scores found for a particular structured question. Keep this fact in mind when you write the report. That statement will be remembered by your audience far better than "a score of 2.62 on a scale of 1 to 5." If you plan to conduct the same

Figure 6.18
PivotTable Dialogue Box

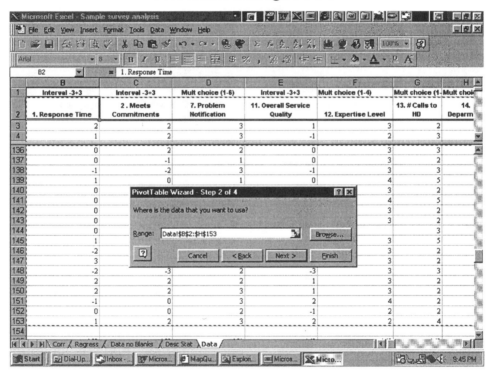

survey again in the future, consider how you might capture this information in a structured question in the future. Perhaps the response categories for a question need to be changed or a new question written to capture some other phenomenon brought out now in the free-form answer.

The way to analyze textual data is through a "distillation" process — you boil down all these words into categories of comments, supplemented with a few well-chosen statements. As you start reading the comments, create a tally sheet and with each open-ended response, try to categorize it on the tally sheet or create a new category. You may find that you need to refine the categories as you proceed and nuances in the responses become evident. The real beauty of open-ended questions is that patterns of reasoning sometimes emerge. Group similar comments together to see if patterns are revealed. Free-form comments can help you to get to the "why" behind some of the feelings that customers have expressed.

When you proceed to writing the actual report, you will want to include some of the more cogent comments in the body of the report. A complete list of quotes, sorted into categories, can also be a very useful report exhibit.[9] Recognize that some comments may address multiple categories. Do remember to be balanced in the way you summarize the textual responses. Because you are presenting anecdotal, rather than scientific, representative data, your judgments about what to present will weigh heavily. Try to be fair. Even if most of the comments are negative, also report the positive ones as well.

Focus Group Research. Although the process of analyzing the textual data from focus groups is similar to what's required for data from open-ended questions, it is far more involved. The semi-structured nature of focus group sessions means that the data will be wide-ranging, making the distillation process more challenging. If you taped the sessions, transcribing key quotes will take some time. A literal transcript of every word is not necessary, but key points and key quotes should be captured. As you listen to the tapes and read through the notes, look for the themes, and copy additional quotes under those theme headings. There will be redundancy within those comments, so reduce them down to the unique points, saving the cogent quotes for the written document.

This analysis will also be an iterative, distillation process. Your challenge is to find the connections across all the themes, identifying the reasoning processes and root sources of customer issues. In addition to categorizing comments across all participants, it may also be useful to describe a few participants more fully. Present an individual story or narration of those chosen people who serve as exemplars of what you have found in the customer base. This tech-

---

[9] Many readers will turn to that appendix *first*. That can be disheartening after investing so much time in the structured survey!

nique allows you to draw all the logical connections for one individual (or company as the case may be), bringing more power to the analysis. The reader may be able to relate to this description and understand the logic connections better than just with the categorized comments. Books on focus group research will present some of the more involved analytical techniques, but they all come down to teasing out the critical pieces of information from among all those words.

Figure 6.19
Pivot Table Dialogue Box

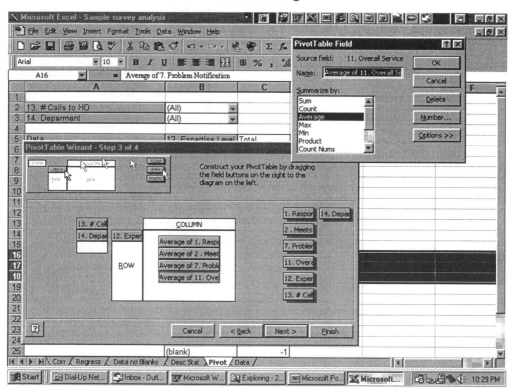

The Written Report and Management Presentation

The last step in a survey project is writing the report of the research findings. What your final report includes will be determined by the nature of your service product and the audience. Always err on the side of being too structured and formal. You may look stuffy, but you'll be considered professional and stuffy.

The report should explain, at a high level, all of the following:

- Why you did the study
- How you did study
- The findings for each question
- The findings for the study as a whole
- Conclusions drawn by you, the analyst
- Your recommendations

Let's take, as an example, a report for an annual survey. The contents of such a report should include:

- **Executive summary.** This should be a crisp, one-page summary of the entire document. Dedicate one to two sentences to stating the nature of the research activity and how it was accomplished. Dedicate a short paragraph to the key findings of the study, and another short paragraph to the recommendations derived from the findings. The executive summary is designed for the executive who does not have time to read the entire document — thus, its name. Do not write this summary purely in a "bullet" style. Using bullets for each major finding is fine, but flesh out those points in well-developed prose.

- **Methodology of the study.** You may feel a formal description of methodology is unnecessary, but the truly incisive reader of your report will decide whether to believe your findings based upon how you performed the study. The goal of the methodology description is to keep the reader focused on the analysis of the data and findings rather than questioning the validity of the study. In your management presentation if no one asks a question about methodology, then you've succeeded.

  If you are performing higher-level statistical analysis of the data, then the methodology becomes critical. Briefly outline how the instrument was developed and tested, how the respondent sample was generated, steps taken to minimize bias from the survey administration, and whatever else you feel is pertinent. This is also the place to present the sample size, response rate, respondent group size, and the overall statistical confidence in the results. Finally, if you have performed any data cleansing outlined at the start of this chapter, describe those actions here.

◆ **Detailed Findings.** Typically, present the findings for each question in sequence from the survey instrument. However, you may

Figure 6.20
Pivot Table Output

	A	B	C	D	E	F
	File Edit View Insert Format Tools Data Window Help					
	Arial	10	B I U ≡ ≡ ≡ ⊞ $ % , ⅛ ⅜ ⊈ ⊈ ☐ ▾ ♦ ▾ ▲ ▾ 2 A			
1						
2	13. # Calls to HD	(All)				
3	14. Deparment	(All)				
4						
5	Data	12. Expertise Level	Total			
6	Average of 1. Response Time	1	0.666666667			
7		2	0.725490196			
8		3	0.597222222			
9		4	0			
10		(blank)	0			
11	Average of 2. Meets Commitments	1	1			
12		2	1.039215686			
13		3	0.680555556			
14		4	0.681818182			
15		(blank)	0			
16	Average of 7. Problem Notification	1	1.666666667			
17		2	2.235294118			
18		3	2.328767123			
19		4	2.181818182			
20		(blank)	2			
21	Average of 11. Overall Service Quality	1	0.666666667			
22		2	0.68627451			
23		3	0.589041096		*Minor formatting done to*	
24		4	0.238095238		*improve readability.*	
25		(blank)	-1			
26	Total Average of 1. Response Time		0.546666667			
27	Total Average of 2. Meets Commitments		0.8			
28	Total Average of 7. Problem Notification		2.258278146			
29	Total Average of 11. Overall Service Quality		0.563758389			
30						

Corr / Regress / Data no Blanks / Desc Stat \ Pivot / Data /

want to open with demographic questions. Refer to appropriate tables or graphs and discuss the meaning of the results. It is best to put data tables and any charts for the question right there with the discussion. Don't make the reader flip back and forth from the appendix to the text. If a skew in responses make the means for a question unreliable, discuss that here. Also, if you have some quotes from open-ended questions, interviews, or focus groups that relate to a particular question on the survey, you may want to present it in the context of that question. Remember to be balanced in what you present.

If you did perform focus groups or other context-rich research to help design the questionnaire or as follow-up research, you should also include the findings from that research as a section of this report. Draw connections between the textual data and the survey data.

After you have covered the findings for the individual questions, next turn to the analysis you performed for the data set overall. For example, present the correlation or regression analysis performed on the survey data to identify the critical elements in the service organization. If this is one survey in a series, then you should also discuss how the findings from this study differed from past research.

◆ **Conclusions.** Given your findings, what do you conclude? What are the strengths of the operation? What are the weaknesses of the operation? Ideally, your research, perhaps in conjunction with other research initiatives, has allowed you to perform some root cause analysis. Research should direct us to the heart or root of any problems, so that steps can be taken or projects initiated to correct those problems. Here is where many of the Total Quality Management tools can be a great help.

◆ **Recommendations.** Given your findings and your conclusions, what direction do you believe the organization should take? What improvement projects should be initiated? What additional research do you believe should be done to pinpoint or clarify the issues needing correction? Be sure to state your recommendations in a positive, professional manner since they may affect many groups within the organization.

The Emperor's Clothes Dilemma

Sometimes writing the survey research report brings the surveyor face to face with an ethical dilemma: Do you report the truth according to the research or what the managers want to hear? Many times the boss doesn't want to hear bad news, but the survey actually reveals much bad news mixed amid the good news. What do you do in such a case? To use the children's story, do you tell the Emperor he has no clothes on?

Hidden between the lines of the original Statement of Purpose, there may have been a different agenda. Was this survey really being done to prove how good things are rather than to identify opportunities for improvement? Did the sponsoring manager already have a draft of conclusions in mind before you even started the first draft of the questionnaire?

As a consultant, the author faces this dilemma. Some clients specifically hire an outside consultant because they have more faith in getting truthful results from an outsider, and the sponsoring manager doesn't want to force an employee to be the messenger of bad news. Occasionally however, a client will show by comments or decisions in the instrument design stages that he really doesn't want to hear the whole truth. Perhaps certain questions will be eliminated from consideration because they cut a little too close. Each of us has to explore his own inner guiding principles in handling this type of situation, and this will test your ethical roots. It may not happen, but you should be prepared for it.

Remember, there is a difference between a critique and criticism. Critiquing is a professional, responsible activity. Avoid loaded language or assigning blame. State the facts as they have presented themselves, and draw honest conclusions that can be solidly defended by fact, not by opinion. The reason for doing the research, hopefully, was in part to identify areas for improvement, so present those opportunities from the rigorous, fact-based critique, and no one should blame the messenger for the bad news.

The Management Presentation

In addition to the written report, you will probably be asked to deliver a presentation to a group of managers about the survey's findings. If you aren't asked, you should offer because a presentation of this kind is your opportunity to make sure everyone is receiving a consistent message. It is also a good opportunity to address the next steps in the process improvement continuum, while you have the decision makers' attention.

A classic consultant's trick, one the author does not practice, is to deliver the final report at the time of the presentation. This avoids lots of hard questions that might arise from a detailed reading of the report. If you work within the organization, you won't get the chance to run anyway, so you might as well deliver the report one to two weeks prior to the presentation. If you have outsourced any of the analysis, be sure you get the report prior to the management presentation.

When developing the presentation, your biggest struggle will be to distill all the work you have done down to a score of slides and a one-hour talk. Focus on the high points. You do not need to present all the detailed findings for every question. You won't have time if it is a long survey. Apply the concept of Pareto Analysis to

Figure 6.21
Sample Data Table for Interval Survey Question

1. Response Time			Percent	Cumulative %
Count	150	High 3	4	4
Blank	1	2	21	25
Mean	0.55	1	27	52
Median	1	0	31	83
Mode	0	-1	7	91
Conf. Interval	0.21	-2	9	99
Std Deviation	1.29	Low -3	1	100

your presentation, and "separate the critical few from the trivial many." However, always have the backup slides to address issues that someone may bring up. Print out a list of all your slides so that you can go right to the critical slide.

In a normal project schedule, you would develop the presentation after the written report. The author finds it is useful to do them concurrently. When you are writing a lengthy report, the logical connections among all the individual points can get muddied. As the writer, you've become so close to the words, you can't see the missing logical links. When you force yourself to develop an oral narration of the material, some of these breaks in logic will become evident. Doing "dry runs" of your presentation may uncover some shortcomings in the written report.

Data Tables

As mentioned below, the detail data can be included with a chart covering one or more questions. However, you are not going to chart every descriptive statistic for every question. You will probably only chart the mean scores and frequency distributions. Resist the temptation to have one massive table that covers a full page in 9-point font displaying all the data. It will be unreadable. Instead, consider putting small data tables in the section where you discuss the findings for each question.

Figure 6.22
Sample Data Table for Nominal Survey Question

9. Order Problems	Count	Percent
Yes	111	17.0
No	543	83.0

10. If Yes, Problem was...	Count	Percent
Not as Expected	5	3.6%
Damaged	25	18.0%
Box Damaged	6	4.3%
Defective	35	25.2%
Wrong Size Shipped	5	3.6%
Wrong Size	5	3.6%
Incomplete Shipm't	24	17.3%
Missing Items	9	6.5%
Not Yet Received	17	12.2%
Other	8	5.8%
Total	139	—

Total will exceed 100% since multiple responses allowed

Figure 6.21 provides an example of a data table you might include with the discussion of the interval survey question, Response Time, from our sample data set.

This format could also be used for an ordinal or ratio question. In a small data table you can present the descriptive statistics, including the frequency distribution and cumulative frequencies. In the introductory paragraph of the detail findings section include an explanation of the chart contents if you plan to use this format repeatedly. You may need to define some of the statistical terminology.

For nominal data, tables are more complex, since you have to present each response choice and show the percent of respondents that chose each. Figure 6.22 presents a table showing two survey questions. The first question is a binary question used to branch to the second multiple-response, multiple-choice question.

It will take some time to develop a format for these tables that is pleasing to the eye. Here are some guidelines that will help:

- Center most column headings and set them apart through boldface type or shading.

- Always align numbers on the decimal point. When formatting a table using a word processor, this is easy since you can set a tab for decimal alignment. When using a spreadsheet for formatting, you can accomplish this by having the same number of decimals for the entire column.

- Show no more than two decimal points and probably only one. For scaled questions, going beyond the first decimal point conveys nothing, since the survey measurement process is not that precise. Look at the accuracy of your results that is plus or minus a certain percent. This will guide you in the number of decimals to display.

- If a large number of cells contain zeros, consider substituting dashes (-) for the zeros.

Charting and Graphing the Data

"A picture is worth a thousand words" according to the axiom. In this case charts and graphs are worth a thousand words. The text of the report should analyze and interpret the data. Charts and graphs should be used to present the data and direct the reader's attention to key findings in the data analysis. In designing your charts you should follow the same principle that was followed for designing the survey questionnaire. Just as the questionnaire is not a test for the respondent, report charts are not a test for the reader. The reader should not have to work to understand the message you are trying to convey.[10]

- **Clearly label your charts.** Use titles, legends, and axis labels that clearly explain what the chart is about. Don't assume and don't force the reader to figure out what the chart is trying to communicate. Make certain the titles and labels are not so cryptic that no one can discern their meaning.

---

[10] For some excellent books on visualizing data, read Edward Tufte's three books, listed in the bibliography. Professor Tufte also presents an engaging one-day seminar that includes copies of his books. See www.edwardtufte.com for more information.

◆ **Develop "short names" for your survey questions.** As stated earlier, you won't be able to put 10 entire survey questions on a chart, and using labels such as Q1, Q2, Q3, etc. conveys the laziness of the graph creator. Create short names for each survey question, such as "Technical Competence," or "1st Fix Quality." Include an exhibit with the survey questions and their corresponding short names.

◆ **Use colors consistently and with a purpose.** Colored charts, rather than gray-shade patterns, are easier to read, but do resist the use of coloring areas of the chart for the sake of coloring. It will create visual dissonance. Be consistent in how you use colors or patterns. This will avoid confusion as the reader progresses through the report. If printing the report in black and white, verify that the "colors" can be differentiated when produced in gray scale. Otherwise, change the patterns or use the black-and-white options available in the Chart Wizard — look for the "Custom Types" tab in Step 1. If you have to create your own black-and-white chart, consider saving it as a User-Defined custom chart type.[11]

◆ **Use three-dimensional charts only if there is a third dimension.** A three-dimensional chart implies that there is a third dimension of data being displayed. If there isn't, the reader will be looking for it.

◆ **Be consistent in your use of chart types.** Use the same type of chart throughout the report to show a specific type of information. For example, use scatter plots for trends and pie charts for demographic statistics.

◆ **Be consistent in the scale of the axes.** When plotting data from interval questions, it is best to show the entire scale, from 1 to 10 for example, rather than just from 6 to 10. The reader may not notice the truncated scale. If you do truncate the scale, always truncate in the same fashion, using a footnote to inform the reader.

◆ **Use notes where appropriate to describe complex data.** If there are some key points you want the reader to note on the chart, don't hesitate to put an explanatory note on the chart. As a rule it is better to place annotations in the same vicinity as the item

---

[11] To do this, select the chart whose format you want to save. From the Chart menu, select "Chart Type…" then select "User-Defined" after which an "Add" button will appear.

being annotated. Don't make the reader flip back and forth from endnotes.

- **Use highlights where appropriate.** Consider highlighting an area of the chart with color, an arrow, or some other symbol to direct the reader to a critical point. For example, you may use this technique to direct attention to a statistically significant difference among groups. Don't overuse highlights, however. If you do, nothing will be emphasized.

- **Include data tables on charts.** Excel allows you to include a data table at the bottom of a chart. That's a nice way of presenting the back up detail data right there with the chart. Be sure to eliminate the legend. It will be redundant.

- **Consistent item ordering.** Arrange the items in a chart in a specific order and continue that logic through all charts. The order may be from greatest to least importance, or it may follow the chronology of the service delivery process, which may be reflected in the order of the survey questions. Don't be tied to one rule. While you should probably present the service performance in their order from the survey instrument, you may want to group all the attitudinal questions together.

Figure 6.23
Pie Chart Example — Respondents by Expertise Level

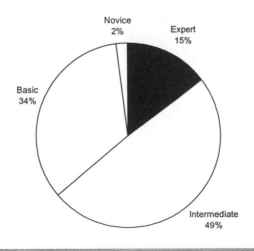

◆ **Resist the urge for an "all in one" graph.** An all-encompassing chart may be clever, and it may be cute, but it is also probably not comprehensible to anyone but the author.

◆ **Anticipate questions.** Try to anticipate inconsistencies in the data presented that may confuse the reader, leading them to focus on their confusion rather than the content. Explain data inconsistencies in a footnote. For example, if blank responses or branching logic lead to different total counts across survey questions, explain the inconsistency to the reader. The reader can then focus on the content of the material, and when you do your management presentation, you won't be distracted from the core focus of the presentation to explain what are probably inconsequential matters.

Pie Charts

Pie charts can depict nominal data. (See Figure 6.23.) They show the proportions of different elements in a whole. Pie charts are most commonly used to show demographic breakdowns or other segmentations applied to the data set. Since pie charts show proportions, they can be used to show frequency distributions for ordinal or interval questions, but that is not the common use for this chart type.

Figure 6.24
Column Chart Example

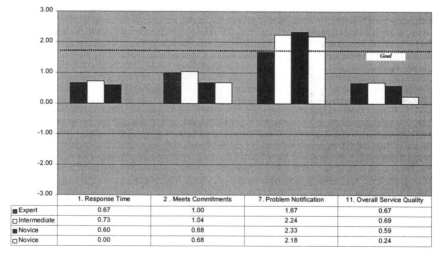

	1. Response Time	2 . Meets Commitments	7. Problem Notification	11. Overall Service Quality
■ Expert	0.67	1.00	1.67	0.67
□ Intermediate	0.73	1.04	2.24	0.69
■ Novice	0.60	0.68	2.33	0.59
□ Novice	0.00	0.68	2.18	0.24

Bar Charts and Column Charts

Bar charts and column charts[12] are ideal for depicting all types of survey data. They can illustrate the proportions from nominal or ordinal data, and they can show descriptive statistics from interval-scaled survey questions. You can show the results for multiple survey questions, and multiple response segments, on one chart. There are limits, however. At some point the number of bars on one chart will make the chart unintelligible. After around 30 bars — 10 questions and three segments, for example — the chart will become very crowded. To show performance against some goal, draw a line showing the goal for those performance indicators.

Figure 6.24 is a column chart presenting the mean ratings for four survey questions segmented along the Expertise demographic question from our sample data set. Notice we've shown the full scale, which is -3 to +3 and added the data table and a "goal" line.

Figure 6.25
Stacked Bar Chart Example

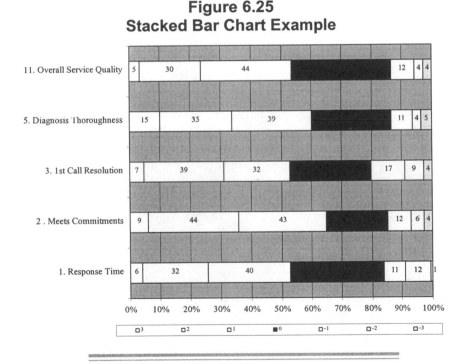

---

[12] Excel uses *bar chart* to refer to a horizontal display of the data. This is also known as a *horizontal bar chart*. *Column chart* refer to a vertical display of the data. This may be known as a *histogram*.

Frequency distributions can be displayed using bar and column charts. Refer back to Figure 6.13, which is a combination column chart and scatter plot, produced using the histogram function. Note that only one survey question can be applied on a chart.

Bar and column charts can also be used to show change. For example, if you have a data table that shows the percentage change in certain performance measures from a previous period, a bar chart provides a more visual presentation. Since there may be negative changes, the zero line might be the center of the chart.

Stacked Bar and Stacked Column Charts

A real challenge for graphing is to bring a frequency table alive for ordinal or interval data. An alternative for the Histogram function just described is to use stacked bar and column charts. Each "stack" represents one survey question, and each segment of the stack represents the frequency percentage for a response category.

Figure 6.26
Scatter Plot Showing Mean and
Standard Deviation Over Time

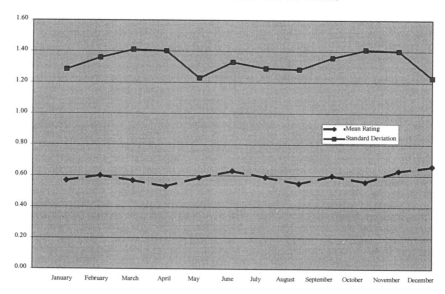

Because they are *stacked bars* or *columns*, the viewer can see the cumulative frequency for some point in the distribution. The viewer can also see the median and other percentile points in the distribution. The advantage of this format over the histogram is that multiple survey questions can be displayed on one graph.

Figure 6.25 is an example of a stacked bar chart. No data table is included since Excel puts data tables at the bottom of the chart, making them far less useful for the stacked bar format. Also, there are seven pieces of data being displayed for each survey question charted, which would make the data table crowded. Instead, we displayed the count on the bar segment. Alternatively, we could have displayed the percentage on each segment. Notice that the distributions for Meet Commitments and Diagnostic Thoroughness are more heavily weighted towards the higher end of the scale.

Stacked bar charts convey considerable information, but they are crowded, so the reader must be directed to the key points. If you use one of these in a presentation, consider having the chart "build" by each category in the distribution.

Scatter Plots

Scatter plots contrast a pair of variables where each axis represents one variable. These plots are commonly used to show trends in some measure over an extended period of time. Thus, "time" is the variable on the horizontal axis. (See Figure 6.26.) A bar chart can also show this information, but a scatter plot with connecting lines conveys to the viewer that this is the same performance measure. Multiple measures can be depicted on the same chart if they share the same scale. Two scales can be used on one chart, with one shown on the left vertical axis and the other on the right vertical axis. Use caution, though. This technique can confuse the viewer.

Many times in analysis we contrast the results from one variable against another, which is bivariate analysis. The classic example of this is to contrast satisfaction and importance for various performance measures. Considerable value can be gleaned by contrasting other measures, such as performance measures between two periods. A very appealing way of presenting such comparisons is using scatter plots. The concept is to have two dimensions, one for each axis, and to plot points for various measures along these dimensions.

Figure 6.27
Scatter Plot Showing Gap Analysis —
Contrasting Importance and Satisfaction

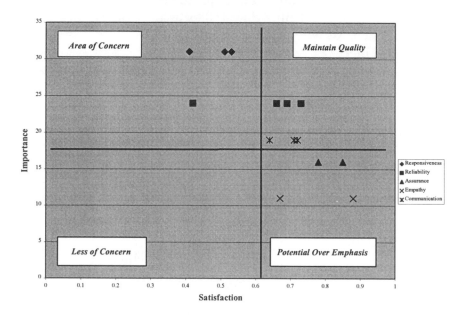

Depending upon the dimensions on each axis, the chart area can be divided into sections, either four quadrants or in half with a diagonal "northeast-southwest" line. If divided into quadrants, each will represent some situation. If the two dimensions are current and previous period performance, the diagonal dividing line will indicate for which measures an improvement versus a decline in performance occurred. Figure 6.27 shows an example contrasting satisfaction as measured by several survey questions with derived importance measures for five major service quality dimensions into which the questions were grouped. The quadrants give management an indication where attention should be focused.

Summary

This chapter has addressed how to analyze the data collected during a survey process and how to present that data in a manage-

214

ment report. Many decisions revert back to the choice of question formats discussed in Chapter 4. Question formats determine the type of analysis that can be performed and the way findings can be charted. Specialized tools can be used for this analysis and presentation, but Excel can do the job. Now with the data analyzed, the next step in a customer loyalty program is to apply the data to improving the operation. That's the topic of the next chapter.

CSCSCS

7 Taking Action

By the end of this chapter, you will know:
- ◆ The importance of service recovery procedures
- ◆ How context-rich research techniques, previously described for instrument design preparation, can be put to further use
- ◆ How to construct statistical process control charts for operational quality control
- ◆ How to use these charts as a tool for continuous process improvement

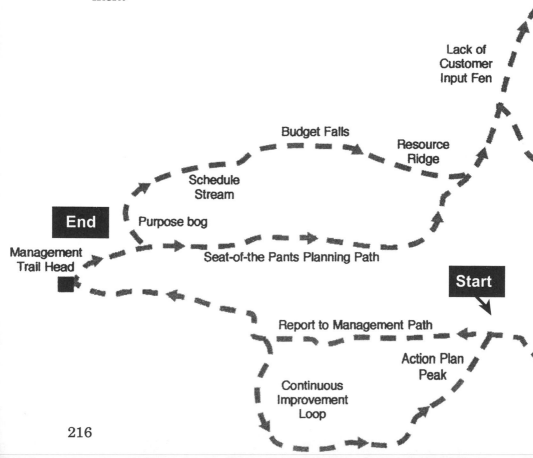

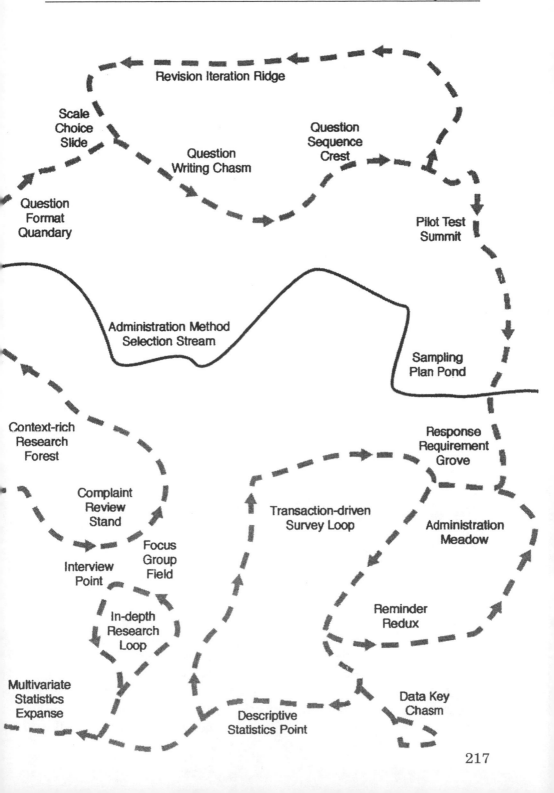

Revision Iteration Ridge

Scale
Choice
Slide

Question
Writing Chasm

Question
Sequence
Crest

Question
Format
Quandary

Pilot Test
Summit

Administration Method
Selection Stream

Sampling
Plan Pond

Context-rich
Research
Forest

Response
Requirement
Grove

Complaint
Review
Stand

Transaction-driven
Survey Loop

Administration
Meadow

Focus
Group
Field

Interview
Point

In-depth
Research
Loop

Reminder
Redux

Multivariate
Statistics
Expanse

Descriptive
Statistics Point

Data Key
Chasm

217

You've now gone through a lot of effort planning and executing the survey project. The final step is actually the next step in another process: taking the findings of the survey and applying that learning to customer retention efforts either through process improvement or fixing some uncovered problem.

Taking some action is truly critical for continued success with a customer loyalty program. You introduced the survey project to your customers as something that was so important that you needed some of their "mindshare." Your customers did their part—they gave you some time. Now you have to do yours. Show them — as well as your own organization — how truly important their feedback was.

Simply thanking them for their input will ring hollow if no tangible changes can be seen. The perfunctory "thank you" we get from store clerks, and even vending machines, has devalued its meaning. No reasonable person would expect fundamental changes within an operation to happen overnight, but the surveying should be seen as the first of a series of communications with the customer. Update customers using existing communication channels, such as newsletters or user groups, about the progress on improvement projects driven by the survey feedback. Early in this book we said that a customer survey is part research and part marketing. Here is the marketing aspect.

The exact form of the action you take obviously will be dictated by the reasons you initiated the survey project, by the type of data you collected, and by the findings in the survey data analysis. The survey findings may spawn projects to streamline service delivery processes, to initiate more personalization in the service delivery process, to revamp service pricing due to the perceived value of the service, or to accomplish a host of other possible objectives.

Follow-up Research

Recognize that the survey data may not prove detailed enough to support process redesign efforts. The survey data may only identify areas that need to be revamped, but not the specific areas to be redesigned. This is to be expected from a high level survey. Thus, the next action for process reengineering would be further data collection. Here's where the context-rich research techniques come into play. Personal interviews and focus groups were advocated as techniques for generating the issues to be surveyed. After the survey, they might also be used to gather granular data in specific areas targeted for improvement projects. Notice on the trail map at the start of the chapter that a side loop goes from data analysis back to these research techniques.

Improvement projects require some organizational momentum. While they may improve processes, they also interfere with transacting business in the here and now. Surveying falls into that category. It can be put off because of more pressing issues, and service organizations always have fires to fight. If you generated enough momentum to initiate and complete a survey project, take a breath, but not a long one. You need to capitalize on the momentum that has been generated. Charge ahead!

Service Recovery Actions

While customers won't expect changes to a service organizational design to happen immediately, they will expect immediate action if they have told you about a service failure. If you are conducting a transaction-driven survey program, then you *must* plan for the action you will take based upon the specific responses, not just the aggregated information. Why? To a good extent a transaction-driven survey is complaint solicitation. You have asked the customer about the service quality of the last service event. If there was something drastically bad about it, the customer is

> What the research indicates is that customers who have had a complaint handled successfully are more loyal to a company than perhaps even those who have had no complaints at all.

going to expect some response to the complaint that has now been filed through the survey process. That seems perfectly reasonable. Specific complaint-handling procedures should be part of a transactional survey program. Plan for this in advance.

This complaint-handling activity is known as *service recovery*. There is much substantial research as well as anecdotal stories about the importance of service recovery.[1] What the research indicates is that customers who have had a complaint handled successfully are more loyal to a company than perhaps even those who have had no complaints at all. Consider your own experiences. Has some vendor made good on a problem quickly and reasonably? How likely are you to do business with that company again? The author re-

---

[1] See for example, Hart, et al. 1990, Zemke, 2000, and Goodman, 1999.

cently stayed at a Courtyard hotel and when checking out, Ali, the front desk clerk, asked how my stay was. I said, conversationally, that everything was fine — except for those noisy people in the hallway at 2 AM. Did I blame the hotel for that? Not really, but Ali, without missing a beat, looked at my bill on her computer terminal and said, "I am sorry about that. I see you had breakfast with us yesterday. How about if I credit you for that meal as a way of making up for the problem?" Courtyard has obviously empowered frontline people to address service complaints. For me, this was an unexpected gesture. Am I more likely to stay at Courtyard hotels in the future — and sing their praises? You bet!

If you identify a customer in need of service recovery, what action should you take? Obviously, the core issue must be addressed, but you also want to offer some compensation as in the Courtyard example. What compensation is appropriate depends upon the nature of the complaint. Ralston-Purina's customer service operation offers compensation for problems with their product, and as Ken Dean, Director of Quality Systems & Resources, stated, "All complaints are not created equal." A broken bag of dog biscuits demands a different response than a damaged oriental rug. They developed a list of possible recovery actions, and some of these go beyond compensation in cash or with free products. They might send flowers or a coupon for dinner.[2]

Is your work done when the service recovery actions have been taken? The question remains: did the service recovery create a satisfied customer? To gauge this you should again turn to surveying, which is something Ralston-Purina does. A brief follow-up survey will let you know whether those actions you took were truly effective.

We mentioned early in this book that a survey program is as much about marketing as it is about operations. That's because in services, marketing and operations are so tightly intertwined. Good operational delivery is good marketing. Transaction-driven surveying and service recovery programs should be considered in that light. There are now tools specifically designed to address complaint solicitation and complaint handling. (See the list of automation tools and outsourcers discussed at the end of Chapter 8.)

---

[2] Interview April 1999.

Operational Quality Control:
Statistical Process Control Charts

If you are creating a transaction-driven survey program, then a primary driver for the program is probably to exercise quality control over the service delivery operation. You probably intend to gather the data both to look for specific customer complaints that need an immediate response and to search for trends. Most likely you will plot the data on a trend chart, that is, a scatter plot diagram with time as the horizontal axis. Depending upon the volume of data you are collecting, you may plot monthly, weekly, or even daily points. In addition to plotting points for the service operation as a whole, you might trend performance for individual support groups. For example, you may have multiple call centers, many field service offices, or you may have your support organization aligned along the product types being supported. The data you plot may be for the overall satisfaction score, and you may also plot some key individual performance characteristics, for example, reliability or responsiveness. (See Figure 7.1.)

> The philosophy behind SPC is that quality should be built into a product, rather than assuring quality through inspection and removal of bad product.

When you construct these charts, of course, you will be looking for overall improvement trends, but you will also be looking for aberrations. If some score drops significantly for a particular time period, you may investigate what caused the drop. You want to do it soon, because the underlying problem may still be there, causing more dissatisfaction for more customers. You are exercising quality control, and perhaps surprisingly, you are only a few steps away from constructing and using statistical process control (SPC).

The philosophy behind SPC is that quality should be built into a product, rather than assuring quality through inspection and removal of bad product. We build quality into a product by sampling the product on a regular basis at various stages of production, checking to be sure that the each stage is operating properly, and creating ongoing processes to remedy, at the source, any correctable problems that are discovered.

SPC was created by Bell Labs back in the 1920s, but its first real application occurred in post-war Japan. Japanese industry, looking for ways to become competitive in their war-torn economy, turned to the late W. Edwards Deming. Deming was instrumental in the implementation of SPC in Japan in the 1940s and 1950s. Toyota was one of the first companies to embrace the quality assurance philosophy behind SPC. While SPC is now widely used in manufacturing around the world, it also can serve useful purposes in services.

To describe SPC requires some statistical concepts. In any task, be it drilling a hole or responding to a service request, there will be some *variation*, which can be considered *error*. Some of that variation is a natural consequence of the design of the task. For example, try cutting paper into one-inch strips with scissors. Cut a number of strips and measure them. You will find that they all won't be exactly the same. The variation may be due to the skills or training of the people, whether it's the start or end of the shift, the quality and sharpness of the scissors, differences in the quality of the paper being cut, or changes in the humidity, which affects the paper.

There will always be some error, and that error can be categorized into two types. The first type is a result of the variability that's inherent with the design of the task. This is called *normal error*. The second type of error is due to *assignable causes*. This is called *abnormal error*.[3] If we eliminated all assignable causes, we would be left with only normal error.

We can't control the normal error without redesigning the operation, but we can reduce the abnormal error. We do that by identifying when abnormal error is present and searching for assignable causes. This is a form of *root cause analysis*. Those factors listed above for the paper-cutting process are potential assignable causes. Knowing these causes, you could construct a fishbone or Isahakawa diagram to focus the quality improvement effort toward identifying and resolving the sources of abnormal error.[4]

When we measure customer satisfaction with various aspects of our service delivery operation we will be measuring both normal and abnormal error — unless you expect to get perfect scores on every question! Statistical process control provides a tool to distinguish between the normal and abnormal error. By isolating the

---

[3] *Normal error* is also called *non-random error* and *abnormal error* is sometimes called *systematic error*.

[4] For a good review of quality improvement tools, see *The Memory Jogger II* from Goal/QPC, 1994. This is a small, pocket-size compendium of the various tools of data analysis and quality improvement. It doesn't provide elaborate detail, but it is a great quick review of the techniques.

latter, we can take steps to identify the assignable causes and improve service delivery.

There are a number of different types of SPC charts that can be
constructed. Here we'll focus on one that is most appropriate for a
service environment.[5] Let's assume we're capturing satisfaction data
using a 10-point scale, and our management team has decided that
any score of 4 or below on the overall service quality question rep-

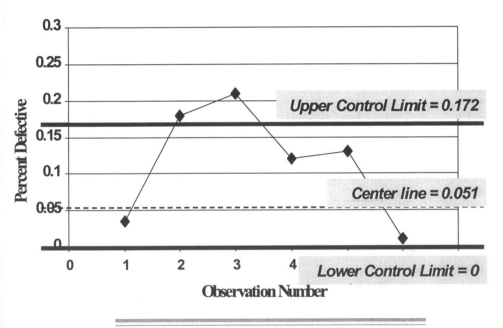

Figure 7.1
Statistical Process Control Charts
Exercising Quality Control

resents a "defective" service transaction. We would expect some
scores or 4 or lower, but we would like to know if the number of
defective transactions has spiked, which would indicate something
has changed in the operation. Our first task is to construct a chart
called a *p* chart, which will help us identify whether the *proportion*
or percentage defective has changed due to some abnormal error.

---

[5] Bob E. Hayes' book, *Measuring Customer Satisfaction*, does an excellent job of outlining how
to construct different SPC charts.

To start the process we have to "prime the pump," that is we need some data. Say we collect transactional survey data for 25 weeks to generate our baseline data. Each week we surveyed 30 people. At the end of the 25 weeks, we find a total of 38 defective service transactions (that is, 38 surveys with a score of 4 or below) out of the 750 surveys, giving a proportion defective of 5.1% or 0.051. With that data we can now construct our control charts.

The p chart has three elements: a *center line*, which is the average scores from the baseline data, and two control limits, an *upper control limit* and a *lower control limit*. After we construct the charts, we'll explain those concepts.

The formula and calculations are:

$$\textbf{Upper control limit} \; = \; \bar{p} + 3\sqrt{\frac{\bar{p}(1-\bar{p})}{n}}$$

$$= 0.051 + 3\sqrt{\frac{.051(1-.051)}{30}} \quad = 0.172$$

$$\textbf{Center Line} \; = \; \bar{p} \qquad\qquad\qquad = 0.051$$

$$\textbf{Lower control limit} \; = \; \bar{p} - 3\sqrt{\frac{\bar{p}(1-\bar{p})}{n}}$$

$$= 0.051 - 3\sqrt{\frac{.051(1-.051)}{30}} \quad = -0.067$$

Where $\bar{p}$ = proportion defective

　　　　n = the number of surveys in each sample (**not** the number of samples taken)

Notice the second term of the equations for the control limits. The calculation under the square root sign in essence represents a standard deviation for that sample size. So, our control limits are approximately three standard deviations on either side of the center line, $\bar{p}$. (For those of you with some training in statistics, you know that "the mean plus or minus three standard deviations" is a recurring theme. Why? Because that area represents almost the entire area under the normal distribution curve. To be specific, it represents 99.73% of the area under a normal distribution curve.)

Here's the concept behind control charts. If a proportion defective in a sample is more than three standard deviations from the long run average for proportion defective, then something unusual is probably happening. An observation that far from the center is very unlikely to be caused by normal error. In fact, in only 27 chances out of 10,000 would the error be a result of normal variation. It's reasonable to assume that some abnormal error has occurred due to an assignable cause.

We construct our control charts as seen in Figure 7.1. Notice how closely it resembles a trend line. The horizontal axis is time, and the vertical axis is the proportion defective. (No vertical axis is explicitly shown in a control chart.) Here's how we use it. Each week when we collect our transaction-driven sample data, we calculate the proportion defective in the 30-survey sample, and we plot it on the chart. (Note that we could do this

> One of the tenets of the Total Quality Management philosophy is that workers should be responsible for their own quality.

for any other time period if we so choose, such as daily instead of weekly.) If the plotted points fall within the control limits, then we conclude that the observed error was purely random. If a plotted point falls outside a control limit, then we conclude that some non-random error has occurred. In the example, we see two points beyond the upper control limit. The operation is said to be *statistically out of control*. We should start the investigation for assignable causes.

In this case we found a lower control limit that is below zero. We truncate that to zero, since the proportion defective can't go below zero. In fact, what if the lower control limit were slightly positive, and we plotted a point that was below the lower control limit? Are we saying that our operation is statistically out of control because it is too good? That flouts common sense. But if the operation ran so smoothly during that week, wouldn't we want to know what factors lead to this statistically unusual circumstance? If we learn why — the assignable cause — then perhaps we can instill that in our ongoing operation.

One other tenet of the Total Quality Management philosophy is that workers should be responsible for their own quality. These SPC charts should be maintained not by management, but by the workers. They should plot the data and have weekly review meetings to investigate any assignable causes. The charts should be used as a tool for process improvement, not as a tool for performance investigation. Ralston-Purina's call center uses this practice. Feedback from the control charts has helped identify when a product needed to be reformulated due to the level of complaints.

The astute reader may ask, "but if we identify and correct several assignable causes, the proportion defective will drop, which is good, but then our charts will show we will always be in control. What value are the charts then?" This is quite true, and periodically we need to recalculate the control charts. Initially, we will identify the major assignable causes of abnormal or systematic error, the "low hanging fruit." Then we need to look more closely for the less frequent or less prominent causes of error. That's what will happen as we recalculate our control charts with, presumably, tighter control limits.

Summary

While the primary purpose of this guidebook is to help you develop a rigorous customer survey program, the survey program is a means to an end, not an end in itself. Survey data, especially with the use of statistical process control charts, will highlight areas that need further review. In Chapter 4 we mentioned ways of garnering some detailed data during the survey process, such as branching to an open-ended question after a low score, but you may need to do more research to get the detailed information necessary for re-engineering projects.

A major purpose of transaction-driven surveys is to track the quality of service delivery in near real time. Disgruntled customers will be identified and a service recovery plan should be at the ready to address these complaints.

cases

8 Survey Automation Tools and Survey Outsourcing

By the end of this chapter, you will know:
- What the different types of survey automation tools are
- Where these can best assist a surveying effort
- Where the hidden dangers lie in use of these tools
- The features to consider in the evaluation and selection process
- Where these tools can be purchased
- Aspects of survey projects amenable to outsourcing

The information technology revolution has hit virtually every business process, and market research is no exception. Automation techniques have been applied to surveying for many years now, but they were only able to address selected areas of the process. The web opened whole new frontiers for improvement of survey processes. Many of these have been addressed in Chapter 5, but in this chapter we will try to pull all the threads together and provide a balanced look at both the pros and cons of survey automation.

Survey Automation Tools

Look over the tasks associated with a survey project. Many of them are repetitive clerical tasks, especially in the area of survey administration. Repetitive tasks in any operation are prime candidates for automation. The survey administrative tasks are the primary targets of automation software, but many of these packages go further and help automate other key areas such as developing the survey instrument and reporting the results.

Survey automation is not a new concept, and many types of survey automation tools exist. (See Figure 8.1.) We all remember taking standardized tests in school, where we had to use a #2 pencil and fill in all those circles properly so the scanning machine could read our answers. Those same machines have been used to scan results from paper-based surveys for quite some time. Scanning automates keying the data. Computer aided telephone interview (CATI) software has also existed for some time. CATI automates the delivery of scripts for telephone interviews, walking the interviewer through the mechanics of the survey including any branching logic. Survey responses are entered directly in the computer as given by the respondent.

Figure 8.1
Types of Survey Automation Tools

♦ Scanable forms and machines for paper-based surveys

♦ Computer Aided Telephone Interviewing (CATI)

♦ Web-based focus groups

♦ Email survey instruments

♦ Web-form survey instruments

The new breed of survey automation tools leverages the network infrastructure of the web economy. These new tools automate the data entry process, but they also address other aspects of survey administration, that is, distributing the survey instruments and collecting responses. Several of the tools also incorporate a host of other productivity enhancements, including the creation of the instrument and reporting the results.

Benefits of Using Survey Automation Tools

Automation tools deliver three main benefits:

♦ **Speed.** Automating the administration of the survey can shave many weeks off the time to complete a survey project. Outsourcing the administrative tasks may save some time, but not as much as performing the administration electronically. The speed of compiling the results may be crucial if you are hoping to identify customer situations that need special attention.

- **Quality.** Repetitive tasks are prone to errors. So, automating the distribution and collection of surveys and data keying will reduce errors.

- **Cost & Scalability.** As outlined in the chapter on survey administration, the use of automation tools changes the cost dynamics of surveying. The cost of doing survey research by postal mail or by telephone is strongly tied to the sample distribution size. Automation tools, which utilize the scalability of the internet, break that relationship and drive the cost of administering incremental surveys to nearly zero.

  That doesn't mean it's free! With the automation tools the operational cost decreases, but there is an investment cost. You have to buy the software, which will run from hundreds of dollars to several thousand, depending upon the features you want. You will also have to learn to use the software. These up-front costs are minor, however, compared to the cost of administering one large-scale survey. With each subsequent survey the return on investment becomes greater.

The Role of Automation Tools in a Survey Project

Below we have recreated the stages of a survey project from Chapter 3, noting the role that survey automation software can and cannot play in each stage. Note that not all software packages have each of these features.

1. Project Management: Plan the survey project

- **Project Management.** The software can assist you, if it includes project planning capabilities or links easily into project management software.

2. Survey Instrument Development

- **Attribute Identification.** Some automation is now available for the baseline research that identifies the attributes to include in your survey. This is found in web-based focus group tools. (See Chapter 4 for more discussion on these new tools.) However, these tools cannot guarantee that the focus group is conducted successfully and the analysis of the data properly identifies critical attributes.

- **Question Instrument Design.** If the automation tool has a library of scales, it may help you design questions more quickly and easily. If it has a library of questions or sample instruments, it may help you design the overall questionnaire. It can also guide you through the development of a questionnaire by prompting you for introductions, instructions, section headings, and summaries. Be aware that the quality of editors for designing questions varies greatly across products.

- **Creation of Instruments.** Automation tools help with the tangible creation of the instrument. Older tools automated formatting printed survey instruments. More recent tools will generate the instrument for administration via email or via a web-form. Some of the tools on the market have mail-merge capabilities for generating customized cover letters.

- **Pilot Testing.** These tools *cannot* conduct pilot tests, which take on even greater importance when using automation tools.

3. Survey Administration: Distribution and Data Collection

- **Sample Generation.** Many automation tools can identify necessary sample sizes and generate random samples from a list of customers (that is, the population) that you provide. Many tools will generate stratified, random samples.

- **Survey Distribution and Reminders.** The biggest benefit of automation tools comes from the ability to distribute the survey electronically simply by hitting the "Send" key. This may be as an email with the survey in ASCII text, as an HTML attachment, or as an invitation to link to a URL for a web-form survey. Some tools can also generate follow-up notices for only those who have not responded. This is very important feature for addressing non-response bias without annoying those who have responded.

- **Survey Security.** Many tools have identification codes included in the invitation to insure that only invited people can take the survey and that they can take it only once.

- **Survey Collection and Data Input.** The second major payback comes from the automated collection of the completed surveys and creation of a data file. The respondent completes and returns the survey electronically, which generally comes as an email to a designated email account. Survey tools can then read the returned emails and load the responses into a data file.

4. Reporting

◆ **Data Analysis.** As with spreadsheet or statistical analysis software, survey automation software can assist with the analysis and presentation of the data. Some products have filtering capabilities to segment the data set along demographic data or along responses to specific questions. Most include the capability to generate descriptive statistics and graphs of the results. The more expensive tools target market research more broadly with a full complement of multivariate statistical capabilities and data collection tools. What these tools *cannot* do is write a report and bring meaning to the data. You, the analyst, must apply your knowledge of the issues being researched to the analysis.

◆ **Distribution of Results.** Some tools have moved into real-time reporting of results via web pages.

Selecting Survey Automation Tools

As with the selection of any technological improvement, you first need to assess what you want from the technology. In your first exposure to this technology, you will not know all the capabilities that various vendors offer, so expect your selection criteria to change as you learn more about these tools. In a first survey project, you won't know all the features you will truly need. This is a maturing process. Consider buying a basic package first. Then with experience you will learn what questions to ask, and you can upgrade to a package that better meets your needs.

The purpose of this chapter in part is to help you ask better questions in your first purchase experience. Figure 8.2 lists features to consider when evaluating and selecting a survey tool. Consider using Figure 8.2 as a checklist when reviewing survey tools. There is a surprising range of differences across the tools on the market. Some differences are outlined below.

◆ **How tasks are automated.** Each tool has its own nuances in how it automates a survey project's tasks. In particular, the editor for creating questions and scales varies greatly across products. You should test drive a product to see if you like the way a vendor has implemented the instrument design process. Strongly consider how intuitive the user interface seems to you.[1] This is a software tool that you will not use every day. A poor

---

[1] The author has used a survey tool where *i.e.* and *e.g.* were misused in the dialogue boxes for creating a survey. That caused considerable confusion until I realized they meant *i.e.*, which means "that is," when they wrote *e.g.*, which means "for example."

Figure 8.2
Features to Consider in Selecting Survey Software

1. Project Management Features

♦ Planning tools—budgets, resources, and schedules
♦ Guidance through a survey project

2. Support for Multiple Question Formats

♦ Open-ended or free-form
♦ Multiple choice, single response, multiple choice, binary choice
♦ Ordinal scale: ordinal, forced ranking
♦ Interval scale: Likert, horizontal numerical, fixed-sum, etc.

3. Survey Instrument Design Process

♦ Wizards for question creation
♦ Ease of creating new questions
♦ Ability to apply one scale easily over a series of questions
♦ Ability to create new scales
♦ Ability to create section headings
♦ Handling of reverse coded questions
♦ Support for randomizing question presentation order
♦ Support of branching
♦ Grammar and spell checker

4. Libraries of Pre-Written Questions and Instruments

♦ Comprehensiveness
♦ Relevance to business issues of interest
♦ Validated reliability

5. Edit Controls on Data Entry

♦ Length of field for open-ended question input
♦ Multiple choice: "Check only one..."
♦ Ordinal: "Please rank order... Only use each number once..."
♦ Fixed sum: "The entries must sum to 100..."

6. Support for Survey Administration

- Generates cover letters—mail merge with survey distribution list
- Generates survey instrument for paper, email, or web surveys
- Generates HTML for email survey (that is, as attachment to the email message, not just as a link to a web page)
- Provides data input screen for telephone interviews
- Operates in a network or client-server environment—very valuable if telephone interviewers are to share a list of respondents
- Determines sample size requirements
- Size of respondent group that can be loaded into survey data file
- Generates random survey sample from distribution list
- Generates stratified survey sample from distribution list
- Generates follow-up notices to non-respondents
- Generates thank you notes for email and web surveys
- Supports multiple (or at least the ones important to you) email clients

7. Interface with Service Management System

- Generates transactional survey sample
- Offers control for repeat respondent selection
- Will ignore those listed as non-responsive
- Able to merge customer information data fields into survey record

8. Data Analysis Supported

- Descriptive statistics
- Multivariate analysis
- Export capabilities

9. Report Output Formatting Options

- Filtering capabilities
- Quality of tables and charts
- Text captions for charts
- Data file export
- Web-based reporting

interface will mean more relearning when you use the tool for the next survey project.

◆ **Support for question formats.** The tools differ in their support for different types of survey question formats. All the tools will support open-ended, multiple choice, and some variation of interval-scale questions. Few tools support true forced-ranked ordinal scales or fixed-sum question formats. Some tools may force you to put an anchor on every point of an interval scale. Before buying a software tool, you should strongly consider the types of questions you want to pose in this survey project and future ones. That's why some knowledge of the survey instrument is useful before you make your tool selection decision.

◆ **Size of response group.** The size of the database that can be analyzed at once will vary across tools. In part, this is how the tool vendors set prices for their products. (See below.) But there is also some limit driven by the underlying database structure. If you are conducting transaction-driven surveys, this could be a concern for you. Will you want to analyze one year's worth of data at once? If so, try to scope the likely size of the response group.

◆ **Range of tasks supported.** Some tools provide assistance with a broader range of tasks. For example, a few have project management tools, and many provide assistance with generating random samples. Most, but not all, will generate follow-up notes to non-respondents. Several have recently developed real-time reporting of survey results via web pages. Some tools support seamless branching by processing the HTML as screens are submitted, which requires a new screen after each branching question. HTML surveys attached to an email survey solicitation is also now available.

◆ **User-friendliness for the respondent.** Be sure to look at the survey from the respondent's point of view. Can you produce clean, attractive surveys, either in a web form or in email text? Are the web forms high in usability through good ergonomic design? If you must do an email survey (as opposed to a web-form survey), then having the survey as an HTML attachment is preferable. The format is much cleaner, more flexible, and less prone to respondent error.

◆ **Degree of customization possible.** What if you want to do something a little out of the ordinary. Can you customize the tool to meet your needs? Will the vendor have to do it?

- **Integration with other applications.** You may not be intending to use the survey tool as an island of automation. Instead, you may be intending to integrate it with your customer relationship management (CRM) system. Can you import data feeds of customer information and transaction histories into the survey tool? Can this be automated?

- **Desktop versus enterprise application.** The basic survey tools run as a stand-alone application on a desktop PC. Some tools are client-server tools while others straddle the fence by allowing multiple users to share files with customer contact information. Consider the mode in which you see your company using these capabilities. Would it be best to purchase a large-scale tool that is enterprise wide, coordinating all interactions with customers?

- **Service versus product purchase.** As with many software applications today, you can rent rather than buy the capabilities. The tool vendors' business models differ widely. Some are strictly product vendors. Others will host survey administration services on their servers. Others provide a full complement of survey services from design through analysis. Consider what best fits your needs.

- **Technical support.** The product bundle you buy is more than the software. It includes services. A survey book designed for customer service managers would be remiss without suggesting you consider the level of technical support offered by the vendors. Is it free? If you have to buy a contract, what services does it cover? Are upgrades included with initial product purchase? If not, are they included in any service contracts? Does the vendor offer training classes? How comprehensive is the user manual? What technical assistance will they provide? Technical support can become important when you're trying to get the web form to process responses properly. How much will the vendor work with your system administrator to isolate problems?

- **Company reputation.** Is the vendor an established company that will be around years from now? You will likely want to upgrade your product. What's the company's history in delivering upgrades? Do they have a satisfied customer base?

Your project team needs to consider what you need the survey automation tool to do for this project – and perhaps for future projects. Which capabilities really matter to you? Don't fall prey to flashy features with little real value. Beyond price, be sure to include the expected impact upon your productivity of the tools. If one tool will save you a full day in generating graphs for the final report, that should be part of the decision process. The largest cost associated with these tools is not the check you will write to the vendor. Rather, it is the time you will spend learning the tool and making it work in your environment. Once you go through this process, you may spend the time and effort to start fresh with a new tool, so it is wise, before you make a purchase decision, to think very carefully about which features are likely to prove critical for you in the foreseeable future.

Pricing of Survey Automation Tools

You will find a wide range of prices in the survey software tools. As you would expect, higher price tags denote greater capabilities. Many vendors will offer different versions of their software. The differences in the feature sets that typically drive the price structures are:

- **Type of administration methods supported.** Some tools will have different versions for hardcopy and electronic survey tools. Pricing will vary on the range of methods supported.

- **Size of respondent pool.** Vendors typically segment their product offerings by the number of responses that can be loaded into the data file for analysis as one set of data. The number of responses will be set as ranges, which will be something like 1 to 100 responses, 101 to 500 responses, 501 to 1000 responses, and 1000 and greater responses. Any demonstration software will likely support up to 10 respondents in a survey.

- **Desktop, enterprise, or hosting.** The stand-alone desktop model will be least expensive, whereas, the enterprise model will have user licenses. In the hosting models, expect a one-time set-up fee and then pricing for each survey based upon the length of the survey instrument, the number of surveys sent out, and the number of responses processed.

- **Extent of services offered.** Many offer services rather than products. Obviously, the extent of the services will drive the pricing.

Hidden Dangers with Automation Tools

While there are tremendous benefits to these tools, there are also some hidden dangers or shortcomings.

Delusions of Research Validity. We've just outlined a number of areas where survey tools can increase productivity. It is important to realize, however, that an automation tool is not a panacea. In fact, these tools can be dangerous in the hands of those without a proper understanding of survey research methodology.

Let's use a very topical analogy. Only a few years ago buying a company's stock required a relationship with a full service broker, who provided advice and executed the stock transaction. Today, anyone with a PC and internet access can trade stocks. Does the ability to trade stocks directly confer knowledge of sound investment philosophy? Obviously, it does not.

The same goes for surveying. Now we have tools that make it possible for just about anyone to conduct survey research. Anyone can execute the *mechanics* of writing a survey instrument, but that ability does not mean the person knows anything about designing a survey instrument. Add to this our society's tendency to accept the results of any survey as fact. News broadcasts report survey findings, and few reporters are knowledgeable enough — or interested enough — to question the methodology. How many managers in your company would truly challenge *how* some research was performed before implementing the findings? This blind acceptance of survey research may be part of reason why so many people think that survey research is simple and straightforward. It is, after all, just a bunch of questions...

While survey automation tools can simplify the tasks of formatting and compiling a survey instrument, *they can in no way guarantee the validity or reliability of the instrument*. The business value of the data is only as good as the weakest link in the chain, which may well be the quality of the questionnaire. If you have read this far into the book, then you should have developed an appreciation for the complexities of properly done survey research. However, survey automation tools can allow us to do the wrong things faster — *and* with more misplaced confidence in our flawed results.

There are two specific blind spots created by survey automation tools.

Lack of Instrument Feedback. As mentioned in Chapter 5 where survey administration methods were compared, one shortcoming of survey automation tools may not be immediately obvious. The medium doesn't readily allow the respondent to give you feedback on the questionnaire. If you have done a paper-based survey, you have likely had the experience of finding comments written in the margins of the returned questionnaires. Some people will put question marks next to questions they don't understand or challenge you in writing on the premise behind a question. Sometimes they'll rewrite the choices given for a multiple-choice question. (The author does this on occasion.) No questionnaire will ever work perfectly for every potential respondent, but a large amount of feedback about the instrument tells you that what you really have is a draft in need of more work. With an electronic survey, particularly on a web form, the opportunity to obtain this feedback is virtually eliminated. Pilot testing your instrument thoroughly is particularly critical with email and web surveys.

Data Entry Errors. Finally, email surveys that present the instrument in ASCII text have a particular weakness in the area of data entry errors. Respondents have to reply to the survey invitation and enter their answers after some special characters that follow each survey question. If they corrupt those special characters, the response cannot be read. Also, typically an identification number is included in the original message as a means of validating the reply email. If a respondent corrupts that identification number, the survey tool won't load the data in the survey data file.

Outsourcing

We have mentioned that many survey automation tool companies also offer services. In fact, many started selling automation software and have transitioned to a business model based on survey services. Why? Many clients prefer to buy services rather than build those capabilities in-house, and the vendors saw the profit potential. So why might you consider outsourcing? There are two distinct advantages. The most obvious advantage is that you are buying expertise. The second advantage is that you are buying capacity. By outsourcing, you are more certain of completing the project on schedule, since the outsourcer has a monetary incentive.

All or part of a survey project can be outsourced. Aspects of a survey project that are most amenable to outsourcing are:

- Moderating focus groups and analyzing the textual data
- Designing the survey instrument
- Mailing the notification letters, surveys, and follow-up notes
- Conducting telephone interviews
- Performing statistical analysis

Of course, the entire surveying program can also be outsourced. As with any outsourcing venture, you need to develop a solid Request for Proposal (RFP). This requires that your project team strongly consider each step of the project and make decisions about what to include in the RFP. You will probably want to know from the vendors:

- Survey instrument design methodology. Their instrument design and validation process.
- Survey administration methodology. The types of administration performed and the controls used to reduce administration biases.
- Number of survey responses completed for a given price.
- Analytical capabilities. Univariate, bivariate, and multivariate data analysis.
- Breadth of research offerings should any follow-up research be desired.
- Background of project team in market research and data analysis.
- Background of project team in your specific business area.
- Client list.
- Your assessment of the trustworthiness and ethical bearings of the company. Remember, these people will be representing you to the customer!

Sources of Survey Automation Tools and Outsourcing Organizations

The list of companies that provide survey automation tools and outsourcing services is constantly changing. Rather than print a list here that will soon be out of date, an up-to-date list is maintained at www.greatbrook.com/surveyautomationtools.htm. If you have a product or vendor you feel should be added please email me at info@greatbrook.com. Note that this is simply a list for your perusal. No endorsement is intended or implied by the inclusion of a product or vendor.

Beyond this list, do recognize that most market research firms will conduct survey research. Also, the marketing or quantitative methods departments of local business schools and the psychology departments in liberal arts schools may have professors who will do instrument design work or statistical analysis. Postal survey mailings can be outsourced to any mailing house, and telephone interviewing can be outsourced to a telemarketing organization.

C3C3C3

Appendix:
Discussion of Exercises

Exercise 1
Critical Incident Study and Attribute Identification

There's no "answer" to this exercise. Attribute identification is something that comes with practice. You can read how to do it, but to internalize the concept, you must practice it. Brainstorming in a group setting is a good way to develop the skills.

Exercise 2
Developing Scales

In my workshops, this exercise tends to set off those light bulbs over people's heads. They begin to see the challenge of designing a good survey instrument. With the endpoints, the question is: how extreme do you want them to be? Should you use *Extremely* or *Very*? The midpoint anchor stumps many people. No one likes the *Neither... Nor...* option, for example *Neither Hard Nor Difficult*, but the other options are *Neutral*, *Indifferent*, or something similar. Many people will quickly find merit in an even-numbered scale to avoid this issue!

Some people try to be creative and use anchors like *Excited* or *Ecstatic*. When administering these, some percentage of respondents will say they can't identify with the anchors. They just don't get excited about the phenomenon behind the question. They won't know how to respond since the dimension for measurement doesn't match their thinking processes. Their responses would probably be lost.

The fully-anchored scales are just an extension of the previous exercise adding anchors for the two midway positions in the second and fourth steps in the scale. For a paper-based survey, this is easy. You just have formatting issues. But for a telephone administration, problems with these scales can be found. Do the anchors take a long time to verbalize? By the time respondents hear the fifth anchors will they have forgotten the first ones?

A final issue is the use of generic scales versus a scale more specific to the phenomena. Can the scale you develop be used for measuring multiple attributes or must a new scale be created for each attribute? Consider how much more space on a survey form this would take and how much more time this would take to deliver verbally. Will the survey now be so long that respondents balk at continuing.

Generic scales, such as satisfaction or met-expectations scales, solve this dilemma, but they pose a new one. Once you've picked a scale, now try writing all your questions. You will find writing the questions to fit the scale will be more of a challenge than you first thought.

Exercise 3

Analyzing Instrumentation Bias

Let's discuss each question individually.

Please answer the following questions. Thank you for your time.
As an introduction, this is woefully brief. If you received a survey with that introduction, how motivated would you be to spend your valuable time completing the survey?

1. Your name and title are:
Demographic questions are the easiest ones to write, and it seems logical to ask them first — to a novice surveyor. However, they set up that mental wall and in no way engage the respondent. Many people will quit the survey right here. Put demographic information at the end of the survey.

2. Please rate the service you received for each support event in the past year.

Very Invaluable	Poor	Fair	Good	Extremely Valuable
1	2	3	4	5

This question is replete with problems! Let's list them.

♦ The anchors aren't balanced. *Very* and *Extremely* are not equal opposites.

- *Invaluable* is ambiguous. Is something that is invaluable so valuable its worth cannot be measured or is it of no value? *Priceless* poses the same problem.

- The spacing between the potential answers is not even. The respondent, consciously or subconsciously, may interpret the distance between 4 and 5 and as a bigger interval than between 3 and 4. If so, then this is not an interval scale. Taking averages will be misleading.

- *Fair* is not a good midpoint. Most people consider *Fair* to be closer to *Good* than it is to *Poor*, which means the intervals aren't equal — even for the three points where visually the separation is equal. The result is a downward bias in the results since more people would pick *Fair* than they would if the intervals were truly equal.

- The anchors don't all describe the same dimension. The endpoints address value while *Poor – Fair – Good* could represent value, but it's not clear.

- Respondents are being asked to condense their experiences with a support organization for a whole year into one response. That's unreasonable recall expectations, and the last experience will likely dominate the answer.

- No basis for comparison has been provided to the respondent. Is it compared to experiences in the prior year, compared to other support organizations, compared to expectations. If each respondent uses a different comparison, then how would the results be interpreted?

- Finally, the question should have line wrap set so that second lines indent allowing the number to stand alone. That's a small formatting thing, but the lack of the line wrap conveys sloppiness.

3. Please rate your satisfaction with the availability of Customer Care.

Very Dissatisfied	Somewhat Dissatisfied	Neither Satisfied Nor Dissatisfied	Somewhat Satisfied	Very Satisfied
1	2	3	4	5

This question also has several problems.

- *Notice that the question is in italics whereas the other questions are not.* Subconsciously, that might change the way respondents treat the question.

- *Availability*, like response time, is an ambiguous term open to interpretation. It could mean the hours when Customer Care is open, how quickly Customer Care answered the phone, or the flexibility Customer Care showed in responding to issues. You might find yet more interpretations for that word.

- "Customer Care" is company jargon. Some respondents might not know what it means without some definition.

- How would you respond to this question if you were just plain *satisfied*, that is, your expectations were just met? Test this scale with a group. Some will say that satisfied lies to the left of *Somewhat Satisfied*. Some will say to the right of *Somewhat Satisfied*. Others will say they think of *satisfied* as a midpoint and might quickly select that option.

- If you're *Neither Satisfied, Nor Dissatisfied*, then what are you? That's an option that is hard to interpret. Why? Let's say you're somewhat satisfied. Doesn't that also mean you're somewhat *dis*satisfied? If so, then the midpoint doesn't make sense.

- The scale lacks good dispersion properties. Assume that *satisfied* lies to right of *Somewhat Satisfied* and *dissatisfied* lies to the left of *Somewhat Dissatisfied*. Almost the entire scale is devoted to measuring midrange feelings. The endpoints will capture extreme feelings but also many people who are just satisfied or dissatisfied.

4. How important is the following? Please use the following scale:

Not Important	Important	Somewhat Important	Very Important	Extremely Important
1	2	3	4	5

Courtesy & Friendliness: _____
Competence & Speed: _____
Thoroughness & Accuracy : _____

Again, there are several problems.

- Yes, the grammar is poor. The opening sentence should read, "How important *are* the following?"

- The instructions don't tell the respondent where to record their answer, though it seems pretty obvious.

◆ The scale order is confused. *Important* should be between *Somewhat Important* and *Very Important*.

◆ This is a truncated scale. Degrees of unimportance are not captured. That may be fine.

◆ The most egregious problem lies in the double-barreled questions. *Courtesy & Friendliness* are fairly close attributes in the United States, but they are very dissimilar in other cultures. *Competence & Speed* and *Thoroughness & Accuracy* are pairs of very dissimilar attributes. How would respondents answer if they thought *competency* was more important than *speed*?

5. Please check the services below that you believe the Association offers members and then rate your satisfaction with each.

		Not Satisfied		OK			Very Satisfied
Affinity credit card	❏	1	2	3	4	5	6
Travel services	❏	1	2	3	4	5	6

The choice of anchors is questionable and the even-numbered scale with *OK* over a non-existent midpoint might confuse respondents. Is *OK* even a good midpoint for this scale? Most importantly, how would a respondent answer if that thought an "Affinity credit card" was offered — assuming they knew what it meant — but did not actually have one? *N/A* should be an option.

6.Do you attend local chapter meetings?

__ Yes __ No __ Sometimes

We have overlapping response categories. What if someone attended half the meetings. Does that deserve a *Yes* or a *Sometimes* response? Also, notice the layout. Someone selecting *No* might check the line to the right of *No*.

7. When using your Platinum Training Membership, what factors influence your decision about which courses to attend? (Please rank, with a 5 being the most significant and a 1 being the least.)

__Training Services Representative __Skills Assessment

__Training Services Catalog __Self

__Certification Learning Path __Manager or Supervisor

__Other_____

What is the respondent supposed to do, *rank* or *rate*? The question says rank, but the presentation of the 1-to-5 scale with seven response options implies rating. If some respondents rated whereas others ranked, what would you do with the data? Could you tell whether they were ranking or rating? As bad as this question is posed, imagine if there were five response options!

8. You recently contacted Frozen Systems' Technical Support Help Desk. In an effort to continually improve our service to you, our valued customer, we would appreciate it if you answer the following short survey. Please rate the following questions using the following scale.

Completely Satisfied	Very Satisfied	Fairly Well Satisfied	Somewhat Satisfied	Somewhat Dissatisfied	Very Dissatisfied
1	2	3	4	5	6

Your call was answered in a timely manner: ____

The analyst was able to answer your questions in the initial call: ____

If a follow-up expectation was set, it was met: ____

The analyst assisted in ultimately resolving your problem: ____

The analyst was courteous and professional: ____

Let's start by examining the instructions. How might the phrase "our valued customer" affect respondents? It's loaded phrasing. How can you say something bad about Frozen Systems after reading that?

Look at the scale here. What does *Fairly Well Satisfied* mean? Is it in the proper rank order? Notice that the creator of this scale wanted to avoid the midpoint problem, and a neutral position would be between 4 and 5. That might be okay, but are the intervals equal across the anchors? We go from Somewhat to Very Dissatisfied in one interval, but Somewhat to Very Satisfied has an extra interval. The scale is also set up such that low numbers represent a better situation. Picture the reader interpreting the charts.

Let's turn to the questions. Are they all written to a Satisfaction scale? A Strength-of-Agreement scale would seem more appropriate. Consider the second question. That is really a binary, Yes/No question that should act as a filter for the third question. Finally, are courtesy and professionalism the same attribute or different attributes?

Exercise 4

Instrumentation and Administration Bias

At first glance the two survey questions would appear to be measuring the same phenomenon even with different wording and different scales. Yet the responses are dramatically different. Some set of factors is causing the observed difference. It may be bias from the instrument or bias from the administration — or both.

Instrumentation bias. Consider the phrasing of the questions carefully.

> *Question 1:* "In general, would you say criminals who commit nonviolent crimes in the US are not punished enough, are adequately punished, or are punished too harshly?"

> *Question 2:* "Please tell me if you agree or disagree with the following statement: We need to change the laws so that fewer non-violent crimes are punishable by prison terms."

In the first question, the term "criminal" is presented up front. This may overwhelm the "nonviolent crimes" part of the question. It's unclear whether the nonviolent crime is what makes the person a criminal. Could some respondents be assuming the question is asking about someone with a violent criminal history? The phrasing also doesn't specify the type of punishment that is too harsh, adequate or too lenient. Did the respondents know the typical punishment handed out for nonviolent crimes?

In the second question, the respondent is not told the percent of non-violent crimes that are punishable by prison terms, but the question implies that the percent is high. It would interesting to see the results if the wording were reversed to ask if *more* non-violent crimes should be punishable by prison terms. Finally, in both questions we don't know if other questions in the surveys may have affected the interpretation of these questions.

Administration Bias. We don't know anything about the administration of the surveys beyond the administration date and the method. How were respondents selected? We can easily envision how bias in sample selection could lead to different results. Because the groups sponsoring the research got the results they wanted, that's a legitimate concern.

CʒCʒCʒ

Bibliography

The following is a list of books on surveying and other books referenced in this book. To see a short review of many survey-related book, please go to www. greatbrook.com and follow the links to the on-line bibliography.

Alreck, Pamela L. and Settle, Robert B., *The Survey Research Handbook,* Homewood, IL: Irwin, 1985.

Barnett, George A., et al., "The Use of Fractionation Scales for Communication Audits," *Organizational Communication,* Communication Yearbook 5, 1982.

Barlow, Janelle, and Claus Møller, *A Complaint is a Gift,* San Francisco: Barrett-Koehler Publishers, 1996.

Dillman, Don A., *Mail and Internet Surveys: The Tailored Design Method,* John Wiley & Sons, 1999.

Fink, Arlene (Editor), *The Survey Kit : How to Analyze Survey Data/ How to Measure Survey Reliability and Validity/How to Sample in Surveys/How to Design Surveys,* Sage Publications, 1995.

Fowler, Floyd J., Jr., *Survey Research Methods,* Newbury Park: Sage Publications, 1993.

Fowler, Floyd J., Jr., *Improving Survey Questions: Design and Evaluation,* Applied Social Research Methods Series, Vol. 38, Sage Publications, 1995.

Goal/QPC Press, *The Memory Jogger II,* 1994.

Goldman, Alfred E., Susan Schwartz MacDonald, *The Group Depth Interview: Principles and Practice,* Englewood Cliffs, NJ: Prentice-Hall, 1987.

Goodman, John, "Basic Facts On Customer Complaint Behavior And The Impact Of Service On The Bottom Line" *Competitive, The Newsletter of the Service Quality Division of the American Society for Quality,* May-June, 1999.

Hamburg, Morris, *Statistical Analysis for Decision Making,* 2nd edition, New York: Harcourt Brace Jovanovich, 1977.

Hayes, Bob E., *Measuring Customer Satisfaction: Survey Design, Use, and Statistical Analysis Methods;* ASQ Quality Press, 1997.

Greenbaum, Thomas J., *The Handbook for Focus Group Research,* Thousand Oaks, CA: Sage Publications, 1998.

Hart, Christopher, et al., "The Profitable Art of Service Recovery," *Harvard Business Review,* July-August, 1990, pp. 148-156.

Holstein, James A. and Jaber Gubrium, *The Active Interview,* , Thousand Oaks, CA Sage Publications, 1995.

Kao, John, "Scandinavian Airlines System," Harvard Business School Press, Case 9-487-041, 1987.

Kaplan, Robert S. and D. P Norton, *The Balanced Scorecard: Translating Strategy into Action,* Harvard Business School Press, 1996.

Krueger, Richard A., *Focus Groups: A Practical Guide for Applied Research,* Sage Publications, 1994.

Lynch, Richard. L. and Kelvin F. Cross, *Measure Up!: Yardsticks for Continuous Improvement,* Blackwell Publishers, 1995.

Naumann, Earl and Kathleen Giel, *Customer Satisfaction Measurement and Management,* Thomson Executive Press, 1995.

Patton, Michael Quinn, *Qualitative Evaluation and Research Methods,* Newbury Park: Sage Publications, 1990.

Rea, Louis M., Richard A. Parker (Contributor), Alan Shrader (Editor), *Designing and Conducting Survey Research: A Comprehensive Guide,* Jossey-Bass Public Administration Series, 1997.

Shostack, G. Lynn, "Designing Services That Deliver," *Harvard Business Review,* January-February, 1984.

Stewart, David W., Prem N. Shamdasani, *Focus Groups: Theory and Practice,* Applied Social Research Methods Series, Vol. 20, Sage Publications, 1990.

Tufte, Edward R., *The Visual Display of Quantitative Information,* Cheshire, CT: Graphics Press, 2001.

Tufte, Edward R., *Envisioning Information,* Cheshire, CT: Graphics Press, 1990.

Tufte, Edward R., *Visual Explanations, Images and Quantities, Evidence and Narrative,* Cheshire, CT: Graphics Press, 1997.

Vavra, Terry G., *Improving Your Measurement of Customer Satisfaction,* Milwaukee: ASQ Quality Press, 1997.

Zeithaml, Valerie A., and Mary Jo Bitner, *Services Marketing,* New York: McGraw-Hill, 1996.

Zemke, Ron, and Chip R. Bell, *Knock Your Socks Off Service Recovery,* New York: AMACOM, 2000.

Index

A

B

C

D

E

F

G

H

I

K

L

M

N

O

P

T

U

V

W

About This Book

Customer Surveying A Guidebook for Service Managers is designed to complement the Questionnaire Advisor ^{SM} product from Great Brook Consulting. Questionnaire Advisor ^{SM} includes the Support Services Questionnaire Library. Questionnaire Advisor^{SM} is also part of the Survey Project Counselor ^{SM} and Survey Project Toolkit ^{SM} from Great Brook.

If you have purchased the *Guidebook* separately and are interested in learning about these other products from Great Brook, please contact us at (978) 779-6312 or visit us at www.greatbrook.com.

ଔଔଔ

Frederick C. Van Bennekom, Dr. B.A.

About the Author

Dr. Van Bennekom is Principal of Great Brook Consulting. He is also a lecturer in Northeastern University's College of Business Administration, where he teaches graduate level Operations Management and Service Management courses. Fred's research and business practice examine the use of customer feedback for organizational improvement, with a special focus on the strategic linkage between customer support and product engineering. He has authored many surveys used by service organizations for service program development and for quality control purposes. Fred has also developed an expertise in the use of the new breed of electronic survey software tools.

Prior to his academic career, Fred served ten years as an information systems consultant for Digital Equipment Corporation's Field Service organization, developing management reporting systems for field management. He received his B.A. from Bowdoin College and his masters and doctoral degrees from Boston University's School of Management.

Fred is a featured speaker at many industry conferences within the US and abroad. He has published in both industry and academic journals and has contributed to several books, including *We're Off to Seize the Wizard* by Jeff Pepper of ServiceWare, *Field Service Management* by Arthur Hill, and *Software by Design: Shaping Technology for the Workplace* by Harold Salzman and Stephen Rosenthal.

Fred has served as an officer in the Association of Support Professionals and AFSMI, and he is a member of Decision Sciences Institute, the Help Desk Institute, and the American Society for Quality. He can be contacted at 978-779-6312 or at fred@greatbrook.com.

CRCRCR